CRITIQUE OF JOURNALISTIC REASON

Critique of Journalistic Reason

PHILOSOPHY AND THE TIME OF THE NEWSPAPER

Tom Vandeputte

FORDHAM UNIVERSITY PRESS   NEW YORK   2020

Fordham University Press has no responsibility for the persistence or accuracy of URLs for external or third-party Internet websites referred to in this publication and does not guarantee that any content on such websites is, or will remain, accurate or appropriate.

Fordham University Press also publishes its books in a variety of electronic formats. Some content that appears in print may not be available in electronic books.

Visit us online at www.fordhampress.com.

Library of Congress Cataloging-in-Publication Data available online at https://catalog.loc.gov.

Printed in the United States of America

22 21 20   5 4 3 2 1

First edition

Contents

Abbreviations

All translations are my own, unless indicated otherwise. The endnotes provide references to the existing English translations whenever these are available.

AJ   Walter Benjamin, "Announcement of the Journal *Angelus Novus*." In *Selected Writings*, vol. 1. Edited by Marcus Bullock and Michael W. Jennings. Translated by Edmund Jephcott et al., 292–96. Cambridge: Harvard University Press, 1996.

Ak   Immanuel Kant, *Gesammelte Schriften* (facsimile of the standard "Akademie" edition published by the Königlich Preußische Akademie der Wissenschaften, 1902–). 29 vols. Berlin: De Gruyter, 1968–.

AP   Walter Benjamin, *The Arcades Project*. Translated by Howard Eiland and Kevin McLaughlin. Cambridge: Harvard University Press, 1999.

APP   Immanuel Kant, *Anthropology from a Pragmatic Point of View*. Edited and translated by Robert B. Louden. New York: Cambridge University Press, 2006.

B   Walter Benjamin, *Briefe*. Edited by Theodor Adorno and Gerschom Scholem. 2 vols. Frankfurt am Main: Suhrkamp, 1978.

BGE   Friedrich Nietzsche, *Beyond Good and Evil*. Translated by Judith Norman. Cambridge: Cambridge University Press, 2007.

CA   Søren Kierkegaard, *The Concept of Anxiety*. Translated by Reidar
          Thomte and Albert A. Anderson. Princeton: Princeton
          University Press, 1980.

CB   Walter Benjamin, *The Correspondence of Walter Benjamin,
          1910–1940*. Edited by Gerschom Scholem and T. W. Adorno.
          Translated by M. R. Jacobson et al. Chicago: University of
          Chicago Press, 1994.

CF   Immanuel Kant, *The Conflict of the Faculties*. Translated by
          Mary J. Gregor. New York: Abaris Books, 1979.

CI   Søren Kierkegaard, *The Concept of Irony*. Translated by
          Howard V. Hong and Edna H. Hong. Princeton: Princeton
          University Press, 1989.

CJ   Immanuel Kant, *Critique of the Power of Judgment*. Translated
          by Paul Guyer and Eric Matthews. Cambridge: Cambridge
          University Press, 2000.

CPrR   Immanuel Kant, *Critique of Practical Reason*. In *Practical
          Philosophy*. Edited and translated by Mary J. Gregor.
          Cambridge: Cambridge University Press, 1996.

EH   Friedrich Nietzsche, *Ecce Homo*. In *The Anti-Christ, Ecce
          Homo, Twilight of the Idols*. Translated by Judith Norman.
          Cambridge: Cambridge University Press, 2007.

EPW   Søren Kierkegaard, *Early Polemical Writings*. Edited and
          translated by Julia Watkin. Princeton: Princeton University
          Press, 1990.

EW   Walter Benjamin, *Early Writings 1910–1917*. Edited by Howard
          Eiland. Cambridge: Harvard University Press, 2011.

FE   Friedrich Nietzsche, "On the Future of Our Educational
          Institutions." In *Anti-Education: On the Future of Our
          Educational Institutions*, edited by Paul Reitter and Chad
          Wellmon, translated by Damion Searles, 3–96. New York: New
          York Review of Books, 2015.

FL   Friedrich Nietzsche, "Fragments sur le langage." Translated by
          Philippe Lacoue-Labarthe and Jean Luc Nancy. *Poétique* 5
          (1971): 99–142.

GM   Friedrich Nietzsche, *On the Genealogy of Morality*.
     Translated by Carol Diethe. Cambridge: Cambridge
     University Press, 1997.

GS   Walter Benjamin, *Gesammelte Schriften*. Edited by Rolf
     Tiedemann and Hermann Schweppenhäuser. 7 vols. Frankfurt
     am Main: Suhrkamp, 1972–91.

GSC   Friedrich Nietzsche, *The Gay Science*. Translated by Josephine
     Nauckhoff. Cambridge: Cambridge University Press, 2008.

GW   G. W. F. Hegel, *Werke*. 20 vols. Frankfurt am Main: Suhrkamp,
     1970.

JN   Søren Kierkegaard, *Kierkegaard's Journals and Notebooks*. Edited
     by Niels Jorgen Cappelorn et al. Princeton: Princeton University
     Press, 2011–.

KK   Walter Benjamin, "Karl Kraus." In *Selected Writings*, vol. 2.
     Edited by Marcus Bullock and Michael W. Jennings. Translated
     by Edmund Jephcott et al., 433–57. Cambridge: Harvard
     University Press, 1996.

KSA   Friedrich Nietzsche, *Werke: Kritische Studienausgabe in 15
     Bänden*. Edited by Giorgio Colli and Mazzino Montinari.
     Berlin: Walter de Gruyter, 1988.

KSB   Friedrich Nietzsche, *Sämtliche Briefe: Kritische Studienausgabe
     in 8 Bänden*. Edited by Giorgio Colli and Mazzino Montinari.
     Berlin: Walter de Gruyter, 1986.

O   *The Origin of German Tragic Drama*. Translated by John
     Osborne. London: Verso, 1998.

Pap.   Søren Kierkegaard, *Søren Kierkegaards Papirer*. Edited by P. A.
     Heiberg, V. Kuhr, and E. Torsting. Copenhagen: Gyldendal,
     1909–48.

PhH   G. W. F. Hegel, *The Philosophy of History*. Translated by J.
     Sibree. New York: Dover, 1956.

PhR   G. W. F. Hegel, *Elements of the Philosophy of Right*. Edited by
     Allen Wood. Translated by H. B. Nisbet. Cambridge: Cambridge
     University Press, 1991.

PR/WS   Søren Kierkegaard, *Prefaces / Writing Sampler*. Edited and
          translated by Todd W. Nichol. Princeton: Princeton University
          Press, 1997.

PS   G. W. F. Hegel, *Phenomenology of Spirit*. Translated by A. V.
          Miller. Oxford: Oxford University Press, 1977.

RL   Friedrich Nietzsche, *Friedrich Nietzsche on Rhetoric and
          Language*. Translated by Sander L. Gilman et al. Oxford:
          Oxford University Press, 1989.

RR   Immanuel Kant, *Religion Within the Boundaries of Mere Reason*.
          Translated by George di Giovanni. In *Religion and Rational
          Theology*, edited by Allen W. Wood and George di Giovanni.
          Cambridge: Cambridge University Press, 1996.

S   Karl Kraus, *Schriften*. Edited by Christian Wagenknecht. 20 vols.
          Frankfurt am Main: Suhrkamp Verlag, 1994.

SV   Søren Kierkegaard, *Søren Kierkegaards Samlede Værker*. Edited
          by A. B. Drachman, J. L. Heiberg, and H. O. Lange. 14 vols.
          Copenhagen: Gyldendal, 1901–06.

SW   Walter Benjamin, *Selected Writings*. Edited by Marcus Bullock
          and Michael W. Jennings. Translated by Edmund Jephcott et al.
          4 vols. Cambridge: Harvard University Press, 1996.

TA   Søren Kierkegaard, *Two Ages: A Literary Review*. Edited and
          translated by Howard. V. Hong and Edna H. Hong. Princeton:
          Princeton University Press, 1978.

TI   Friedrich Nietzsche, *Twilight of the Idols*. In *The Anti-Christ,
          Ecce Homo, Twilight of the Idols*. Translated by Judith Norman.
          Cambridge: Cambridge University Press, 2007.

UM   Friedrich Nietzsche, *Untimely Meditations*. Translated by R. J.
          Hollingdale. Cambridge: Cambridge University Press, 1995.

Z   Friedrich Nietzsche, *Thus Spoke Zarathustra*. Translated by
          Adrian del Caro. Cambridge: Cambridge University Press, 2006.

CRITIQUE OF JOURNALISTIC REASON

Morning News

Kant, Hegel

The *newspaper reading* of the early morning [*das* Zeitungslesen *des Morgens früh*] is a kind of realistic morning prayer [*Morgensegen*]. One orients one's attitude towards the world either through God or through that which the world is. The former gives as much security [*Sicherheit*] as the latter, in that one knows where one stands [*wie man daran sei*].

—HEGEL, *JENA APHORISMS*

"The *newspaper reading* of the early morning"—with these words a certain to-pos is, perhaps for the first time, introduced into the philosophical tradition: its preoccupation with journalism.[1] The comparison between newspaper reading and the morning prayer appears in the margins of Hegel's writings, amongst the miscellaneous fragments, notes, and reflections collected in his notebooks of the Jena years—texts written before the publication of any of his major books and only published posthumously in a local newspaper in the 1840s.[2] Also the form in which this comparison is elaborated—that of an aphorism—may suggest that it bears no relation to Hegel's systematic writings.[3] But even though it is consigned to this apparently marginal place, the scene of newspaper reading is presented here with a distinct emphasis. Set in italics and placed at the start of the first sentence, the word *Zeitungslesen* suggests that it is invested with a special significance: that this word and the scene of reading it evokes mean something more than the reader may initially assume. The emphasis on this scene is brought out only further by the resonance be-tween the two compounds around which the aphorism is organized, *Zeitung-slesen* and *Morgensegen*, both of which are composed of the same amount of syllables, similar in sound and meter, and only the slightest step removed from rhyme. If this play of emphasis and resonance suggests anything, it is that this remark is not just a pithy reflection on the accidental resemblance of two all too familiar scenes from everyday life at the start of the nineteenth century—that there is more at stake in this aphorism than the provision of a witty observation that exists at a safe remove from Hegel's philosophical work of those same years. In their emphatic introduction, the scenes juxtaposed here rather seem to serve as two of those "abbreviations" (*Abkürzungen*) in which, as Hegel writes later, thought shows itself to be the "most powerful epitomist": scenes in which thought compresses the insights it has reached, albeit not in a language of concepts but one of figures and images.[4]

If it is possible to understand the comparison of the scenes of reading and praying presented in Hegel's notebooks as an *Abkürzung* in this sense, this is because these two scenes, taken together, epitomize the conception of history in which the planned introduction to his philosophical system—the *Phenomenology of Spirit*—would culminate. In order to grasp the precise philosophical significance with which the scene of *Zeitungslesen* is endowed in this aphorism, one would first need to turn to the scene to which it is juxtaposed: that of the Lutheran *Morgensegen*. As is well known, religious experience plays a decisive role in Hegel's philosophical writings of the preceding years, especially in their account of the absolute.[5] In the *Systemfragment* of 1800, Hegel had argued that the absolute—or what is there called "infinite life"—must remain strictly inaccessible to reflective thought and its inherent opposition of subject and object.[6] Even though reflection is destined to strive for the "elevation of the finite into the infinite life," such elevation could only be accomplished in the domain of religion. In religious experience, the subject renounces its own absoluteness and instead takes hold of the absolute, which precedes both subject and object as their common source. History and nature are both grasped as manifestations of the absolute, but insofar as this absolute remains strictly separated from its reflected image in consciousness, it does not have a historical character itself—it knows no development. The juxtaposition of the morning prayer and newspaper reading in Hegel's Jena notebooks draws on this earlier understanding of religious experience but also points to a shifted conception of the absolute. This shift is suggested by the prayer that is here supposed to capture religion's privileged relation to the absolute: the Lutheran *Morgensegen*. As an exemplary expression of what Hegel refers to in the *Phenomenology* as "manifest religion," this morning prayer is oriented toward a God that becomes incarnate in the world it has created and, after having sacrificed itself, is resurrected as holy spirit.[7] If the Lutheran prayer orients itself toward the absolute, it is an absolute being that has entered the world and actualizes itself in space, time, and history. To say the morning prayer is thus, for Hegel, to take hold of the absolute as the holy spirit that is at work in time and history—and to grasp oneself as a moment in its development. More than any other prayer, it is the *Morgensegen*, undertaken at the dawn of every new day, that most acutely exemplifies the relation to this absolute being, which Hegel describes in the *Phenomenology* as "the spirit who dwells in his community, dies in it every day, and is daily resurrected [*in ihr täglich stirbt und aufersteht*]."[8] Insofar as it is grasped as spirit, the absolute being of the *Morgensegen* is no longer merely an absolute that manifests itself in history while remaining separate from it. Instead, history turns out to be the movement of alienation and reconciliation by which the absolute realizes itself in the world, day after day.

A *Zeitungslesen* that is comparable to the *Morgensegen* in this precise sense is thus not a newspaper reading in the familiar sense. A "newspaper reading of the early morning" that may be compared to the morning prayer cannot be satisfied with the inventory of accidental occurrences that is offered to it on a daily basis; it would have to be a reading that is oriented toward the absolute. Only insofar as it is oriented toward the absolute could this reading find the same *Sicherheit*, the same security that the morning prayer finds in its orientation toward God. But rather than representing this absolute being as a God that may dwell in the world but is still other to it, the reading that Hegel conjures up here would discover the absolute in the being of the world itself—in "that which the world is" (*was die Welt ist*).[9] Like the *Morgensegen*, such reading puts its faith in the absolute as a spirit that is at work in the world; but rather than apprehending the absolute as a holy spirit, the faith of this reader is perhaps closer to what Hegel calls a "faith in the world spirit" (*Glauben an der Weltgeist*)—a term that appears in the introduction to his lectures on the history of philosophy of the same years.[10] What distinguishes this "faith in the world spirit" from its religious counterpart is captured by the laconic phrase with which Hegel here characterizes this credo: *es geht vernünftig zu*—things go about rationally.[11] A newspaper reading that can be called a "realistic morning prayer" would be a reading that has discovered the absolute spirit that "dies every day, and is daily resurrected" to be nothing but the movement by which reason unfolds itself in the real.[12] The task of the newspaper reader would be to recover this movement from the inventory of accidental occurrences presented in the pages of the newspaper—to read the *Zeitung* as the report of the movement by which the absolute moves outside itself and returns to itself, day after day.[13]

Written in the years directly preceding the publication of the *Phenomenology of Spirit*, it is difficult not to read the aphorism from the Jena notebooks as a condensed expression of the speculative identity of the ideal and the real that will organize Hegel's philosophical system and the conception of history that underpins it.[14] The juxtaposition of newspaper reading and *Morgensegen* would then anticipate one of Hegel's famous later formulations of this identity, the proposition that "the task of philosophy is to comprehend *that which is*, because that *which is*, is reason"; and by capturing this comprehension as a *Zeitunglesen*, it would also evoke the counterpart of this proposition, the claim that philosophy is "its time, apprehended in thoughts" (*ihre Zeit in Gedanken erfaßt*).[15] Despite its apparently marginal place, the aphorism would then capture the decisive insight around which Hegel's philosophical system is organized. But while many of the other aphorisms in the notebooks return in the preface to the book that was conceived to be the introduction to this system—the *Phenomenology*—the comparison between newspaper reader and morning prayer remains curiously absent. Despite the continued importance that Hegel attached to images of daybreak, the scene of reading that is conjured up here, that of the *Zeitungslesen des Morgens früh*, will not return in any of his published writings. Is this a mere coincidence—or did he suspect that this scene would work against the system it is supposed to epitomize?[16] Did the Jena philosopher, who would go on to briefly act as editor of the *Bamberger Zeitung*, sense that there something in this scene of reading that undermines the immanent movement of the concept—the same movement that is supposed to guarantee the possibility for an identification of the real and the rational, of divine providence and historical development?[17] Does this comparison pose a danger to the system—the danger that it would render the speculative identity that it ought to exemplify into a laughing matter? Does the scene evoked here not present a lapse of the most serious of matters—the comprehension of history as the unfolding of spirit—into mere jest?

"The *newspaper reading* of the early morning"—before Hegel explicitly introduces this scene of reading into the philosophical tradition, it already makes a more modest appearance in a brief but important text by Kant that was itself originally written to be published in a newspaper: the essay "A Renewed Question: Is Humankind Constantly Progressing?"[18] The figure of the newspaper reader plays a decisive role in Kant's response to the question that is raised in the title of the essay: whether there is a secure ground to hope that *das menschliche Geschlecht* continually approaches its moral destination—or whether history is, as Kant points out in the first sections of the text, a mere *Possenspiel*, a farce without a final goal or progression toward it.[19] Despite the fact that this question is raised in a seemingly marginal piece of writing, an occasional piece that appears to be no more than an appendix to the Kantian system, it stands in a close relation to a problem that is of fundamental importance to the critical enterprise: the problem of the possibility of history.[20] Like his other writings of the early 1790s, Kant's essay on progress is an attempt to elaborate the consequences of a thought that had remained latent in the first two *Critiques*: that the realization of the supreme end of practical and theoretical reason, the "highest good" (*das höchste Gut*), cannot be restricted to the realm of personal morality alone but must extend to the creation of a moral community—a community whose realization, ultimately, requires the reshaping of the empirical world in accordance with the demands of morality.[21] The moral duty that is expressed in Kant's final formulation of the moral imperative—"Act to promote the highest good"—thus implies a task can only be developed through a concrete development in time that extends beyond the individual and must encompass the *Menschengeschlecht* in its entirety. Such a task could be called "historical" in the precise sense of the word: for it is with this task—its *Aufgabe* or "assignment" to the human being—that history first opens up as the domain of its possible fulfillment.

In the essay on historical progress, Kant is not only concerned with the manifestation of this imperative—that is to say, how the task to realize the highest good is given to the human *Geschlecht*—but also with the conditions under which it can be effective. If the historical imperative is to make an effective claim on a rational being endowed with freedom, it must not only manifest itself as a "fact" of moral consciousness; in order for this imperative to express a duty, there must also be grounds to expect that it is *possible* for the individual to contribute to its realization. This is where the question of progress comes into play: for if history would indeed be a *Possenspiel*, which Kant describes here as a play in which good and evil, moral lawfulness, and lawlessness effectively neutralize one another, there would be no way for the individual to ensure that its actions are not merely a Sisyphean effort.[22] If the historical imperative is to maintain its purchase on the subject addressed by it—if there is, in other words, to be history at all—the individual must have grounds to expect that humanity progresses toward its final moral end: for it is only in the secure expectation of progress that each human being finds itself subjected to the duty to contribute to humanity's advancement toward its ultimate destination. If Kant's "historical imperative" is not to collapse, there must be grounds to hope that history progresses toward the better. But as the essay on progress and the other historico-philosophical reflections of the early 1790s never cease to point out, securing such a ground and predicting the future course of events raise serious difficulties insofar as the history under consideration here is a moral history. Because the subject of this moral history—a subject famously described by Kant in the opening sections of the essay as a "diviner who creates and contrives the event he announces in advance"[23]—must be a rational being endowed with freedom, it is not possible to find this ground *a posteriori* by identifying the rules and regularities of prior experience. Because the one who "creates and contrives" this moral history is also a finite being—a being that, as Kant had shown in the sections on "radical evil" in the *Religion*, not only finds itself addressed by the moral law but also possesses an "innate" and "inextirpable" propensity toward evil[24]—there is no way to decide *a priori* whether such a being will tend to obey the moral law or not, no basis to expect whether it "finds itself on the good (though narrow) path of constant progress [*Fortschritt*] from the bad to the better."[25]

It is in the context of this problem, which is laid out in the first half of his essay on "A Renewed Question," that the figure of the newspaper reader will make its appearance. The introduction of this figure is, not by chance, staged in a passage of the text that is concerned with the encounter with a historical occurrence that is referred to by Kant simply as the "event of our time" (*Begebenheit unserer Zeit*): the French Revolution.[26] In an unexpected move, however, the essay does not concern itself with the event of the Revolution itself to substantiate the hypothesis that history is continually advancing toward the better. Instead, it turns to its "spectators" (*Zuschauer*) who do not directly participate in this event but see it taking place from a distance: spectators whose model is certainly not found in the onlookers of the events in the streets of Paris but rather in the newspaper readers who, from across the Rhine, witness the unfolding of a spectacle without personal or partisan self-interest and allow their partiality to "betray itself in the open" (*sich öffentlich verrat*).[27] If the display of this affective participation with the Revolution demonstrates that there are grounds to expect a moral tendency in the human *Geschlecht*, this is because the "mode of thinking" (*Denkungsart*) that allows this participation to betray itself must belong to a "moral disposition" (*moralische Anlage*):

> The revolution of a gifted people which we have seen going on in our
> day may succeed or founder; it may be filled with misery and atrocities
> to the point that a sensible human being, were he boldly to hope to
> execute it successfully the second time, would never resolve to make
> the experiment at such cost—this revolution, I say, nevertheless finds in
> the minds of all spectators [*den Gemüter aller Zuschauer*]—who are not
> implicated in the game [*Spiel*] themselves—a wishful *participation*
> [*Teilnehmung*] that borders closely on enthusiasm [*die Nahe an
> Enthusiasmus grenzt*], the very expression of which is fraught with
> danger; this participation, therefore, can have no other cause than a
> moral predisposition in humankind.[28]

Not the revolution itself, but the participation that this event finds in the *Gemüter* of its spectators thus intimates the moral disposition in which Kant will find the ground for the slow but uninterrupted progress of humankind toward its moral destination. The name that Kant reserves for this participation is "enthusiasm"—a state of the *Gemüt* that is here initially described as a "wishful participation" (*Teilnehmung dem Wunsche nach*). If enthusiasm is an affective participation "after the wish," this wish is not to be mistaken for an empirical desire; it must rather be understood in the precise sense in which Kant had conceived of the wish in *Religion*, the book that he had finished right before his reflection on the revolution. In the third chapter of the book, Kant had identified the idea of the kingdom of God with the highest good as the final goal of practical and theoretical reason—and as in the case of Hegel, the relation of reason to its supreme end is here associated with a prayer: "The wish of all the well-disposed is thus: 'that the kingdom of God come, that his will be done on earth [*auf Erden geschehe*]'; but what preparations must they make in order that this wish come to pass among them [*mit ihnen geschehe*]?"[29] This conception of the wish informs Kant's account of enthusiasm, of which he writes in the essay that it is "directed only toward what is ideal and indeed purely moral."[30] Enthusiasm begins as a "wishful participation" but cannot be reduced to it; for Kant, it designates that state of the *Gemüt* in which the realization of this pure, moral ideal in the empirical world is not only wished for but held to be possible. That the spectators who witness this event unfolding without being implicated in it express their "sympathy with the players on one side [*Teilnehmung der Spielenden auf einer Seite*] against those on the other" is at first the expression of a mere wish: the as yet unfounded desire that the "play of great transformations" (*Spiel großer Umwandlungen*) is not the *Possenspiel* evoked in the first half of the essay but a progression of humankind toward its moral destination.[31] Yet it is exactly the expression of this unfounded wish by the spectators of the French Revolution that, in Kant's reading, turns out to provide the ground for the expectation of its realization. Insofar as this wishful participation is "universal," felt without exception by every human being; insofar as it is "unselfish" (*uneigennützig*); and, most importantly, insofar as the spectators of the revolution even endanger themselves in expressing this feeling, it will turn out not to be a mere wish at all. For if this wishful participation is an incentive that is in itself sufficient to determine the power of choice, if it can outweigh even the natural disposition toward self-preservation, its universal expression points not only to a moral "constitution" (*Beschaffenheit*) but also to the "capacity" (*Vermögen*) of humanity to reach it.[32] The wishful reader who encounters the universal, dangerous expression of this wish on the pages of the newspaper thus discovers that there is reason to expect that humankind is capable of reaching its destination. The feeling of enthusiasm is the medium of this discovery; it is the initially groundless wish for the realization of the moral idea that, by its sheer force, provides the ground to expect its real-ization and opens up the possibility for the individual to contribute to the progression of humankind toward its final goal.

But even though Kant's account of this "wishful participation" with the French Revolution is unmistakably modeled on a newspaper reader, the im-agery he employs in the essay derives almost without exception from the sphere of the theatre: the relevant passage does not speak of readers, but draws on a vocabulary of spectators and actors, of the stage and the play, of the unfolding of history as a *Spiel* of great revolutions. Through this imagery, the essay, how-ever, alludes to a quite different mode of experience—an experience of reading and writing captured in the images of newspaper readers feverishly devour-ing the latest news, of reporters and journalists frantically scribbling down commentaries, of rumor and gossip reverberating within the crowd.[33] In earlier drafts of the "Renewed Question," the figure of the newspaper reader is still explicitly presented as the model of the spectators whose enthusiasm will provide a ground for historical progress. The participation of the "mere spectators" (*bloße Zuschauer*) with the French Revolution is here said to find its characteristic expression in a "warm desire for newspapers" (*heisse Begierde nach Zeitungen*)—newspapers whose sole purpose would be to provide the "material for the most interesting [. . .] conversations."[34] This addition is impor-tant, for it suggests that this desire for newspapers does not serve any empiri-cal interest: this *Begierde* does not stem from the reader's natural drives, nor is it merely an intellectual desire for the advancement of this reader's own in-sights. These readers desire their newspapers only as the material for the "most interesting" (*den interessantesten*) conversations—that is to say, those conver-sations that are concerned only with what Kant had referred to, in the second *Critique*, as the "supreme interest" of reason.[35] This is why Kant, in his draft for the essay of 1793, will add that even a "reasoning, enlightened" (*räsonnier-enden aufgeklärten*) being feels this desire: the *Begierde* described here does not originate in the human being qua natural being but expresses a purely ra-tional interest, which is unselfish and completely independent of anything outside of reason itself.[36] The feverish desire for news about this "game of great revolutions" turns out to be the expression of a need that emerges from a con-versation of the most interesting kind, a wish that originates from a *Räsonnie-ren* in pursuit of its supreme interest—the realization of the highest good. Not only the ragged phenomenal expression of the revolution but also the *Zeitungs-fieber* that accompanies it are thus salvaged and put to work in a history that advances toward its moral destination.

Kant had made a similar argument in that other study of a world-historical event that took place earlier in Kant's lifetime and that was, like the French

Revolution, inseparable from the endless commentary, rumor, and chatter it incited amongst its contemporaries: the Lisbon Earthquake. Like the *factum brutum* of the French Revolution, an event that is, by the time Kant discusses it in the "Renewed Question," incontrovertibly stained by the suffering and atrocities of the preceding years, the 1755 earthquake makes itself felt as a world-historical occurrence in front of which the whole conceptual apparatus supporting the belief in progress threatens to collapse. As in his later text on the Revolution, the study of the earthquake is written as a newspaper article; and also here, Kant's attempt to neutralize the brute facticity of this event is accompanied by a parallel attempt to curtail its experience—an experience that is, once again, figured in the newspaper reader. "Great occurrences that concern the fate of all human beings," so Kant begins his first article, "rightfully incite that renowned desire for novelty [*diejenige ruhmreiche Neubegierde*], which awakens in response to everything exceptional and tends to be accompanied by the question as to what caused it."[37] Not only are we presented here with the attempt to curtail the destabilizing effects of the earthquake on a certain conception of history, to purge natural catastrophe of moral significance; but the other tremor that takes place in response to it, the "inciting" or "stirring" (*Erregung*) of the "desire for novelty" is consigned to its rightful limits and secured for the purpose of methodical questioning, observation and reasoning. Like Kant's later article on the French Revolution, his earlier article on the earthquake does not merely ward off the threat posed by this *Begebenheit*—the tremor on the scene of world history and the tremor within the reader—but aims to extract opportunity from the wreckage, interpreting the experience of these occurrences as the sign of a disposition that can guarantee the consistent progression of humankind toward its supreme end.[38]

Despite its central role in the early draft, the "desire for newspapers" of the spectators of the revolution will disappear from the final, published version of the essay, together with the reference to the "most interesting conversation." In the published version, the figure of the newspaper reader unmistakably provides the central model for the key passage on the spectators and their affective participation with the "event of our time"—but all direct references to this figure have now been removed. At certain points in the text, the description of the spectators still contains traces of the mode of reading and writing on which it is modeled. When Kant speaks of the Revolution as an event unfolding "in our days" (*in unsere Tagen*), this wording bears the mark of an experience whose rhythm is dictated by the daily news; when he explains how the mode of thinking of the spectators "betrays itself *in the open*" (*sich öffentlich verrät*), this does not evoke the space of the theatre but rather that of *Öffentlichkeit*, of publishing and publicity; and when he claims that these spectators have a disposition that "lets their participation become loud" (*laut werden läßt*) the words he uses to describe this self-publishing recall the German idiom for erupting rumors—*laut werdende Gerüchte*.[39] Apart from these traces, however, the published version of the text no longer contains any explicit reference to a "warm desire for newspapers"—even if this desire had already been integrated into the Kantian system by interpreting it as a need that arises from that "most interesting conversation" by which reason sets itself its highest goal.

Even though these references have been removed, Kant has not abandoned his initial model for the "affective participation" in the French Revolution. Throughout the essay, it is clear that the description of the *bloße Zuschauer* and their encounter with the "game of great revolutions" is modeled entirely on the figure of the newspaper reader and the experience of history exemplified by it. The very possibility of the central metaphor of the theatre, the play, and the spectator is predicated precisely on this experience: only for the newspaper reader has it become possible to speak of world history as something that appears as a drama unfolding in the present; only for a newspaper reader has it become possible to relate to history not just as a game of great revolutions, but one that "can be *seen* unfolding [*vor sich gehen sehen*] in our days."[40] And only for the newspaper reader, not the onlooker in the streets of Paris, does it become possible to relate to this drama as a spectator who looks at the stage "without selfishness" and "without the least intention of assisting"—both aspects of these spectators that are crucial if their wishful participation is to be understood as a pure enthusiasm.[41] Indeed, the very distinction between *Zuschauer* and *Anschauer* rests on the assumption that these spectators are not immediately affected by the *Begebenheit*, that they do not see the event that is given to them as an object of intuition but relate to it as readers. It is only the reader immersed in the daily papers who could be portrayed as a spectator that is defined at the same time by a constitutive absence from the stage of world history and by a sense of proximity that borders on presence.[42] The figure of the newspaper reader is constantly alluded to in this vocabulary, together with the scenes of reading, writing, and conversation that accompanied it in the earlier drafts of the essay—but only indirectly, avoiding all direct reference. In doing so, the theatrical imagery employed by Kant not only evokes but also conceals a scene of reading. In the passages of the essay on the Revolution, experience is consistently transposed from the sphere of reading and writing to the sphere of seeing and thinking. The reader turns into a *Zuschauer*; the event is seen rather than read about, construed as an "event before the eye" (*Eräugnen*) rather than an encounter with a text, while the participation (*Teilnehmung*) of the spectators takes the place of an imparting (*Mitteilung*). The newspaper reader is transformed into a figure that conforms to the abstract concept of an enlightened *Leserwelt* that had made its appearance earlier in Kant's writings.[43] The literal reading that is captured in the early draft of the essay as an "impatient, warm desire for newspapers" is idealized and abstracted to the point where it becomes almost indistinguishable from seeing, just as the movement of the "most interesting conversation" that gave rise to this desire is turned into an inner movement of thought.

This transformation of the figure of the newspaper reader and the removal of direct references to reading, writing, and conversation from the published version of the essay is striking—especially because Kant certainly understood *Zeitungen* and *Zeitschriften* to be the exemplary site of his own experience of the "great game of revolutions" unfolding in his time. In a letter to Fichte, written in the year in which the *Conflict of the Faculties* was prepared for publication, Kant portrays himself as a thinker whose communication with the world only becomes possible through the *Blätter* delivered on a daily basis to his study. "For the last year and a half, my poor health and frailties of age have forced me to give up all my lecturing. Now and then I still send news of my existence [*gebe ich Nachricht von meiner Existenz*] through the channel of the *Berliner Monatsschrift* and recently also through the *Berliner Blätter*, which I do as a means of preservation, agitating the little life force I have left."[44] But despite the awareness that both the news of the *Begebenheiten* of the world and the news that is issued by Kant himself depend on *Schrifte* and *Blätter*, all direct references to reading, writing, and conversation are actively kept out of the essay on progress that will finally be published in that same year. The same question that was asked about the absence of the scene of *Zeitungslesen* from Hegel's systematic writings thus arises with regards to its concealment in Kant's reflections on history. Is there something about the figure of the newspaper reader that threatens to undermine the attempt to find the grounds for a conception of history that progresses consistently toward its destination? What made it necessary for Kant to purge the experience of history exemplified by this figure from its linguistic dimension—to turn a reader into a spectator and conversation into mode of thought?

A provisional response to these questions can be found in a text that Kant wrote between the early drafts of his essay on progress and its publication several years later: the *Anthropology*—and in particular the theory of "conversation" (*Unterredung*) that is found in the concluding sections to its first part. Here, at a safe remove from world-historical questions, Kant will allow himself an analysis of the movement of dinner-table conversations that spiral around the occurrences of the day. Any such conversation has its natural point of departure in the "novelties of the day" (*die Neuigkeiten des Tages*)—novelties that are "first domestic, then from elsewhere, having flowed in through private letters and newspapers."[45] The conversation around such novelties follows three stages: those of "narration" (*Erzählung*), "reasoning" (*Räsonnieren*), and "jest" (*Schertz*).[46] Nothing could be more different from the slow but uninterrupted progress toward the supreme end of reason that is described in the "Renewed Question" than the movement of *Unterredung*: a movement in which reason elevates itself from the empirical world only to prepare its ineluctable lapse into jest. "The conversation," Kant writes, "naturally falls down into the mere play of wit [*das bloße Spiel des Witzes*]."[47] Not the constancy of advancement toward a final goal but the fateful lapse into jest describes the dramatic movement of *Unterredung*: a lapse that Kant, in the *Critique of Judgment*, presents precisely as an unforeseen fall into nothingness, a "sudden transformation of a suspenseful expectation into nothing [*einer gespannten Erwartung in nichts*]."[48] What corresponds to this nothingness is the collapse, in the "news of the day," of all distinctions between the important and the trivial, the great and the small. In the *Neuigkeiten des Tages*, world-historical occurrences here enter into the fabric of *Alltag* and become virtually indistinguishable from it; conversations about the "revolution of a gifted people" exist in seamless continuity with those about the most mundane occurrences and ultimately, as Kant writes, the most elementary form of news—bad weather. Weather talk is, as Kant points out on various occasions in the *Anthropology*, the beginning and the end of all *Unterredung*.[49]

Perhaps Kant's reluctance to introduce the figure of the newspaper reader into his historico-philosophical reflections of the 1790s may be understood in connection to these passages from the *Anthropology*, which stem from the same years as his essay on the "renewed question" as to whether humanity can hope for a constant progress toward its moral destination. The substitution of a scene of reading and writing with one of seeing and thinking in Kant's account of the "participation" in the French Revolution might derive from the suspicion that there is something about the linguistic character of this experience that undermines his attempts to find a secure ground for the expectation of progress. Perhaps Kant realized that the *Mitteilung* of the "game of great revolutions" does not just provide the condition of possibility for the *Teilnahme*, which will, in turn, provide the ground for a steady progression toward the supreme end of practical and theoretical reason; perhaps he sensed that the same *Mitteilung* which renders this participation possible also harbors an element that undermines the teleological conception of history that it is supposed to sustain. As the theory of *Unterredung* in the *Anthropology* suggests, Kant's removal of the references to the "warm desire" for newspapers and conversation may be no accident; instead, it might point to the suspicion that there is something about the linguistic dimension of reason that never ceases to threaten its as-

cension to lofty heights with a lapse into jest. Maybe the disappearance of the
figure of the newspaper reader from Hegel's work may be understood in this
light. As in the case of Kant, Hegel initially invests this figure with a central significance in his philosophy of history: even if the scene of reading the newspaper conjured up in the Jena notebooks no longer discloses history as the realm
in which an ultimately unreachable idea is constantly approached, but rather
exemplifies the discovery that history is nothing but the rational development
of the real toward its immanent telos—a development that is completed only in
its full comprehension. And as in the case of Kant, Hegel will omit the scene
of newspaper reading from his systematic writings after it has made an appearance in his notebooks. Is this disappearance perhaps driven by the same
suspicion that Kant had articulated in his later writings—the suspicion that
there is something about this scene and its irreducible linguistic dimension that
threatens to ridicule the same teleological conception of history that it ought
to exemplify? What happens to the unfolding of spirit in time when it turns
out to be nothing but the unfolding of the newspaper?

   "The *newspaper reading* of the early morning"—this book will examine how
the topos that is here emphatically introduced into the sphere of philosophy
will resurface in the work of three thinkers who, each in his own way, may be
understood to write "after" Hegel: Kierkegaard, Nietzsche, and Benjamin. The
writings of each of these three thinkers are punctuated by images of messengers, reporters, and newspaper readers, scenes of announcements and proclamations, reflections on rumor, chatter, and the talk of the day—but the significance
of these dispersed remarks and passages has nevertheless remained largely overlooked or misunderstood.[50] My study of these images will start from a simple
premise: that the recurrent concern with journalism of these three thinkers
can be neither separated from their philosophy "proper" nor treated as a sup-
plementary application or extension. Quite the contrary: as I will attempt to
show, the critical engagement with journalism plays a pivotal role in their
philosophical work, in particular their reflections on history, time, and language. Examining this role will require a particular mode of reading: one
that understands philosophical thought to unfold not merely in concepts and
propositions but just as much in a language of figures, types, images, and
scenes. This figural language would have to be understood not as an "illustration" of thoughts that have already been formulated, nor as a device used to
communicate them more effectively. A philosophical reading of the images
of journalists and newspaper readers scattered through the work of Kierkegaard, Nietzsche, and Benjamin would attempt to grasp how their thought is
first articulated in and through these images. Such a reading would have to show
how these images, even where they are ostensibly presented as illustrations, may

exceed and outdo the concepts of which they are never mere applications or appendices.

The special significance of journalism within Kierkegaard, Nietzsche, and Benjamin's philosophical reflections on history hinges on its exemplary status. Journalism is treated here as the expression of an experience of time and history that each of these thinkers will take to be characteristic of the time in which they are writing. In different ways, all three will examine the newspaper as a form in which the *Geschichtsbetrachtung* and *Geschichtsauffassung* of their time, its mode of perceiving and comprehending history, become available for inspection and susceptible to philosophical scrutiny. "To seize the essence of history," Benjamin writes in a hyperbolic proposition that will provide a starting point for the final chapter of the present study, "it suffices to compare Herodotus and the morning newspaper."[51] All the characteristic features of modern historical experience, everything in and through which this experience would differentiate itself from its ancient counterpart, figured by Herodotus, are here taken to be concentrated in the form of the newspaper. And just as the figure of Herodotus marks a limit point—that of the most ancient, "first" historian—so the *Morgenzeitung* appears here as a sheet of paper at the other extreme of history, at the end of the modern age of which it brings the news. It is this special status of the newspaper, the journalistic form par excellence, that points to the pivotal role journalism would have to play in any philosophical inquiry into the conditions and possibilities of historical experience. Any attempt to grasp how historical experience is constituted today—and *geschichtliche Erfahrung* is meant here not only as the experience of history but also, in a stricter sense, as that experience in and through which history first becomes possible[52]—would require a study of journalism: a study of its characteristic sense of space and time, its concepts and tropes, its modes of reading and writing, its subjective types and figures.

If journalism may be taken to exemplify the time in which Kierkegaard, Nietzsche, and Benjamin understand themselves to be writing, it does so by presenting this as a time marked by the crisis of the philosophy of history. In different ways, each of these three thinkers grasp the pages of the newspaper as a place where all teleological and totalizing representations of history are destined to founder, together with the conceptions of progress and development that sustain them. The figures of the journalist and newspaper reader appear in their writings as representatives of progress and perfection, of approximation and development, of the overcoming of the old and the dawn of the new—but the history of which they bring the news will invariably amount to stories of stalled conversations, of permanent confusion and restless inertia, of unreliable accounts and disputed facts, of fateful progression and endless deferral. As the following chapters will show, the announcement of the new tends to lapse here into a repetition of what has already been; and it is precisely the *Morgenzeitung*—the sheet of paper that was supposed to bring the news of a history of constant progress or continuous development—that becomes a stage where history fails to take place at all. The study of journalism and its characteristic experience of history is thus, for Kierkegaard, Nietzsche, and Benjamin alike, tied together with the critique of the conceptions of history of which the journalist and newspaper reader act as the unreliable representatives. But if the pages of the newspaper are treated here as a stage where history as a philosophizable concept reaches its end, this end will turn out to remain inconclusive. In journalism, the philosophy of history continues to lead a life after its own demise—a life that Kierkegaard describes as that of an "inanimate body which still performs the usual functions."[53]

The study of journalism is, however, not only interwoven with the critique of the philosophy of history and the scrutiny of its inconclusive demise; for Kierkegaard, Nietzsche and Benjamin alike, it also plays a crucial role in their attempts to think time and history in its wake. The reflections on journalistic writing and newspaper reading are, in each case, bound up with a radical rearticulation of historical experience: its form, structure, and conditions of possibility. What is at stake in these reflections is, first of all, the attempt to articulate an experience of history that is no longer governed by the teleological and totalizing schemes underpinning the modern representations of history—a mode of perceiving and comprehending history that breaks decisively with notions of progress and development. Articulating this experience of history, however, implies and presupposes another task—namely, to rethink the historical character of experience itself: to ask how it is that the domain of history and its distinct configuration of time, rather than appearing as a simple given, first open up out of the structure of experience.[54] Thinking the historicity of experience in this stricter sense revolves around the question of how every experience is structurally exposed to another as yet impossible experience—a non-conceptual and imperceptible other that refers all given history to a wholly differently structured future. Journalism plays a double role in Kierkegaard, Nietzsche, and Benjamin's renewed engagement with this question. The experience of history of which the journalist and newspaper reader are the emblematic figures is, on the one hand, the most "improperly temporal" (*uneigentlich zeitlich*), to borrow an expression from Benjamin.[55] For all three thinkers, it is here that the ahistorical tendencies of the modern conception of history are pushed to an extreme, that experience congeals into rigid forms, history turns into an endless succession of facts, and its time is reduced to an unbroken homogeneous continuum. And yet it is, nevertheless, also in journalism that the elements for another experience of time and history must be sought—one that breaks down the generality of forms of experience and interrupts the homogeneity of the temporal continuum. If journalism will occupy a special place in this search, this is first of all because language plays a decisive role in the constitution of the experience of history it exemplifies.

To treat journalism as an emblem of the experience of time and history characteristic of the "present age"—Kierkegaard's expression—means to grasp this experience as one constituted in language. The experience captured in the figures of the journalist and the newspaper reader is not so much communicated by means of language but, rather, an experience that first comes into being in language. In the modes of writing and reading exemplified by these figures, the apparent immediacy of the here and now—the sense that the newspaper reader can see world history unfolding in the present—is inseparable from its linguistic mediation; the Kantian a priori appears here as if it were a fact of language.[56] This is implicit in Kierkegaard, Nietzsche, and Benjamin's references to the newspaper as a "form of communication" (*Form der Mitteilung*), an expression that appears in different variations in the work of all three thinkers;[57] yet it is Karl Kraus, the Austrian writer whose critique of journalism is central to the chapter on Benjamin, who formulated this thought in unsurpassed hyperbole in his claim that "time and space have become forms of cognition of the journalistic subject [*Erkenntnisformen des journalistischen Subjekts*]."[58] Indeed, tracing the reflections on journalism through the writings of the three thinkers under consideration here points to the key role language plays in their attempt to recast the concepts of experience inherited from German Idealism and to rearticulate the relation between experience and history. In different ways, each of the three will undertake what Benjamin calls a "philology of the newspapers" (*Philologie der Journale*): a meticulous scrutiny of the language of journalism that starts from the assumption that the experience of history characteristic of their own time is condensed in the forms of the fact and the rumor, the report and the phrase, the announcement and the warning, opinion and chatter.[59] These philological studies take on a special significance in the context of their respective analyses of the crisis of the philosophy of history. For Kierkegaard, Nietzsche, and Benjamin alike, it is precisely in the pages of the newspaper that a dimension of language persistently manifests itself, which refuses the mastery of a rational subject and fails to obey the immanent movement of the concept. But the *Philologie der Journale* does not stop at recovering an aspect of language that interrupts the movement of gradual progress and continuous development; for each of these three thinkers, the language of journalism, together with its characteristic modes of reading and writing, will also furnish the models for their attempts to think time and history differently. *Zeitungslesen* and *Zeitungsschreiben* appear here as the models for a different conception of historical time: one in which time does not precede experience as an empty form but is produced in and as the moment of reading and writing.

The experience of history that is exemplified by the writing of the journalist and the reading of the newspaper does, indeed, not only have an emphatically linguistic character but also is characterized by a distinct temporal structure. As the following chapters will show, the recurrent engagement with the theme of journalism in the work of Kierkegaard, Nietzsche, and Benjamin is closely related to their respective attempts to think time within and against the modern philosophical tradition, in particular what may be described as its tendency to prioritize the present in its thinking of historical time.[60] In different ways, each of the three thinkers discussed here call into question conceptions of time as a homogeneous continuum in which past and future are reduced to different modalities of the present. What Kant and Hegel are here accused of sharing with one another—despite their obvious differences as well as the tensions within their work—is the failure to rid themselves from a conception of time as just such a continuum, where the past is thought as a present that has already passed and the future as a present that is yet to come. Such a conception of time may be used to describe the time of mechanical change, but as Kierkegaard, Nietzsche, and Benjamin will each point out in different ways, it is not the time of history. In their critique of traditional conceptions of time, journalism plays a double role. On the one hand, the newspaper is understood as a hyperbolic example of the imposition of the time of mechanical change onto history: on the pages of the newspaper, the time of history is represented as an inexorable succession of dates, reported one after another, ordered in a homogeneous continuum. On the other hand, the figures of the newspaper reader and the journalist harbor the germs of a different conception of time, one in which time is no longer thought as a homogeneous continuum but, rather, as a configuration of different times in a "now" that can no longer be thought as a point on a line. The attempt to think this "now" is at the heart of the concepts that will provide the focal point for the three chapters that make up this book: Kierkegaard's "instant" (*det Øieblik*), Nietzsche's "untimeliness" (*das Unzeitgemässe*), and Benjamin's "actuality" (*Aktualität*). The significance of the figure of journalism in the work of each of these thinkers can be grasped only in relation to these concepts, just as any exposition of these concepts must be accompanied by an interpretation of this figure. As we will see, these three concepts play a crucial role in the attempts of Kierkegaard, Nietzsche, and Benjamin to rethink how the time of history is constituted; but they are also central to their respective endeavors to rethink philosophical thought itself. The "instant," the "untimely," the "actual": each of these concepts marks a renewed attempt to conceive of philosophy in terms of a singular relation between thought and its time. As such, these three concepts may be understood as distinct attempts to radicalize and recast the proposition advanced by Hegel: the proposition that philosophy is "its time, apprehended in thoughts" (*ihre Zeit in Gedanken erfaßt*).[61]

1

Talking Machines
Kierkegaard

Nothing, nothing at all happens without passing through the
journalist.
— KIERKEGAARD, *WRITING SAMPLER,* SAMPLE NO. 9

Hegel begins his *Lectures on the Philosophy of History* with the presentation
of three figures, juxtaposed and arranged in successive order: the chronicler,
the historian, and the philosopher of history.[1] These figures not only capture
three specific modes of historical experience—Hegel speaks of them as
the three most basic "ways of observing history" (*Arten der Geschichte zu
betrachten*)—but also mark the three distinct moments toward its full comprehension. While the chronicler—who is, like the historian and philosopher,
rendered by Hegel as a male figure—restricts his attention to the particular
occurrence when writing the "original history" of an age to which he immediately belongs, the historian attempts to write a history as a whole, reflecting
on the historical life of epochs that are not his own; the philosopher of history, finally, marks the sublation of both modes of observation into the full
comprehension of world history, history in its totality, as the progressive development of the concept. "The only thought that philosophy brings with it,"
Hegel proposes in the introduction to the lectures, "is the simple thought of
reason, that reason governs the world, that also world history has taken its
course rationally [*daß es also auch in der Weltgeschichte vernünftig zugegan-
gen sei*]."[2] Under the thoughtful gaze of the philosopher, world history shows
itself to be nothing but a "stage" (*ein Schauplatz*) for the progressive unfolding of the *logos*.[3]

To the three *dramatis personae* that together summarize Hegel's account of the comprehension of history, Kierkegaard counterposes another figure: the journalist. The significance of this figure, grasped in its relation to the Hegelian philosophy of history, will be the focal point of this chapter. If the journalist is understood here as an addition to a cast of characters that seems complete in itself, a sequential staging of three figures that seems to have already arrived at a conclusion, this is because Kierkegaard will reserve a specific role for this figure: namely, to enact a parody of the idea of history that finds its culmination in Hegel's philosopher of history. On the pages of the newspaper—and this is the thought that will be elaborated in the following examination of Kierkegaard's preoccupation with journalism—every conception of history as a progressive movement toward an immanent end must turn into a *parody of itself*. For Kierkegaard, journalism will mark the dissolution of history conceived as a logical development of the concept and mock the categories on which it rests—not least that of the *logos* itself, which will lead a strange afterlife in the language of the newspapers. But this parodic repetition of the Hegelian philosophy not only enacts a comic conclusion but also, as we will see, provides the starting point for Kierkegaard's attempts to articulate his own conception of historical time and experience.[4]

To approach Kierkegaard's engagement with journalism in this way—that is to say, to understand the journalist as a figure with a special significance in the context of the critique of "philosophy" insofar as it is supposed to have come to a culmination in the Hegelian system—means to diverge from the standard interpretations of the theme and its position within his corpus. Even though the continued importance of the theme for Kierkegaard has often been noted, most commentators tend to interpret this interest in narrowly biographical terms—a tendency that does not come as a surprise if one takes into account the reception of his writings, which has been consistently burdened by an obsession with the empirical facts of his life.[5] In the rare cases where the theme is seriously addressed, it tends to be overshadowed by its relation to the *Corsair* affair of the mid-1840s, Kierkegaard's polemic against the local press that emerged out of a confrontation with a satirical newspaper. Consequently, the countless hyperbolic attacks on journalists scattered throughout the journals and published writings of those years—a hyperbole that is perhaps best exemplified by Kierkegaard's later remark that "the 'journalist' is the epitome of the deepest apostasy of humankind [*Slægtens*] from God"[6]—are often mistaken for the mere expression of a personal feud with a local newspaper. In its emphasis on empirical facts, the biographical reading of Kierkegaard's polemical portrayals of journalists is the pendant of an equally reductive historicist reading, which mistakes the significance of his interest in journalism for a commentary on the political life of Copenhagen in the early nineteenth century.[7] There is, indeed, no doubt that the medium of Kierkegaard's thought is experience—albeit not of the empiricist or positivist kind—and that it is determined to think only what had become concretized in it. But any reading of his work that would overlook how this experience is transfigured or, to use Kierkegaard's own term, "transubstantiated" (*Erfaringens Transsubstantiation*) in thought and writing would miss the philosophical significance of his ongoing preoccupation with journalism.[8]

Rather than being constructed through empirical procedures, the journalists, editors, reporters, and "absolute trumpeters" of historical progress that populate Kierkegaard's writings are perhaps closer to the *Gestalten*, the shapes or figures of consciousness that play a crucial role throughout Hegel's philosophical work, especially in the dramatic play of personae staged in *The Phenomenology of Spirit*. Like the *Gestalten* called to the stage here, Kierkegaard's figures are no mere illustrations, but a necessary moment in the presentation of thought—a manifestation without which thought would have nothing to think.[9] They hover between the sensible and the ideal, the abstract and the concrete, the individual and the generic—but always in a more hyperbolic manner than their Hegelian counterpart. Kierkegaard constructs his cast of characters out of historical material that seems most trivial and contingent, least worthy of the idealizations of philosophy: he derives his personae from local newspaper articles rather than great novels, from small-town gossip rather than the canon of philosophical thought. In doing so, these figures exaggerate the dramaturgical elements that remain largely implicit in their Hegelian counterpart: the *dramatis personae* in his writings—and the journalist may serve here as their exemplary protagonist—will consistently enter his work as actors on a stage, overtly performing their work of personification and presentation. In this exaggerated form, however, Kierkegaard's figures unmistakably begin to resist the classical rhetorical determination of figuration that still dominates Hegel's *Gestalten*.[10] If the latter are ultimately reduced to the status of representation, separated from and subordinated to the presentation of the concept, the figures in Kierkegaard's work always seem to resist their designated function as well as the economy of externalization and return that depends on it.[11] Whether it is the hyperbolically portrayed journalists or the personifications of abstract concepts that are followed through *ad absurdum*, there is a sense in which these figures are always at the point of tearing themselves loose from the explicit, literal meaning that they are supposedly meant to convey and, instead, lead a life of their own.

In this impulse to lead a life of their own, Kierkegaard's figures anticipate the reflections on language and history that will be elaborated in the texts that

provide the main focus of this chapter: the "early writings," all produced before the commencement of Kierkegaard's self-proclaimed "activity as a writer"
(*Forfatter-Virksomhed*).[12] The theme of journalism plays an important role in
these texts, especially in the three newspaper articles of 1836 in which Kierkegaard engaged in a series of attacks on journalists and newspaper editors of his
time and the unfinished draft for another important unpublished polemical
article that was written in the same year. Apart from these articles, which will
be central to the first part of this chapter, this theme also appears in a number
of other texts from the same period, ranging from the unfinished comic drama
The Comprehensive Debate Between Everything and Everything to the notebooks Kierkegaard began to keep in those years and would later refer to as his
"journals" (*Journaler*) and his first longer published text, the book review *From
the Papers of One Still Living* of 1838.[13] In each of these texts, which have still
hardly received serious consideration,[14] the theme of journalism surfaces in
the context of an ongoing polemic against his time—or what Kierkegaard will
later call "the age" (*Tiden*)—that takes reporters, feuilletonists, editors, newspaper articles, phrases, and headlines as its privileged target. That none of these
texts are included in the "writerly activity" proper, as it was strictly defined and
delineated by Kierkegaard in his later writings, is not surprising if one appre-
ciates that the boundaries of this activity are intimately connected with the
form of the book. Whenever the theme of journalism resurfaces in Kierkegaard's later writings, this will happen in texts that cannot be reduced to the
book form, or exist in its margins, ranging from his countless prefaces, his book
review *Two Ages* and the brief essay "The Present Age" (*Nytiden*) lodged into
it, and his unpublished *Writing Sampler,* whose pseudonymous author is the
journalist A. B. C. D. E. F. Rosenblad, to the broadsheet that Kierkegaard published in the last years of his life and which will be the focus of the second
part of this chapter: *The Instant*.[15] That the theme of journalism consistently
makes an appearance in these writings is no coincidence: for there is a sense
in which all of these writings can be said to have an eminently journalistic
character in and of themselves.

This journalistic character is especially clear in the case of Kierkegaard's
early writings, which can be read as a work of journalism even when they are
not written with a view to being published in newspapers or circulated as
ephemera. Whether they take the form of a newspaper polemic, a comic play
or a philosophical reflection, all of these texts are written in response to an
"occasion" (*Anledning*) that is, without exception, provided by the occurrences
of the day. Just as the pages of the diary are for Kierkegaard a place where
thoughts can "emerge with the umbilical cord of their first mood intact," so
the philosophical elements of the polemical articles appear together with the

invariably ephemeral and fleeting occasion that prompted them.[16] This particular relation to the "occasion" characterizes Kierkegaard's newspaper articles as much as his unfinished comic drama, the extensive unpublished fragments in his diaries as much as his book review of 1838. Not only are these texts permeated by the short-lived novelties, current events, recently published texts or the latest gossip that occasioned them; they are also conceived as interventions into the talk of the day—that peculiar amalgam of chatter, gossip and rumor that, for Kierkegaard, was exemplified by the newspaper. If Kierkegaard's early writings seem to have grown old in a way that others have not, if they seem more distant to us than his books, this is probably due to this distinctive journalistic character and their intimate relation to the moment in which they are written. In order to grasp the peculiar topicality of these texts today, it would be necessary to unpack how these texts spring from the occurrences of the day without, however, ever being reducible to their occasion. This would require us not only to trace Kierkegaard's consistent attempts to weave philosophical reflections into these occasional writings, in particular an early critique of the philosophy of history, but also to examine how this journalistic writing may be read as a historico-philosophical work after the philosophy of history—a work that emerges out of the attempt to capture an experience of language and history that Kierkegaard thought to be specific to "the age."

Morning Observations

On February 18, 1836, the twenty-two-year-old Kierkegaard publishes a short article in a local paper, the *Flying Mail of Copenhagen*, by the title "Morning Observations in the *Copenhagen Mail*, No. 34."[17] The article presents itself as a response to a text that had recently been published by Orla Lehmann, a newspaper editor, as the concluding piece in a series of articles making "the case for freedom of the press" in his own *Kjøbenhavnsposten*, one of the prominent liberal voices among the many newspapers, journals, periodicals, and pamphlets proliferating in Copenhagen in the beginning of the nineteenth century.[18] Lehmann's piece interpreted this proliferation of "journalistic literature" as a manifestation of the "progressive spirit" that had come to light at the end of the previous century and defends the press against the accusations it suffers from various sides, especially those trivial complaints about "a word that one finds not entirely felicitous."[19] But Kierkegaard's "Morning Observations," like the two other pieces that will follow on it in the coming months, does not engage with the arguments employed in the text to which it responds—at least not in a straightforward or direct sense—nor does it endeavor to take a position in the context of the debate to which Lehmann's article had made the latest contribution.[20] What is at stake here is, as will become clear, not a contribution to a debate at all, not the weighing of arguments or expounding of viewpoints, but rather the performance of a reading and a misreading that shows how every "conversation"—and with it every concept of history that puts its trust in its progressive movement—is inevitably exposed to its own impossibility.

With this in mind, it is only fitting that the occasion that prompts the "Morning Observations" is not an argument or a proposition that its author attempts to counter but, as its title suggests, a familiar historico-philosophical trope that appeared in the newspaper article under consideration: the announcement of the new day. In characteristic hyperbole, the whole conceit of Kierkegaard's article and the protracted polemic that it will unleash revolves around three words that are lifted from his opponent's observations on the age and cited as evidence in a footnote: "it is dawn" (*det er Morgendæmring*).[21] That Kierkegaard lifts exactly these words from the article under consideration is no accident, for the announcement of the new *day* evokes not only a specific historico-philosophical trope but also binds it to the figure of the journalist, here instantiated by a contemporary newspaper editor. "These people call themselves after the day: *jour*nalists," Kierkegaard will write in a later note.[22] If journalism, for Kierkegaard, designates all writing that has its proper place in the myriad of papers, pamphlets, and other ephemera circulating at the time—the broad sense in which the term was also used by its contemporaries— it does so because it names a specific relation between this writing and the *jour*, the day.[23] But if journalism is that writing defined by its relation to the *jour*, the title of the "Morning Observations" presents this day after which journalism "calls itself" in a specific way: as a day that is not yet present, a day that is about to begin. If the proposition *det er Morgendæmring* may be taken to exemplify the writing of the journalist, if this writing can be characterized in summary form as a *Morgenbetragtning*, a morning observation, then this is because all journalism is a writing at dawn, at the break of day—a writing that exists between a day that has already passed and a day that is yet to begin. Only this exemplary status could legitimize the excessive importance that Kierkegaard attaches to the declaration "it is dawn" that is lodged into an insignificant newspaper article; only the fact that every journalistic observation is a morning observation could give the title of the article its full significance.

But this relation to dawn does not just characterize the writing of the journalist; it also places this figure in a special relation to the philosopher of history. Journalism manifests itself most clearly as a repetition of the philosophy of history exactly where its thinking and writing shows itself to be a thinking and writing that is caught between two days, a "morning observation" oriented toward a day that is yet to begin. The occurrence of the minimal proposition "it is dawn" can provide the occasion for Kierkegaard's "Morning Observations" precisely because it recalls another declaration at daybreak—a declaration whose most famous iteration is found in a dense paragraph in the preface to Hegel's *Phenomenology of Spirit*, a paragraph that twists and turns through various metaphors in order to culminate in the image of sunrise (*Aufgang*):

> It is not difficult to see that our time is a time of birth and of transition into a new period [*eine Zeit der Geburt und des Übergangs zu einer neuen Periode*]. Spirit has now broken with the world that it has hitherto existed in and represented [*der bisherigen Welt seines Daseins und Vorstellens gebrochen*] and stands at the point to submerge it into the past. Indeed, spirit is never at rest but is to be grasped in an always progressive movement [*in immer fortschreitender Bewegung*]. But just as the first breath drawn by a child after its long, quiet nourishment breaks the gradualness of merely quantitative progression—a qualitative leap—and the child is now born, so the spirit in its formation matures slowly and quietly into its new shape, dissolving bit by bit the structure of its previous world, whose tottering state is only indicated by isolated symptoms: the frivolity and boredom which unsettle the existing, the indeterminate presentiment of something unknown [*die unbestimmte Ahnung eines Unbekannten*] are the heralds that something other is approaching. This gradual crumbling, that does not alter the physiognomy of the whole, is interrupted by a sunrise [*wird durch den Aufgang unterbrochen*] which, in a flash, puts in place the form of the new world [*das Gebilde der neuen Welt hinstellt*].[24]

The image of sunrise marks the conclusion of this dense passage at the same time as it returns to its beginning. The *Aufgang* that is proclaimed in the last sentence of the paragraph recalls the *Übergang* of its first sentence: it is presented both as the end and as the completion of the "time of transition," which had been announced only shortly before. This "time of transition" is introduced at a specific moment, namely the moment in which Hegel attempts to characterize the time in which this preface is written. What is evoked here is not merely a formal notion of time—the conception of time as the "existent concept" that is introduced earlier in the preface[25]—but a time that is empirically and historically determined: what Hegel describes here as "our time" (*unsere Zeit*).[26] Insofar as it is conceived as a time of transition, this time has little to do with an "age" in the familiar sense of the word; if Hegel's descriptions of this time deserve to be called "morning observations" this is because they recall the time of dawn, a time caught between two days or ages—one that has already passed and one that has yet to begin. Spirit has already broken away from the world of its *Dasein* and the world of its *Vorstellen*, from itself insofar as it has come to know itself and from the object of its knowledge; but despite this dissociation from a world that is now at the point of being determined as the past, the "form of the new world" has not yet emerged.[27] Spirit may have already dissociated itself from the old, but the new world has yet to break forth. But even though this new world is described emphatically as an "unknown," and even though its entrance is portrayed as a "leap" and an "interruption," the image of *Aufgang* suggests that the transition of spirit and the world that it is about to discover are far from indeterminate. As a repetition and completion of the *Übergang* that is declared at the start of the paragraph, the *Aufgang* refers to not only the image of sunrise but the rise of spirit itself; this *Aufgang* in which the transition finds its end and completion evokes to elevation of the *Aufhebung*, to the ascension of spirit to a higher state. But the sublation that is captured here in the image of sunrise has a more specific historical determination: for what is announced in this preface, which follows the fiction of every foreword by positioning itself before the text that has already been written, is nothing but the elevation of spirit toward its ultimate and final goal, the sublation par excellence, namely the *Aufgang* of spirit to the state of complete and total illumination for which Hegel reserves the name "absolute knowledge." Hegel's morning observations do not just capture the time of historical transition in the general sense, a time of transition that could serve as the paradigm of the time of history itself; they also describe the specific transition by which spirit comes into its own and its history is concluded.[28] Not only does the transition announced here proceed according to an already given schema; also the outcome toward which it is directed—an outcome that is described only a sentence before as "an unknown" of which only a "vague foreboding" can be sensed—has already been comprehended by the philosopher at the time of its announcement. When the sunrise is declared in the final sentence, it is declared with absolute certainty, in the present tense, as if it had already happened.

Only when it is read against the background of this announcement does it become clear why Kierkegaard has the anonymous author of his "Morning Observations" attribute such significance to his encounter with the apparently innocuous declaration "it is dawn" in a local newspaper.[29] Kierkegaard takes the recurrent appearance of this trope in this newspaper article, which refers elsewhere to the "dawn of the life and freedom of the people,"[30] as an occasion to stage a scene in which the philosopher's announcement of sunrise is ardently repeated on the pages of the newspaper—but not without being reconfigured in the process. In a language suffused with images and metaphors, the first sentences of the "Morning Observations" conjure up the scene of a town at the break of day, populated by journalists and newspaper readers, organized around a tower watchman and a chattering crowd, its atmosphere filled with errant reports and announcements. Kierkegaard's anonymous author writes:

> It is not the first time [*det er ikke første Gang*] that the *Copenhagen
> Mail*, probably because it is on friendly terms with the tower watch-
> man of political life, has communicated to us that it has not yet become
> day but still continues to be dawn [*ikke var blevet Dag vedblev stadigt
> at være Morgendæmring*]. We have to some extent been confirmed in
> this observation through incessantly hearing the political cockcrow
> of the *Copenhagen Mail*. It is probably also this dawn that has given
> the *Copenhagen Mail* the occasion [*Anledning*] for producing a great
> number of farces [*Possen*] and journalistic conjuring tricks [*journalistiske
> Taskenspillerkunster*].[31]

The scene evoked in these opening sentences repeats the time of transition that is captured in the preface to the *Phenomenology*. Central to the scene is a "communication" (*Meddelelse*), an announcement that is made in the newspaper and evokes the same temporal situation as Hegel's morning observations: the announcement that "it has not yet become day but still continues to be dawn." But even though this announcement seems to be situated in the same time as the announcement of the philosopher—*Morgendæmring*, dawn as the metaphor for a time of transition that finds its end and completion in the sunrise—this time is here structured in a wholly different manner. This much is already suggested by the opening words of the article, which point out that "it is not the first time" (*det er ikke første Gang*) that the newspaper has made this announcement. That the image of dawn is repeated again and again in the announcements of the newspaper causes its meaning to shift: instead of an imminent sunrise, the proposition "it is dawn" comes to designate a repeated deferral. Each time that dawn is proclaimed and sunrise is announced, this deferral repeats itself. In an ironic inversion, every announcement of the arrival of the new day comes to mean that "it has not yet become day" (*ikke var blevet Dag*); likewise, the dawn that is declared by the newspaper must appear with every repetition of the trope as an endlessly protracted dawn, the dawn before an ever-deferred sunrise—and thus the proposition "it is dawn" is paraphrased by the author of the "Morning Observations" into the declaration that "it still continues to be dawn" (*stadigt at være Morgendæmring*). The dawn that Kierkegaard evokes at the start of his early writings is thus a dawn that does not merely continue but "still" continues—a dawn that continues to continue, that continues yet again. This image of an ever-prolonged dawn and an ever-deferred sunrise is reiterated in one of the central images in the opening paragraph: the reference to the "incessant [*idelig*] cockcrow" of the newspapers—a cockcrow that, as yet another instance of the announcement, is *idelig*, incessant in the sense that it never ceases to repeat itself. Like the philosopher's announcement in the preface to Hegel's *Phenomenology*, this cockcrow is situated in the moment of dawn, the space between the day has passed and the day that is yet to begin; but in the incessant repetition of this announcement, its relation to the *Aufgang* has been reconfigured. If the dawn evoked at the start of the "Morning Observations" is the image of a transition, this would be a transition that never quite comes to a conclusion; a suspended transition figured by the ever-renewed deferral of a day that never breaks.

Contradictions Out of Work

The suspension of time that is evoked at the start of the "Morning Observations" is closely connected to another suspension that is also associated with journalism but plays out in the domain of language. In the early newspaper articles, Kierkegaard's attempts to portray this suspension crystallize around the category of contradiction (*Modsigelse*).[32] When the anonymous author of the "Morning Observations" refers to the journalism's daily repeated "communication" that "it has not yet become day but still continues to be dawn," he appends an extensive footnote to his reference to this announcement—a footnote that presents an inventory of contradictory propositions regarding the time in which the newspaper under scrutiny is written, lifted from pages of the *Copenhagen Mail* and served up as evidence:

> The observer to whom the *Copenhagen Mail* has appealed is, so it seems, not entirely reliable [*paalidelig*], for otherwise one would probably not find such confusion [*Forvirring*] in his utterances: "It is dawn," p. 169, col. 2, line 9 up; "The rays of truth dispel their vague phantoms," p. 170, col. 2, line 6 down.—"Life is in its early childhood," p. 169, col. 2, line 13 up; "the universal faintheartedness matched hardly at all the universal reforming spirit one otherwise regards as the salient feature of our time," p. 170, col. 1, line 4 down.[33]

In his second newspaper article, the much longer *On the Polemic of the Fatherland*, which picks apart the reception of his first polemical piece, Kierkegaard refers once more to this footnote and its list of contradictory propositions.[34]

In a passage that reflects on the occasion for his *Morning Observations*, he writes:

> An odd criterion must surely be used for such a piece to be considered "well written," a piece in which, without seeking or hunting, one can produce an assembly of contradictions [*Assemblee af Modsigelser*] that look in amazement at one another without comprehending how they have come together, a display of contradictions [*Udstilling af Modsi-gelser*] that is still conveniently on view in the *Copenhagen Flying Mail*, no. 76.[35]

That the category of "contradiction" (*Modsigelse*) is introduced in the context of Kierkegaard's portrayal of an endlessly prolonged dawn may be understood against the background of Hegel's account of historical movement, which reserves an important role for this category. The "unfolding of spirit in time" is, for Hegel, essentially a movement of contradiction, *Widerspruch*—the exact cognate of the Danish *Modsigelse*.[36] Contradiction is not a negative criterion of truth: taken in isolation, any finite concept and any finite thing involves a contradiction—and it is precisely the impulse to overcome this contradiction that sets spirit into motion. Contradiction is a category of logic not in the formal but in the specific Hegelian sense of the word: logic understood as the *logos* that pertains both to the subjective and objective manifestations of the concept. Contradiction propels both the immanent movement of thought and of being, of the concept and of substance with which it will find itself to be identical. This is articulated most rigorously and rigidly in the lesser *Logic*, where the relation between movement and contradiction is summarized in a formula: "What moves the world as such is contradiction" (*Was überhaupt die Welt bewegt, das ist der Widerspruch*).[37] The *überhaupt* must be understood here in the dual sense of the word: contradiction is not only that which moves the world in general but also that by which there is properly historical movement at all—contradiction is that which drives forward the movement of the concept and guides it toward the absolute.

In order to better understand the role of contradiction in the suspended dawn conjured up in the "Morning Observations," it is important to underline the linguistic character of Hegel's concept of contradiction. That thought and language are inextricably interwoven in the *Widerspruch*—as in the *logos* itself, as the unity of word and reason—is already implied in the term, which presupposes a relation between a *Sprechen* and a *Widersprechen*, the alternation of a *dictio* and a *contradictio*, a saying and a saying-against. The concept of contradiction is indeed closely related to the problem of manifestation, the

Aussage or externalization of thought in language that is followed (and accomplished beforehand) by the moment of return, of reinternalization without loss.[38] In the *Differenzschrift*, the concept surfaces in the context of a discussion of the complications that arise in thinking of the absolute insofar as this thinking must also involve a "saying."[39] Contradiction is here claimed to emerge necessarily whenever the absolute is spoken of, whenever it is captured in the form of a *Satz*, a proposition or sentence. Every propositional sentence on the absolute, conceived as an identity of the subjective and the objective, must split itself into two: a proposition of identity that must be accompanied by one of non-identity if the unity it posits is not to remain abstract. The *Satz* must therefore double itself, turn into *zwei Sätze*—and it is these two sentences that begin to speak to and against one another, inaugurating a conversation that will unfold out of and through a mutual *widersprechen*.[40] As soon as there is talk of the absolute, every sentence must split in two and enter into a conversation with itself; the task for the thinker is merely to immerse oneself in this conversation and follow its immanent development. The account of this conversation and its development is further elaborated in Hegel's famous analysis of the speculative proposition in the preface to the *Phenomenology of Spirit*, where it is shown to emerge out of the contradictions that inhere in the formal-grammatical structure of the propositional sentence itself.[41] Here it is the separation between subject and predicate that must dissolve in propositions on the absolute, insofar as the subject of such propositions—Hegel uses the example "God is being"—encounters its substance rather than something accidental. In the movement set in motion by this dissolution, the immobile, fixed subject of the formal-grammatical sentence will turn out to be a divided whole that engenders a constantly renewed production of other sentences.[42] The monological structure of the grammatical sentence here gives rise to a conversation that will not unfold in fixed terms, but produces ever-new concepts and interlocutors as it learns to speak about itself. What guides this conversation is not an absolute speaker directing the conversation toward its proper end, but a *telos* that arises from the immanent movement of language considered as *logos*. What Hegel describes here as a "dialectical movement" (*dialektische Bewegung*) is nothing but the movement of language as it learns to speak about itself, criticize itself, and carry itself toward its own fulfillment.[43] Contradiction does not just propel this conversation of the *logos* with and about itself; it also guarantees that it is guided toward its necessary conclusion.

When Kierkegaard claims that the occasion for his "Morning Observations" was the flagrant "display of contradictions" on the pages of a local newspaper, this must be understood in light of the role that Hegel reserved for the contradiction in his account of the immanent development of the concept. That

Kierkegaard's reference to these contradictions is not without irony and must be approached with care is already suggested by the excessive precision of the extensive footnote appended to the first paragraph of the article, which is supposed to expose the contradictions that supposedly permeate the newspaper article under consideration. "'It is dawn,' p. 169, col. 2, line 9 up; 'The rays of truth dispel their vague phantoms,' p. 170, col. 2, line 6 down"—the evidence is presented here with a meticulous precision that recalls the orthographic complaints of a discontented newspaper reader: a neat list, supported by page numbers and bibliographic references, provided by a reader who insists on standards of correctness and proper usage. There is something excessive about this list, which seems to be out of proportion with regards to the apparently trivial inconsistencies in the newspaper article that Kierkegaard's anonymous author cites from. More important, however, there is a sense in which the evidence listed in the footnote, despite its emphasis on correctness and propriety, seems to be the result of a faulty reading of the text—a reading that somehow misunderstands the intentions of its author. The contradictory phrases cited here and examined with regard to their logical consistency are, without exception, rhetorical figures; the fragments of text that are accused of breaching the law of non-contradiction are not logical propositions but images and tropes, metaphors and metonyms. The evidence served up in the footnote concerns the coincidence of the assertion that "it is dawn" (*det er Morgendæmring*) in one sentence with a reference to "rays of truth" (*Sandhedens Straaler*) in another; the assertion that "life is in its early childhood" (*Livet er i sin første Barndom*) in one and the "spirit of reform" (*reformatoriske Aand*) typical of the age in another. On both occasions, a sentence that seems to be easily identifiable as a rhetorical figure, a mere illustration of conceptual content, is treated by this reader as if it were a logical proposition that can be probed for its consistency. While Kierkegaard's author, the complaining newspaper reader, claims to detect a confusion in the utterances listed here, the contradictions he presents in this footnote evoke a certain confusion themselves: one that affects the classical separation between logic and rhetoric, between concept and representation. In applying the principle of non-contradiction to rhetorical figures, the accusation of a flagrant "display of contradiction" thus turns out to be based on a misreading—a misunderstanding of figures that could have been understood to represent a propositional content if they had only been adequately identified as such, if their proper meaning had only been correctly deciphered. This confusion of the logical and the rhetorical and of the literal and the figural is only further exacerbated by the list of citations provided by this anonymous author. In the case of both of the contradictions identified here, the author cites and isolates rhetorical figures to the point that their structure resembles that of predicative sentence: most notably "it is dawn." Lifted out of the text and removed from their context, it becomes uncertain whether the appropriate reading of phrases like these would be of a literal or a figurative kind; it has become impossible to decide whether these descriptions refer to a person or an epoch, to a day or an age. Read in this way, the excessively meticulous reading performed here does not just ridicule the flowery language of the newspapers; rather, it takes this language as an occasion to complicate and ridicule the very possibility of distinguishing with absolute certainty between conceptual content and rhetorical ornament—and, with it, the possibility of deciding on *a* meaning or even a controlled polysemy of meanings.[44]

Unreliability of Words

This uncertainty with regard to the figural or literal status of these sentences is summarized in the suspicion that leads Kierkegaard's anonymous author to present this display of contradictions in the first place: the suspicion that the observations attributed here to a tower watchman are "not entirely reliable" (*ikke ganske paalidelig*).[45] If this "unreliability" is demonstrated by the list of citations in the footnote, it is not merely the accidental unreliability of a tower watchman whose observations may be correct or incorrect; instead, it is the structural unreliability that is at work in every *Udsage*, every thought insofar as it must externalize itself in language. Language would be "unreliable" in the sense that words have a way of saying things that are not at all what the speaker had intended them to say. The demonstration that is undertaken in the footnote, supposedly in the name of the correct use of language, inadvertently provides evidence for this more profound and dangerous unreliability through its own misunderstanding of the propositions cited here—a misunderstanding that is, above all else, a *misreading*, a reading that fails to distinguish between literal and figural meaning, between concept and trope. In doing so, the list of citations in the footnote may be taken as a model for the mode of reading that is at the center of all of Kierkegaard's early newspaper articles. Throughout these newspaper articles, Kierkegaard will consistently attempt to read his opponents' words in such a way that they come to say something else than they were intended to say—to lay bare places in the text where words can be made to say something entirely different from their supposedly manifest meaning, where figural language can be read literally and vice versa, where the most insignificant can be mistaken for the most significant—up to the point where not a single word or sentence can be relied upon to do its work.[46] Unwittingly—at least in appearance—the orthographic complaints of

Kierkegaard's anonymous author, who insists on standards of correctness and propriety, demonstrate precisely that there is no reliable way to set up such a standard. In his suggestion that "an odd standard [*en egen Maalestok*] must surely be used for such a piece to be considered 'well written' [*velskrevet*]"— that is to say, written according to the highest orthographic standards—he inadvertently points to this impossibility: if his inventory of contradictions lifted from this text suggests anything, it is that every such *Maalestok* must be odd, in the sense that there is no standard that could ever be reliable. "What is unclearly said [*uklart Udtalte*] is what is unclearly thought [*uklart Tænkte*]," Kierkegaard's anonymous author writes in the second newspaper article.[47] But rather than insisting on the proper usage of words, this quote takes on a different significance when read in light of the suspicion of a structural unreliability of language. If what is said unclearly is thought unclearly, and if nothing that is said can be sufficiently secured against the risk of being misunderstood, if nothing that is said can ever be sufficiently clear, then there is no thought that can secure the possibility of being correctly understood.

The contradictions that Kierkegaard's anonymous author ostensibly complains about thus turn out to be incompatibilities between figurative expressions—a "mere matter of style," as his polemical opponents will later retort, rather than genuine inconsistencies in the logical argument "proper." But out of this complaint another disjunction emerges, a disjunction that is more fundamental than the one between incompatible propositions: the irreducible disjunction between what is meant and what is said, between *logos* and *lexis*, between what a certain statement means and the way in which the statement is meant to mean.[48] This disjunction affects not only any conversation between already established subjects, but also the conversation through which the concept is supposed to realize its immanent development. If the immanent movement of thought involves a necessary moment of manifestation, that is to say, the *Aussage* of conceptual content in language, then this manifestation—without which there would be nothing to think—also exposes the necessary development of the *logos* to the contingent relations of the *lexis*. It is no accident that Kierkegaard's exposition of the unreliability of the *Udsagen* of the newspaper crystallizes around the category of contradiction, as the propelling agent of "development."[49] As the reference to a "display" (*Udstilling*) of contradictions in the newspaper already suggests, the contradictions presented here do anything but propel; rather, they are described as if they were objects in a market stall—inert, laying side by side, indifferent to one another. What makes this display particularly "striking" (*paafaldende*) is precisely that apparently contradictory sentences are brought together without ever contradicting one another in the strict sense of the word, without ever participating in the self-propelling conversation between *Spruch* and *Widerspruch*. "'It is dawn,' p. 169, col. 2, line 9 up; 'The rays of truth dispel their vague phantoms,' p. 170, col. 2, line 6 down"[50]—the propositions gathered here may contradict one another and yet it would be absurd to even attempt to reconcile or sublate them. Rather than resulting from logical inconsistencies between concepts and propositions, the contradictions presented here result from contingent relations between rhetorical figures; what the ostentatious numbering of pages, columns, and lines included here bring out, is that these relations emerge not from the sequential movement of the argument but rather play out between metaphors and images in the most disparate places of the text. The logician that follows the movement of these contradictions and their sublation is led astray: for these contradictions do not emerge out of the "self-generating, self-developing, self-returning path" that guides the immanent movement of the concept in Hegel's account, but rather develop out of the contingent relationships that are necessarily introduced over the course of its presentation.[51]

The inoperative character of the contradictions that Kierkegaard's author finds on the pages of the newspaper is highlighted in another image that he offers in the same passage of his second newspaper article: the image of a suspended conversation, an "assembly of contradictions [*Assemblee af Modsigelser*] that look at one another without comprehending how they have ended up in each other's company [*komne i Selskab sammen*]."[52] The relation between the contradictory utterances cited in the footnote is here presented in the image of a conversational setting: a gathering of personified contradictions that, insofar as this gathering takes place under the sign of an "assembly," would have to be understood as a conversation directed toward a common purpose. In the scene conjured up by Kierkegaard, however, the conversation through which this assembly is supposed to unfold fails to begin: in this mute prosopopoeia of contradictions, the same contradictions that for Hegel act as the propelling agent that set a dialectic in its motion are portrayed as if they merely stand opposite one another, speechless and immobile—"without comprehending [*begribe*] how they have ended up in each other's company." But if the contradictions listed in this footnote do not "comprehend" what brought them together, this is precisely because what brought them together is incomprehensible from the standpoint of the concept. It is not the necessary development of the concept that has yielded these contradictions and placed them in opposition to one another; it is the mere contingency to which logical presentation is exposed insofar as it has an irreducible linguistic character. The mute "assembly" presented here was never called for by the propositions that attend it, nor by the immanent movement of the concept—it is a gathering that has been convened by language itself. Kierkegaard's anonymous author summarizes this in his second polemical article when he points out that the evidence presented here is proof of a "complete lack of any logic" (*fuldkomne Mangel paa al logisk*) in the phrases cited here.[53]

Confusion

The language of journalism whose "unreliability" is at once identified and performed in Kierkegaard's early newspaper articles is thus a language in which the contradictions that were supposed to propel and guide the historical movement of the *logos* cease to be at work. In their scrutiny of the local newspapers, these articles point to a dimension of language that is not reducible to its semantic or referential function: just as there would be something in language that thwarts every attempt to reduce the word to a vehicle of the concept, so there would be something in language that resists and disturbs the orderly development of the *logos* learning to speak about itself. In these newspaper articles, Kierkegaard reserves a special name for this resistance and its tendency to suspend the immanent movement of the concept: *Forvirring*, "confusion." But even though the term surfaces at key moments in these texts—most notably in the claim that the aim of the "Morning Observations" was to "draw attention to a striking confusion" encountered on the pages of the newspapers[54]—it will be elaborated elsewhere in Kierkegaard's early writings: in the unfinished draft for another newspaper article, which was also written in 1835 but remained unpublished. This important fragment, which remains untitled in Kierkegaard's manuscripts, places the concept of confusion at the center of a warning that is proclaimed at the start of the text—an announcement of an exceptionally dangerous threat that is evoked in a long, protracted sentence:

> In this instant [*for Øieblikket*], people are afraid of nothing so much as the total bankruptcy which seems to threaten Europe; meanwhile they forget the much more dangerous and apparently inevitable spiritual bankruptcy that stands at the door—a linguistic confusion [*Sprogforvir-ring*] which is far more dangerous than the old Babelic (symbolical) one, far more dangerous than the confusion of nations and dialects following from the Babelic attempt of the middle ages, namely a confusion within languages themselves [*en Forvirring nemlig i Sprogene selv*], a rebellion more dangerous than all others, namely a rebellion of words [*Ordenes Oprør*] that, torn loose from human dominion [*Menneskets Herredømme*], as it were rush upon one another in despair, and out of this chaos the human being reaches into a sort of grab bag [*Lykkepose*], taking hold of whatever word arises first in order to express his supposed thoughts.[55]

As in the case of the published newspaper articles, the opening sentence of this unfinished fragment ties its reflections on language to the occurrences of the day. The *Sprogforvirring* that is announced by Kierkegaard's author as a "spiritual bankruptcy" (*Fallit i aandelig Henseende*) is introduced as the pendant of another bankruptcy of which there was much talk at the time: the threatening depletion of the Danish treasury. Kierkegaard's author does not hesitate to draw an analogy between the sphere of finance, money, and speculation on the one hand, and the sphere of language on the other. Just as the treasury is threatened by a complete draining of its resources, Kierkegaard's author argues, so there is the threat of a bankruptcy of language, an "apparently inevitable" bankruptcy that would involve the draining from language of that which is supposed to breathe life into the letter: spirit. It is through the announcement of this "spiritual bankruptcy" that this dramatic warning arrives at its true topic: the threat of a *Sprogforvirring*, a linguistic confusion. This "confusion" is placed in a close relation to the exemplary account of such confusion, the Babelic confusion of tongues, at the same time as it is distinguished from it. The confusion whose threat erupts "in this instant" is, so the author of Kierkegaard's article writes, not only "far more dangerous than the old Babelic [. . .] one" but also "far more dangerous than the confusion of nations and dialects following from the Babelic attempt of the middle ages." The confusion that is at stake here, the confusion that is decisive for understanding the crisis marking the time in which this article is written, is not restricted to the fragmentation of a single human language into multiple ones, or even its further fragmentation into a variety of national languages and dialects. The confusion that erupts in this moment is not the confusion *between* languages but a confusion "within languages themselves" (*i Sprogene selv*)—a confusion that is, in other words, not just at work within every language but in human language *as such*. It is here that the article recalls the reflections on language of a thinker who is always in the background of Kierkegaard's early writings: Johann Georg Hamann. The Babelic confusion of tongues is a recurrent trope in the work of Hamann, where it is tied directly to his analysis of the divisions and disjunctions that mark human language as fallen. The alarm that Kierkegaard's author sounds over a confusion "within" language brings to mind Hamann's famous definition of human speech as "translation," *Übersetzung*—a transposition between spheres that are ultimately incommensurable. "To speak is to translate [*reden ist übersetzen*]," Hamann writes, "from an angelic language into a human language, that is to say, thoughts into words—things into names— images into signs."[56] If all speaking is translating, if all human language is marked by the same divisions and disjunctions that traverse human languages, then the movement of the *logos* itself, as a composite of thought and word, would be threatened by a confusion not unlike the one that befell those constructing the tower of Babel.[57] Even the all-encompassing conversation in which the *logos* progressively learns to speak about itself—the accomplishment of which separates the *Øieblik* in which Kierkegaard's author is writing from Hamann's ruminations on language—would be threatened by a confusion that is "more dangerous" than its ancient predecessor because it is more profound, erupting not from a disjunction between languages but rather from an inadequacy of language to itself.[58]

Kierkegaard's author defines this "most dangerous" confusion as a "rebellion of words" (*Ordenes Oprør*). This confusion that arises out of the basic structure of the language of a fallen humanity is conceived as a *røre*, a movement of stirring and disturbing that would seem to spring from words themselves. What is disturbed by this movement is summarized in an image that captures the role assigned to language after the fall: the "human dominion" (*Menneskets Herredømme*) of words, a relation of dominion that humanity will never cease to set up over language.[59] When Kierkegaard characterizes the relation between human beings and language in these terms, he again refers to a familiar motif in the work of Hamann: the thought that human language after the fall is characterized before anything else by the reduction to its semantic function. The "dominion" of words by human beings refers to the reduction of language to a means of communication.[60] After the fall, words are supposed to communicate something—that is to say, *something else*, something other than themselves and outside of themselves. It is also in this way that language is characterized in the account of the construction of the Tower of Babel in Genesis. Here language appears first and foremost as an instrument that serves intentional activity ("let us build us a city, and a tower, whose top may reach unto heaven") just as the shattering of the unity of human language not only completes the separation of a fallen humanity from paradise but also disturbs the function that it will assign to the word as a carrier of the concept ("and the lord said, [. . .] let us go down and confuse their language, so that they may not understand one another's speech").[61] When Kierkegaard's author describes this instrumental character in terms of a "dominion," this recalls Hamann's references to the *Knechtsgestalt* of words: words shaped like servants, put to work as means toward an end that is not their own, an end imposed on them from outside.[62] Like the servant, the word is made to carry something that is external to itself: it is turned into a mere means, an instrument to carry concepts and refer to things to which it has no intrinsic relation. And just as the ideal servant undertakes his tasks without ever being noticed, so the instrument of language is supposed to be wielded with such control and efficacy that it would disappear entirely after it has accomplished its task, dissolving completely into the things of which it speaks. Supposed to—for this instrumental conception of language would have failed to take into account that there is something in language that resists the disappearance of words after they have completed the task assigned to them.

Loquacity of Language

The *Sprogforvirring* for which the author of Kierkegaard's unfinished newspaper article warns is the same confusion that is at the same time performatively denounced and repeated in his articles in the *Flying Mail* of the same year: it names a structural resistance of language to its semantic function. When Kierkegaard's opponents complained that his pieces may show a "powerful language" but that the intentions of the author remained opaque, they unwittingly described the decisive motif of these texts.[63] The linguistic confusion that is described in Kierkegaard's fragment as a "rebellion of words" against their "dominion" by human beings would concern a resistance that is always at work within "fallen" language—language reduced to a means of signification, an instrument that is supposed to be controlled by a speaker. This resistance is, if we take the description of this rebellion seriously, a disturbance that arises out of language itself—an *Oprør* that emerges out of an impulse in words that resists their reduction to a carrier of the concept. Kierkegaard refers to this impulse in a marginal note to the opening paragraph of his unpublished newspaper article: "One speaks [*man taler*] after the association of ideas—the *Selbstsucht* of words [*Ordenes Selbstsucht*]."[64] What drives this rebellion of words is not the "intention" of the speaker or the "drive" of the concept to overcome contradictions—the *Trieb* that propels the Hegelian dialectic[65]—but rather some impulse in words themselves. The specific sense of the German *Selbstsucht*, which is left untranslated in the original Danish, is not exhausted by its usual translation as an "egoism." When Kierkegaard speaks of the *Selbstsucht* of words, this must be understood in the double sense of the word: as an urge (*Sucht*) of words themselves, an impulse that has an affinity with a searching (*suchen*)—but rather than being directed to anything outside of themselves, this impulse of words would also be directed only toward words themselves. Words "themselves," *selbst*: that is to say, words stripped from their semantic function or conceptual content. What stirs these words into motion would not be the "drive" of the concept but an impulse that is at work within language as such, an impulse that must disturb any purpose or intention imposed on it from the outside. Even though this motif of *Selbstsucht* and its relation to the "association of ideas" are not elaborated here, they both return in another journal entry written in the same period. Kierkegaard writes here:

> There are people who speak after associations of ideas, but far under-
> neath this one finds a standpoint that I would like to call the *Selbst-*
> *sucht* of words, where one word pulls another with it [*river det andet*
> *med sig*], where words, that often come together, search one another
> [*søge hverandre*], more or less like words in a lexicon would do as soon
> as they would come alive.[66]

When Kierkegaard speaks of the *Selbstsucht* of words as a viewpoint that is to
be placed "far below" the "association of ideas," this should be taken less as a
normative assertion than as a reference to a more basic viewpoint. The mode
of speaking it designates could not be further removed from one where language is made to function as a vehicle of communication. If speaking after
the "association of ideas" refers to a movement of speech where what is said is
not determined by the intention of an already established subject, but rather
follows the habitual groupings of ideas, so *Ordenes Selbstsucht* names a mode
of speech that propels itself onward even though it has been entirely dissociated itself from the sphere of thought—whether it is the immanent development of the concept or the intention of a speaker. In the *Selbstsucht* of words,
one word drags the other along, without regard for the intentions of a speaker
subject; the subject is not constituted before the act of speaking; the subject is
an impersonal "one" (*man*) which is here said to speak "after" (*efter*) this impulse within language itself. This impulse of words would exceed any possible conceptual determination, any meaning that could be fixed in a lexicon;
language would follow its own "logic," if it is still possible to use this term: a
logic of loquacity, where language would continue to speak even when it has
ceased to fulfill its semantic function.[67]

The announcement of a threatening *Sprogforvirring* in Kierkegaard's unpublished newspaper article thus distinguishes between two distinct dimensions of language that cannot be reduced to one another. On the one hand,
there is the word in its relation to the concept, the word as the carrier of a determinate meaning; on the other, there is the word in its relation to other
words, a *Selbstsucht* of words that is irreducible to their semantic function. This
double relation is evoked toward the end of the protracted opening sentence
of the article, where Kierkegaard's author specifies the *Ordenes Oprør* as "a
rebellion of words that, in despair, as it were rush towards one another."[68]
This "despair" (*Fortvivlen*) of words may be read literally. If words are *fortviv-*
led, the cognate of the German *verzweifelt*, this is because the confusion at
work in language disrupts every simple unity between word and concept; words
find themselves torn between two different, irreconcilable relations. The word
still refers to a concept, but no longer simply that; it also enters into another

relation, a relation that plays out not between word and concept but amongst words, words that "rush towards one another" (*styrte ind paa hverandre*), that is to say, words are driven by an impulse that cannot be controlled by an intention. The image that Kierkegaard's author appends to the end of his warning— "and out of this chaos the human being reaches into a sort of grab bag [*Lykkepose*], taking hold of whatever word arises first in order to express his supposed thoughts"[69]—may be read as an attempt to capture what it would mean to speak under the condition of this double, *fortvivlede* character of words. Against the image of a speaker who is in complete control over every word uttered, Kierkegaard conjures up an image of a speech where the speaker does nothing but reach inside a grab bag, a *Lykkepose*—a term that, like the German *Glückssäckel*, points to the sheer arbitrariness of whatever word arises out of it. If the speaker chooses words, this is a choice that is predicated on an "arising" of words that is arbitrary in the sense that it does not obey pre-established intentions or the laws of conceptual development—only the *Selbstsucht* of words themselves. Under the conditions of this rebellion, any manifestation of thought would be merely the "expression of a supposed thought [*formeentlige Tanker*]"; thoughts that, insofar as they first manifest themselves in language, can at best be "supposedly" attributed to a speaker insofar as they are always predicated on this arbitrary play between words.

Hastværks-Pressen

If the movement of history can be understood on the model of a conversation, then this would have little to do with the conversation of a *logos* that learns to speak about itself, that criticizes itself and guides itself toward its own immanent fulfillment. The very support that would render such a conversation possible—the "words" whose resistance to conceptual determination is already exposed in the "Morning Observations"—would never cease to disturb this conversation. The "confusion" that is always already at work in language throws the orderly movement of the concept into disarray; the *Selbstsucht* of words pulls thought away from that "self-generating, self-developing path" by which the concept returns into itself. Any conversation through which the concept could be brought to its immanent fulfillment would constantly be interrupted by another conversation: a conversation that is not propelled forward by the drive of the *logos* to overcome the contradictions that inhere in all finite things or thoughts, but only by the impulse of language to continue speaking—even if it has nothing to say. The unpublished comic play that Kierkegaard wrote in the following years, and for which he considered the title *The Comprehensive Debate Between Everything and Everything*, could be shown to stage precisely such a conversation—and to do so in the form of a curious repetition of the Hegelian dialectic, populated by journalists and other characters representing a speech without a speaker or a language without a concept, ranging from "a ventriloquist" to "a horn" and to a certain "Mr. Phrase."[70] In Kierkegaard's unpublished newspaper article, as in the case of the *Morning Observations*, where the language of the newspapers is treated as a privileged site of this linguistic confusion in which every contradiction must become inoperative, the author who warns of a threatening *Sprogforvirring* turns to the sphere of journalism to find an emblematic image of the curious self-propelling conversation that emerges from this confusion. Toward the end of this unpublished fragment, in its final paragraphs, Kierkegaard's anonymous author writes:

> In everything one can detect the invention that is so characteristic of the age [*Tidsalderen*]: the rapid printing press [*Hastværks-Pressen*]— even in the curious reflectiveness [*Reflexion*] that has entered our age, with the effect that it, while constantly limiting its expressions through reflection, never really gets to say something. This curious verbosity [*Vidtløftighed*] has also suppressed the usage of sayings [*Ordsprog*] which save so much time and talk [*Tid og Tale*] and has instead encouraged the emergence of a sort of oratorical chatter [*oratorisk Passiar*], which has indeed even taken over our meals [*Maaltider*].[71]

Nothing thus better characterizes this time, "the age," than the intervention that was at the heart of the production of newspapers at the time this fragment was written: the so-called *Hastværks-Pressen*, the rapid printing press of which descriptions and images circulated on the pages of newspapers in the first decades of the early nineteenth century. While the manual Gutenberg press had a special relation to the book form, this recent invention owed its name— *Hastværk* literally means "hasty work"—to its role in the production of newspapers and other journalistic ephemera. It is no accident that one of the journalists that appear in Kierkegaard's unpublished comic play of 1837, *The Comprehensive Debate Between Everything and Everything*, "Mr. Holla Hastværksen," is named after the same machine.[72] In contrast to the different types of printing presses that preceded it, the invention that is "so characteristic of the age" was driven by pressure cylinders. The *Hastværks-Pressen*, in other words, provides the image of an automaton: a machine that moves itself, no longer in need of a subject that operates it, spitting out pages and pages full of text. This machine prints words on the page in the absence of a speaking subject or even a subject who reproduces this speech by operating the press; words are inscribed, that is to say, printed on sheets of paper, without a speaker whose presence would endow these words with their original meaning. The words that are spat out by this automaton have an irreducible exteriority, one that exceeds the exteriority characteristic of the scene of writing or even the scene of printing. The machine therefore anticipates the image of a "talking machine" (*Talemaskine*) to which Kierkegaard refers later in his work—a machine "could say the same thing that spirit had said, but does not say it by virtue of spirit."[73] In its production of words in the absence of a speaker, the *Hastværks-Pressen* not only exemplifies the exteriority of words, emphasizing the dimension of language that is devoid of all conceptual content or referential function; it also conjures up the image of speech that continues even in the absence of a speaker, of words that continue to be uttered without spirit, of language that propels itself onwards even though it no longer functions as a vehicle for either concept or meaning. If this invention can be detected "in everything," this is not because of the speed of its production or because of its name, which is easily mistaken to suggest the insipid critique of the "hasty times" that had already become a worn-out cliché in the early nineteenth century; this machine owes its all-pervasive character to the image it conjures up, namely an image of language as something that speaks and moves by itself. In this rare reflection on the emerging world of technical mediation, it is language, pictured as a machine, evoked in the context of a warning for a fateful Babelic confusion, that Kierkegaard presents as the paradigmatic instance of the instrument that overpowers its supposed master.[74]

Because of this "automatic," self-moving character of language, all speech risks falling prey to a "curious verbosity" (*Vidtløftigkeit*).[75] The speech of language is a verbosity par excellence: for the tendency of the verbose speaker to use more words than necessary in order to convey a meaning is driven to an extreme in the speech of language, which speaks in words that are utterly devoid of referentiality or conceptuality. If the "saying" (*Ordsprog*) says a lot in the least amount of words and "saves time and talk" because it is saturated with meaning, the verbose speech of language expends time and talk without ever saying anything, without conveying any meaning. If no speaker—even spirit—could bring language fully under control, if this verbosity always plays out in language, then every utterance risks becoming *Vidtløftig*—the cognate of the German *Weitläufig*—in the sense that it never moves straight, could never determine its meaning with complete efficiency. All speech, even the conversation through which the *logos* learns to speak about itself, is marred by this verbosity and must risk ending up in "oratorical chatter" (*oratorisk Passiar*). Such chatter is oratorical in the sense that it has nothing to do with logic and can never be brought under the control of the concept; it plays out in the relationship between signs, while their respective meaning has become of secondary importance. This movement of language—the *Selbstsucht* of words—always draws the movement of the concept off its course, leads it astray, keeps it from reaching a conclusion. This verbosity affects not only the presentation of the concept, the moment where the concept must externalize itself in order to appear for itself, the moment of writing that must be marred by the impossibility to ever say what is thought with complete efficiency; it must also affect the moment where this is taken back up into the concept, the moment of reading or appropriation—and it is for this reason that Kierkegaard will claim that this verbosity has even "taken over our meals" (*Maaltider*).[76]

If this "oratorical chatter" is characteristic of the time in which the author of Kierkegaard's unfinished article is writing, this is because it stands in a special relation to what Kierkegaard calls the "whole newer development"—the "development" of philosophical thought that spans from Kant to Hegel. This chatter does not just affect the speculative philosophy, in which this development finds its conclusion; it is first brought to light by the *Reflexionsphiloso-phie* from which this development had originated—but not without corroding the foundations that it had set up to secure itself from it. For this reason Kierkegaard points out that the image of the rapid printing press, the image of language that speaks of itself without a speaker, is already manifest in "the curious reflectiveness [*Reflexion*] that has entered our age." It is in the *Reflexionsphilosophie* that Kierkegaard's author locates the beginning of the conversation through which speech is supposed to learn to speak about itself, for it is here that it discovers that its reference to particular things relied on a naïve faith in their independent subsistence.[77] Instead, speech will refer to the speaking self; but because this reference to the self requires a reference to things from which it distinguishes itself, it can never secure its distinctness. In this speaking about the one who speaks, language is emptied to such an extent that it no longer refers to the things determined in speech; its referential function is suspended altogether. Before speculative thought has attempted to find a ground in pure conceptual language, the *Reflexionsphilosophie* has already amounted to empty talk, a language utterly devoid of its referentiality—the price that speech has to pay for being secured is that it "never really gets to say something" (*egenlig ikke faaer sagt* Noget).[78]

If the "age" to which Kierkegaard refers is defined by this development, the moment in which the unpublished newspaper article is written—the "instant" with which its opening paragraph began—is located *after* the conclusion of this development in the speculative philosophy of Hegel. If the *Hastværks-Pressen* presents an image of the ineluctable conclusion of the "whole newer development"—a development that is itself supposed to be the final stage of the development of spirit where the concept comes into its own—this would be a conclusion of a strange kind: a conclusion that does not quite manage to come to an end, an end that does not quite manage to conclude. The early newspaper articles were already punctuated by references to such failed conclusions. In Kierkegaard's third article, which responds to his opponent's response to the "Morning Observations," extending a polemic that never moves on but keeps on straying into misunderstandings, the author rejects all responsibility for the "dragging on of the conflict" and instead complains about conversations that do not come to an end but "force us to repeat what we have expressed clearly enough."[79] If Kierkegaard's unpublished newspaper article of the same year can illustrate this same impossibility by evoking the image of the *Hastværks-Pressen*, this is because this press captures a peculiar kind of movement. Driven by a mechanism of pressure cylinders, this "invention so characteristic of the age" presents a spectacle of turning wheels and rotating cylinders, an image of an endless spinning on the spot. Yet it is the word that was commonly used to describe the workings of this machinery—the *Eisenbahnbewegung*—that draws out the concrete historical form of this movement without an end. In its entire machinery, the operations of the *Hastværks-Pressen* resemble the movement of the train, Kierkegaard's preferred allegory of the self-propelling spirit that progresses along the "systematic world-historical railroad"; but if this printing press resembles the movement of a locomotive, it is that of a locomotion at a standstill, caught on the spot even if its machinery is running at full speed.[80]

In its resemblance to a train that is running on the spot, the automatic printing press offers an emblem of the age in which the "whole newer development"— and, with it, the entire history of the unfolding of spirit—is supposed to have come to a conclusion. The spirit has come into its own, the concept has fully comprehended itself; and yet words continue to be spoken, language continues to lead a life of its own. The name that Kierkegaard reserves for this stage that follows the conclusion of a development—a "stage" that no longer deserves to be called as such, insofar as it is no longer part of the "development" that precedes it—is parody. "Every development usually ends with a parodying of itself and such a parody is an assurance that this development has outlived itself [*overlevet sig selv*]," Kierkegaard writes in his dissertation.[81] What "outlives" the development par excellence, namely the immanent development of the concept, is that which exceeds its "logic": language as such, empty language, without meaning or a qualified speaker. The newspaper would be the emblematic site of this "outliving," a site where the *logos* lives on after it has come into its own. The conclusion presented in this image is marked neither by pleromatic presence nor by a definite absence: the development of the *logos* ends in a ghostly presence, where speech continues even though there is nothing left to say. This image of the "age" anticipates a passage that will be included in the second part of *Either/Or*: "Our whole time [*tiden*] is at once comic and tragic—tragic because it is perishing [*gaaer under*], comic because it persists [*bestaaer*]. If it were possible to imagine that an inanimate body could still perform the usual functions for a little while it would be comic and tragic in the same way."[82] The persistence that Kierkegaard speaks of here is comic only to the extent that it persists despite perishing, to the extent that it persists after perishing: that the age is tragic and comic at the same time would mean that its tragic elements are ultimately absorbed into a comedy. In the "inanimate body" that is described here we see the image of an empty, purely self-referential language whose appearance Kierkegaard finds to be so characteristic of the age: a language of words that keeps being spoken even when spirit no longer breathes life into it, a language that is ultimately devoid of concept or meaning. The "spiritual bankruptcy" announced by the author of Kierkegaard's unfinished newspaper article is perhaps nothing but the ghostly life that is conjured up here in a dramatic form: the life of an inanimate word that somehow still continues to perform its old functions in the absence of a speaker to animate it.[83] It is no coincidence that this same morbid image also appears—perhaps for the first time—in Kierkegaard's "Morning Observations," where the figure of the journalist performs this ghostly life of a language that lives on without spirit. "One day in the future," its pseudonymous author writes, "just as in England one sells one's corpse to the dissecting room, so here one will sell one's body to be used as editor of the *Copenhagen Mail*."[84]

Retrieval of Words

The *Sprogforvirring* that the author of Kierkegaard's unfinished newspaper article warns against in the strongest possible terms thus finds its exemplary expression in the language of journalism. The disjunction between word and reason that traverses the *logos* from within may be a structural trait of human language, the confusion it gives rise to may have been at work in all human language since time immemorial, but it is in the pages of the newspaper—the instant in which the authors of Kierkegaard's articles are writing—that this confusion finally erupts and disturbs the entire order and progression of the conversation that learns to speak about itself. The language of the journalists, editors, and tower watchmen populating the farcical scenes evoked in these articles marks an extreme point: a language that shows itself not merely to be an unreliable carrier of meaning but also to harbor a dynamic that destines every conversation to end up in a curious "chatter" in which words have ceased to mean anything at all. What Kierkegaard in an early note calls the "deficiency"

(*Mangelfuldhed*) that stamps the human *logos* after the fall is pushed to an extreme in the language of journalism as it is portrayed in the early writings;[85] but as this word already suggests, in that it literally designates a "fullness of lack," it is also at this extreme point that language calls with most intensity for relief from this deficiency and shows, to use a phrase from his unpublished newspaper article, an "urge towards redemption" (*Trang til Forløsning*).[86] Exposing the defective character of fallen language would then turn out to be such a crucial aspect of the early writings because it is only out of a sense of this deficiency that the need for its redemption arises. Only against this background it becomes possible to understand an otherwise obscure remark that Kierkegaard makes toward the end of the same article that had begun to warn against the threat of an all-pervasive confusion of tongues: the assertion that journalism has a special relationship to the concept of "redemption" (*Forløsning*). After having discussed a number of concepts that threaten to be dissolved in the confusion that is at work in all language after the fall, Kierkegaard's author concludes:

> And I still have not even mentioned the concept which has not only been made nebulous [*forflygtiget*] like the others but has indeed been profaned: the concept of redemption [*Begrebet Forløsning*]—a concept which journalism in particular has adopted with a certain preference [*Forkærlighed*] and is now attributed to everyone, from the greatest hero of freedom all the way down to the baker or butcher, who bring redemption to their neighborhood insofar as they sell their wares a tiny bit cheaper than others.[87]

The concept of redemption would have a special place in the language of journalism because it is precisely in journalism that the "confusion of tongues" that affects all language after the fall manifests itself in an unprecedented manner. Nowhere is this confusion more pronounced, more ironically evident, than in the very concept that is supposed to signify the relief from sin and the renewal of paradise in an unforeseeable and unknowable future. The "evaporation" of the concept of redemption, the "profanation" of exactly that concept which Kierkegaard in his diary entry of 1835 had considered "one of the most essential features of Christianity" is driven to a ridiculous extreme in his portrayal of its application in the language of journalism. The concept is, first of all, applied within the sphere of world history, here captured in the figure of the "hero of freedom" (*Frihedshelt*) and thus stripped of its status as a limit concept—a concept that, in the last instance, designates the end of historical development and points to a future that must remain inaccessible from within the sphere of history. But beyond this application, the radical discontinuity that the concept is supposed to designate gives way to a description of the most incremental, quantitative change—wares that are sold a "tiny bit cheaper" than before. In the erasure of these distinguishing characteristics, the concept of redemption ceases to have a determinate meaning: once the concept has "evaporated" entirely, what is left of it is a mere word. But even though this word—*Forløsning*—would no longer be able to bring that of which it speaks to conceptual determination; it would, as a mere word, still harbor an indeterminate *Trang* to mean something; the word would still harbor the promise of a meaning that is as yet outstanding.

In the same unpublished newspaper article where Kierkegaard has his anonymous author warn against an all-pervasive confusion, there is one passage that refers—obliquely, in passing—to the promise of a retrieval of a lost fullness of words. Toward the end of this fragment, Kierkegaard's author raises the question of what is to be done in the light of this threatening confusion, how this dangerous loquacity of language can be kept at bay, in order to provide the following response:

> Undoubtedly it would be best if one could bring to silence the jingling clocks of our time [*Tidens Sangklokke*]; but because this will probably not succeed, we can at least join our financial men by shouting to the people: savings, energetic and bold savings [*Besparelser*]! [. . .] Besides this we could wish [*ønske*] that forcefully equipped men will make their appearance, who would win back [*gjenvandt*] the lost force and meaning of words [*Ordenes tabte Kraft og Betydning*], like Luther has won back the concept of faith for his time [*gjenvandt for sin Tid Begrebet Tro*].[88]

The response begins from an extreme. Confusion would be brought to a halt when there is no more speech, when *Tidens Sangklokke* would be brought to silence. If this silence is "probably" not going to happen, if one cannot count on it, this is because the constant ringing of these clocks is not just connected to the *Tid* in the sense of the "times"—it is not merely the conversation of a particular age that would need to be silenced—but to *Tid* in the sense of time as such. As long as time passes, language will continue to be spoken and continue to speak. The only available option thus seems to be a compromise. What remains is the task to be sparing in speaking, according to an economy that would resemble that of the "financial men" in the crisis evoked at the beginning of the letter—to cut back one's speech, to speak efficiently, to never say more than is strictly necessary.[89] But such sparing speech could never secure itself from the confusion that is at work in all language; it could never guarantee that it does not say too much or nothing at all, and it would still be stamped by the defective economy that is thematized throughout the early writings. It is certainly no accident that the exhortation that Kierkegaard's author uses here—"savings, energetic and bold savings"—is recited directly from a newspaper article on the financial crisis published shortly before and hovers between literal and figural meaning. As soon as this exhortation has been uttered, speech has already exposed itself to the loquacity of words, has already begun to say more than it was meant to say, has already been confronted by the impossibility of ever adequately conveying meaning, without remainder. It is within this defective economy that Kierkegaard's author introduces another possibility—the possibility of "winning back the lost force and meaning of words." Like the insistence on a certain efficiency of speech in the previous sentence, this phrase seems to insist on the retrieval of a proper meaning—a meaning that words originally possessed but that has now been lost. If speaking "sparingly" is impossible because words always say more than what they are meant to say, an adequate economy of speech could only be established if the meaning of words could be determined without ambiguity. On this reading, the example that Kierkegaard's author provides would suggest that the model for such retrieval of meaning is a return to scripture, a primal text in which a proper meaning is fixed once and for all.

But like the orthographic complaints that punctuate Kierkegaard's newspaper articles of the time, this remark is not without irony. This is already intimated by the reference to the odd authority that would suppress the rebellion of words, the "forcefully equipped men" who would retrieve and stabilize a lost meaning—an image that evokes the many references to a policing of language that will return in Kierkegaard's later writings. Such a rescue operation already carries its own impossibility within itself, insofar as the confusion it attempts to suppress precedes all intentional activity. But it is especially the reference to Luther's undertaking that destabilizes the call for a retrieval of the "lost force and meaning" of words and suggests the possibility of a different reading. For if Luther contributed anything to retrieval of the lost meaning of a word—faith, *Tro*—it is precisely that it is not reducible to a concept: insofar as faith is that which escapes understanding and communicability, it must retain a resistance to conceptuality. If the word "faith" would have lost a certain "force and meaning," this is not the loss of strict conceptual delimitation but rather a loss that is inherent in the reduction of faith to a concept—a loss that is inherent in conceptuality itself. Insofar as Luther is taken to be the one who uncovered the resistance of the concept of faith to every attempt at conceptual clarification, the example provided by Kierkegaard's author unwittingly reverses the ostensible meaning of the preceding sentence. The retrieval of the "lost force and meaning" of words would not involve the unambiguous determination and permanent fixation of meaning but rather a retrieval of that which keeps on being lost in language insofar as it is irreducibly conceptual. What is retrieved here is something in language that precedes the imposition of conceptuality and can never be reduced to it. Such retrieval would therefore also have to remain inaccessible to conceptual language: it would be a retrieval that cannot be represented as a determinate occurrence and brought about through intentional activity; it can only be intimated as an indeterminate possibility that may be "wished" for.

Kierkegaard does not elaborate on this schema of loss and retrieval in his unpublished article of 1835. But the outlines of such a schema are implied in the reflections on language of the thinker whose influence of Kierkegaard's early writing for newspapers was already apparent in the warning of a confusion "within languages themselves" in the opening lines of the article. When Hamann, in the famous passage already cited, describes speech as a "translation" or "transposition" between incommensurable spheres, here figured by an "angelic language" and "human language," this *übersetzen* is not to be mistaken for the conscious activity of an already constituted speaker—the translator— who translates one already given language into another. The angelic language of thought only becomes manifest in its transposition into a human language of words—but not without being lost in the translation. There is no access to this purely spiritual language prior to its translation into a language of words. Thought first manifests itself in the *Knechtsgestalt* of human language; before it takes this form, the thought is, as Hamann writes elsewhere, an "invisible embryo."[90] Only in speech does the thought become visible; but it does so only by having already been translated, transformed into a word, that is, something other than itself. The word simultaneously reveals the thought and conceals it; it is an *Offenbarung* that at the same time denies access to what is revealed. The thought is not made present in language; it manifests itself only as something that is irreducibly anterior to speech. If speech is a transposition from an angelic into a human tongue, this means that it is stamped by a structural loss: The thought needs to be translated into the word in order to become manifest, but in doing so it will have already been lost.

Kierkegaard alludes to this anteriority on at least one occasion in his unpublished article. In the margins of the same unfinished fragment that referred to a "lost force and meaning of words," he adds the following note: "Just as there are certain people who smooth out every little wrinkle in a sheet of paper [*Ujævnhed i Papiret*] with an instinctive vigor [*instinctmæssig Heftighed*], so are there people who blurt out a name as soon as they hear it."[91] What Hamann described as a transposition of an angelic into a human tongue returns here as an interplay of hearing a name and blurting it out. The "certain people" (*visse Mennesker*) of which Kierkegaard's author speaks may be read not as a reference to this or that person but rather to human beings in general, just as the image of hearing and speaking offered here may be read as an attempt to capture a basic structure of human speech. The words used to describe the transposition from hearing to speaking, *instinctmæssig* and *Heftighed*, suggest that this transposition precedes every conscious intention: that a name is blurted out as soon as it is heard is beyond the control of any speaker. As the comparison to the smoothing out of a piece of paper suggests, what is heard and blurted out—the name (*Navn*)—does not remain intact; just as the wrinkles and creases of a piece of paper are smoothed out in order to secure its evenness and homogeneity, so the singular character of the name would have been effaced when it is blurted out, the name would have turned into a concept. But the speaker is not conscious of the name that has been effaced. Not only is the name blurted out "instinctively," before the speaker would have become conscious of it, but this blurting out is also said to occur as soon as the name has been heard—*strax*, "instantaneously." Before the speaker could have become consciously aware of the name that is heard, the name has already been spoken; the speaker is denied access to the name that was heard, but only hears itself blurting out a name that is always already stripped of its singularity, like a piece of paper whose wrinkles have been smoothed out.

What emerges from Kierkegaard's unpublished newspaper article is, then, a strange economy of speech: to speak is to be confronted with a loss while being denied the knowledge of exactly what has been lost. The insight that is already at work in Hamann's writings but pushed to its extreme by Kierkegaard in the early writings is that the word that the speaker is left with, the word that is "blurted out," is, in the end, utterly indeterminate—an empty word that no longer acts as a vehicle of a determinate meaning. But just as a word cannot be reduced to its semantic function, it also cannot help to mean or refer. On the one hand, this word points to a thought that has already been lost as soon as it has been spoken and manifests itself only as pure anteriority; on the other hand, it promises the possibility of retrieving this meaning.[92] One feels that one has lost something, but does not know that it is; only in its retrieval— that one can only wish for—will what has been lost make itself known. The *Betydning*, whose loss and recovery Kierkegaard alludes to, never manifests itself in the present, only in the past and the future—but here it manifests itself as something indeterminate, something that must remain unsayable in the present but intimates itself as the promise of a future that cannot be reduced to any present. It is exactly this promise that will be at the center of the reflections on time and history that Kierkegaard will undertake in his writings of the following years—reflections that will play out around the same schema of

loss and repetition that had already structured his early engagement with the
problem of language.

The Instant

Kierkegaard's reflections on historical time are organized around a concept to
which he clearly allocated a central importance but which retains an enigmatic
character: that of the "instant" (*Øieblik*).[93] That this category stands in a certain relation to his preoccupation with journalism is suggested by its conspicuous appearance in the title of his last published work: the self-published
polemical pamphlet *The Instant*, of which ten issues appeared until his death
in 1855.[94] The title of the publication and Kierkegaard's reference to it as a
Blad, a "paper" or literally a "sheet," imply an intimate relation between writing
and time. The writing that is to unfold on its pages—the famous polemic
against *det Bestaaende*, which is usually translated as "the establishment" but
is more accurately rendered as "the subsisting," for what is attacked here is at
bottom what endures, what claims to maintain itself in its presence[95]—would
have an emphatically ephemeral character: it would be a writing that is not
meant to endure but instead to enter into a certain relation to the moment in
which it is written. And yet, when Kierkegaard announces this "paper" in an
"extra paper" (*Følgeblad*) that is appended to its first issue, he begins precisely
by pointing out that it is in the last instance not concerned with the ephemeral, not with something passing, indeed not with anything pertaining to time
as such:

> In my work I have now got so near to the contemporary [*Samtiden*],
> the instant, that I cannot do without an organ by means of which
> I can instantly address myself to the contemporary; and this I have
> called: *The Instant*. [. . .] I call this organ *The Instant*. Yet it is nothing
> ephemeral [*noget Ephemert*] that I want, just as it was nothing ephemeral
> I wanted before; no, it was and is something eternal.[96]

The "organ" announced here will certainly address ephemeral matters; it will
come as close as possible to its own time, the contemporary and it will do so in
a language that accommodates to the "life of the weekday"[97]—a prompt language
that will be elaborated in the form of concise reflections, usually no more than
two pages long, or pithy observations and anecdotes of only a few sentences gathered under titles such as "brief notes" or "brief and to the point."[98] But even though
this *Blad* is written for immediate consumption, it is not interested in the passing,
fleeting moment as such, taken in isolation. It will only be concerned with
Samtiden, its own time, insofar as this time stands in relation to another time,

a time that is no time at all, at least in the sense of a passing time that can be called "ephemeral," but is described here as "eternal." *The Instant* will be the name for a paper concerned with the relation between these two yet to be determined temporal dimensions: the ephemeral and the eternal. This is already intimated by the form and tone of the writing, which oscillates between current journalistic and older religious genres, from the parable to the sermon or the list of theses.[99] Whenever this *Blatt* will speak of ephemeral matters, these are always treated in their relation to the eternal. That this relation is not without its complications is suggested by Kierkegaard's choice of words in his *Følgeblad*: for as soon as it is measured against the eternal, the ephemeral seems to be reduced to a *noget*, a nothing, without however being replaced by something else—at least not something that has a positive presence, as is indicated by the term that is repeated twice in order to prepare the appearance of the eternal in this passage, a "wanting" (*villen*): a term that introduces the "eternal" as something that, despite having been wanted before and being wanted yet again in the moment in which this *Følgeblad* is written, remains outstanding.

In the announcement of *The Instant* one could recognize the outlines of Kierkegaard's programmatic reflections on the *Øieblik* in a book that was published around ten years earlier, *The Concept of Anxiety*, whose central chapter will revolve around a constantly renewed attempt of its pseudonymous author, Vigilius Haufniensis, to define this concept in terms of a relation between *Tiden* and *Evigheden*. When it appears in Haufniensis's treatise, the concept is emphatically related to a problem that remains implicit in the announcement of his paper even though it will motivate the polemic that will unfold on its pages: the problem of the possibility of history.[100] In *The Concept of Anxiety*, the category of the instant is introduced in the context of an examination of historical time—an examination that does not make reference to actual occurrences but is only concerned with the exposure of the field in which history can become possible. That Kierkegaard's most intense engagement with the problem of historical time takes place in this book hardly comes as a surprise if one recalls that "anxiety" (*Angest*) here serves first and foremost as the name for the inherent disquietude of spirit—an "unrest" (*Urolighed*) that determines its necessarily historical character.[101] The model for this disquietude is provided in the famous first chapter of the book, where Haufniensis interprets the story of the fall as a story of an anxiety to which even Adam and Eve are exposed in their otherwise tranquil satisfaction. Anxiety is here interpreted along the lines of Hamann, who had already spoken of anxiety as an "impertinent unrest" (*impertinente Unruhe*) that traverses even the bliss of paradise.[102] In Kierkegaard's account, this impertinent unrest is set in relation to the problem of the possibility of history. Anxiety is here construed as the unrest that draws spirit out of its dream-like state of "innocence" and brings about the fall into history. Anxiety names the disquietude that pervades spirit even where it seems to be completely at rest—a disquietude that never ceases to set spirit in motion and thus provides the precondition for the commencement of history itself.

What Kierkegaard calls *Angest* therefore serves as a name—derived from the Christian tradition—for the disquietude that Hegel had discovered to be constitutive of spirit.[103] The implicit polemic with Hegel's understanding of this disquietude will be that it is not restless enough, that it seeks relief from this restlessness in the concept and, first of all, in the conception of time to which its movement gives rise. With this in mind it is not surprising that *The Concept of Anxiety* reserves a special place for the problem of historical time. If time is, for Hegel, precisely the self-manifestation of the concept in its absolute restlessness—a restlessness that is implied in the definition of time as the "existent concept itself" in the preface to the *Phenomenology*[104]—then Kierkegaard's attempts to rethink this disquietude would have to be accompanied by an alternative conception of time. This alternative conception of time is developed in the middle chapter of the book, where Haufniensis abandons the account of spirit he has carefully built up around the concept of anxiety and its related concepts of innocence, sin, and fall, in order to then begin his exposition once again, from scratch, but now in strictly temporal terms. The analysis of the "impertinent unrest" that is history's condition of possibility is no longer organized around the concept of spirit but around a temporal concept: that of the *Øieblik*, Kierkegaard's name for a time that stands in a yet to be determined relation to "eternity," or what Haufniensis will call "the restless disturber."[105]

Empty Time

The pseudonymous author of *The Concept of Anxiety* starts his exposition of the instant from a critique of the classical conception of time. Not only is this a conception of time to which Hegel, if we trust Haufniensis's hints, still remains indebted; it is also a conception of time that governs and determines what may be called the ordinary experience of time—an experience of time in which the future is thought in a continuity with the past, the past in a continuity with the future and the present as an intermediary of the two.[106] Haufniensis begins his critique of this classical conception by recalling what he refers to as the "correct" (*rigtig*) determination of time—that is to say, a definition that may seem to be correct at this point of the exposition but will show itself to have only a partial truth in the temporal experience that will be articulated over the course of the chapter. "Time, correctly determined, is infinite succession [*uendlige Succession*]," Haufniensis posits—only to add directly that it would be incorrect to assume that this provides a sufficient ground for further determining time in terms of a past, present, and future.[107] If it is understood as infinite succession, no ground could ever be found within time itself to distinguish between a present, past, and future. Recalling one of the aporias that has haunted discussions of the problem of time throughout the philosophical tradition, Haufniensis points out that such a distinction would seem to require finding a "foothold" (*Fodfæste*), a point that would provide secure support for this distinction: especially if such a foothold would have to be something present (*Nærvarende*), a moment that would act as a dividing point between past, present, and future. "Precisely because every moment [*Moment*] as well as the sum of moments, is a process (a passing by), no moment is present, and in time there is accordingly neither a present nor a past nor a future."[108] The terms Haufniensis uses here are significant: just as the procession of the *Proces* of time is determined as a passing by, a *Gaaen-forbi*, so the *Moment* invokes the classical "atom of time" as a now that eludes presence to the extent that it is always on the move. The now, as the form in which time must be given according to the classical conception of time, is also the form in which time can only be given as that which it is not; but if time is given in the now, it has always already vanished, is always already no longer.[109] Insofar as it is impossible to find a foothold in a now, a moment that is present, it would therefore also be impossible to find a secure ground for the distinction between a past, present, and a future within time itself.

Whoever nevertheless insists on positing a present, a past, and a future from within time can only do so by betraying time—and its infinite succession—by spatializing it. Haufniensis points out that time is not genuinely thought in this spatialization but merely subjected to *Forestilling*, representation: "Thinking that this division can be upheld is due to the *spatialization* of a moment, but this brings the infinite succession to a halt; it is through introducing representation, by allowing time to be represented instead of being thought. But also this is to go about it incorrectly, for the infinite succession of time is an infinitely contentless present [*uendeligt indholdsløst Nærværende*] even for our powers of representation."[110] The implicit target here is not merely the classical Aristotelian conception of time but above all Hegel's account of the emergence of time-consciousness in the opening section of the *Phenomenology of Spirit*. Haufniensis alludes on several occasions to this section, which provides an exposition of the release of the absolute in time through the dialectic of "sense-certainty." In the first paragraphs of this exposition, Hegel demonstrates that the experience of time only becomes possible on the condition that spirit has moved through two stages, which roughly correspond to the two moments that Haufniensis refers to as time "thought" and time "represented." The section famously begins by unfolding the dialectic of the This of which sense-certainty finds itself to be immediately aware—a sensuous This, which is, in turn, considered in the "double shape of its being, as the *Now* and the *Here*."[111] In this initial stage, no experience of time in general is as yet possible: the immediate self that corresponds to the sensuous This is only certain of a particular Now of which it is immediately aware. When it is asked about the now of which it is immediately certain ("What is the now?") it can only answer by enunciating a determinate time ("The now is the Night"). Before gaining a representation of time, the immediate self will first have to go through the attempt to preserve the truth of this now by writing it down, only to discover that this truth has, as Hegel famously writes, become "stale" (*schal*) the moment after it has been written down.[112] Writing, which is supposed to preserve the truth of the "now"—and to demonstrate its permanence and persistence in the process—turns out to expose its untruth. But by being written down, this now also gives itself over to being read. By being inscribed on a surface together with another now, writing has spatialized now-points and thereby rendered it possible for the various nows inscribed on a surface to be compared. In this comparison—which Hegel models on reading—various inscribed nows are contracted into a spatial simultaneity. By comparing these now-points in their simultaneity, sense-certainty comes to the discovery that the particular content of each of these now-points is insubstantial and untrue; it grasps only the universal form of the now. This universal form—the now that persists as a perennial moment—imposes its primacy on the particular now-points sublated in it; as particular nows, however, they still cannot be simultaneous. Only on the condition of its abstract externalization in space does the experience of time in general become possible: only on the condition of the spatialization and contraction of now-points, here modeled on a reading of writing, can time be conceived in terms of the non-simultaneity of its moments and the persistence of its form.[113]

Haufniensis's reference to an "infinitely contentless present" (*uendeligt indholdsløst*) may be read in reference to this universal now that emerges out of the comparison of particular now-points.[114] Time is represented but only at the cost of reducing it to an empty form—a form that is taken to stand outside of time insofar as it maintains its own presence despite the infinite vanishing of its content. What exactly is implied in this emptiness is illustrated by Haufniensis in the following sentences, which evoke a seemingly innocent example:

> The Indian people tell the story of a line of kings [*Kongerække*] who ruled for 70,000 years. About the kings one knows nothing, not even their names (so I presume). If we would take this as an example of time, then these 70,000 years are an infinite vanishing [*uendeligt Forsvinden*] for thought, but for representation it expands, spatializes itself into the illusory view of an infinitely contentless nothing [*uendeligt indholdsløst Intet*].[115]

This story offers an image of time as a sequence—a *Række*, a row or line—in which the infinite, endless perishing of particular now-points is absorbed into the constancy and persistence of a universal but empty form. That the names of the individual kings in this sequence of hereditary rulers are said to remain unknown—"that one knows nothing of these kings, not even their names (so I presume)"—would point to the price that is paid for establishing this continuum. As an empty form, this continuum would have nothing but an accidental relation to the particular nows that it absorbs: time is reduced to an empty form indifferent to its content. That this "example of time" (*Exempel paa Tiden*) exemplifies not only a classical conception of time, but also the one that underpins the "whole newer development," is suggested by the fact that this story is not merely told by Haufniensis but retold, recited from the pages of Hegel's *Lectures on the Philosophy of History* and mobilized against its author. In the passage from which Kierkegaard cites this story, Hegel introduces this story as an example of a time in which history proper fails to take place because of the inaccuracy with which history is written—an epoch that fails to become an epoch in the strict sense of the word, passed time without history:

> Indian writings indicate epochs and great numbers that are often of astronomical size and even more often are completely arbitrary. It says of kings that they ruled for 70,000 years or more; Brahma, the first figure in cosmogony, who created himself, was said to have lived for 20,000 million years, et cetera. [. . .] It would be ridiculous to take writings like these for something historical [*es würde lächerlich sein, dergleichen für etwas Geschichtliches zu nehmen*].[116]

The small adjustments Haufniensis makes to the story—the replacement of the "kings" by a *Kongerække*, which implies not only the line of time but also the succession in the sense of a seemingly inexorable succession of hereditary

rulers; the additional remark on the "unknown names" of these kings—
repurpose it and tear the story away from the illustrative function that it ful-
fills for Hegel. But when Haufniensis recites this story and presents it as an
"example of time" represented as continuum, the story still carries the charge
that it was supposed to have in Hegel: that it would be *lächerlich* to take the
time of this epoch as *etwas Geschichtliches*. Time spatialized and represented
in this way might allow one to distinguish a past, present, and a future; it might
lend itself to being measured and calculated, to serve as a homogeneous medium in which the movement of daily existence can be reckoned and organized; but the time exemplified here is not the time of history. In stabilizing
the empty form of the now as an "infinitely contentless present," this conception of time might have provided a first refuge against the work of time, an
initial relief against time in its passing dimension, something permanent that
can withstand its infinite vanishing. But in doing so, it will have already relin-
quished the relation through which history in the strict sense of the word becomes possible and the division between past and future can acquire its
significance—the relation between time as a pure, unrelieved "passing" (*for-
bigangne Tid*) and the possibility of the restoration of its "fullness" (*Tidens
Fylde*).[117] As Haufniensis will continue to demonstrate, the emptiness of the
time that is reduced to a continuum is also the emptiness of a time that no
longer bears a relation to the possibility of its fulfillment.

Doubled Now

Haufniensis thus returns to his claim that time itself—that is to say, time correctly thought as infinite succession, the time that passes—provides no "foothold" for positing a past, present, and a future. To posit a past, present, and
future by resorting to a spatial representation of time would fall short of thinking the past, present, and future in their heterogeneity, insofar as the future is
conceived as a mere continuity with the past. This represented time might provide a basis for anticipation and prediction, but it has nothing to do with the
time of history. Time represented as a continuum of now-points is not historical time; but neither could the time prior to this representation, the time that
is correctly determined as an infinite passing-by, deserve this name by itself.
History—and this is the central thought of Haufniensis's reflections on historical time—could only ever emerge out of a relation between "passing time"
and another time—a time that is absolutely different, incommensurable to the
time that passes. This differential relation would precede any distinction between past, present, and future; these distinctions could, indeed, only ever
emerge out of this relation between two absolutely different times.

The "instant" (*Øieblik*) is the name that Kierkegaard reserves for this relation between two incommensurable times. "History first begins with the instant [*først i Øieblikket begynder Historien*]," Haufniensis writes in *The Concept
of Anxiety*.[118] The possibility of history opens up in the instant: that is to say,
spirit is first permeated by the restlessness that will constitute it as spirit when
passing time enters into a relation to another time. To the extent that this other
time would have to be absolutely different from time correctly determined as
the time that passes, this other time could no longer be called time at all—
least of all by the pseudonymous author of *The Concept of Anxiety*, who never
ceases to insist on the strictest conceptual distinctions. For this other time, absolutely different from the time that passes, Haufniensis thus reserves the name
"eternity" (*Evigheden*).[119] Haufniensis will therefore consistently define the
instant as a relation between "time" and "eternity"—a relation that is for the
first time defined directly toward the end of the section in the form of a proposition that is, in fact, a constellation of figural expressions:

> The instant is that ambiguity [*Tvetydige*] in which time and eternity
> touch [*berøre*] each other; with this the concept of temporality [*Time-
> lighed*] is posited whereby time constantly cuts off eternity [*afskærer*]
> and eternity constantly permeates [*gjennemtrænger*] time.[120]

To understand what is at stake in this definition of the *Øieblik*, it is necessary
to specify what "eternity" means in the context of Haufniensis's discussion of
the problem of time. When Haufniensis defines the instant as a relation between the temporal and the eternal, he draws on the tradition of thinking eternity that revolves around the distinction between *aeternitas* and *sempernitas*,
together with the different relations between the eternal and the temporal
implied in both concepts. Haufniensis will keep on reiterating the irreducible
difference between the two times that enter into relation in the instant: he will
write that time and eternity are "incommensurable" (*inkommensurabelt*) with
one another, thus emphasizing the inadequacy of any conception of the eternal in terms of the temporal, that is to say, in terms of time conceived as a
passing-by.[121] In doing so, he distances himself from every understanding of
eternity as *sempernitas*, which reduces eternity to everlasting duration in time
and thereby thinks it according to a temporal measure. Instead, Haufniensis's
concept of eternity draws on doctrines of divine timelessness—in particular
that of Boethius, with whose texts Kierkegaard was preoccupied in the period
that he worked on *The Concept of Anxiety* and the *Philosophical Fragments*.[122]
Boethius distinguishes the everlasting duration that could be found in the
world—or at least represented in terms of temporal existence—from the *aeternitas*
that is only enjoyed by God. The distinction he draws between time and eternity

revolves around two different conceptions of the "now": time is constituted by the *nunc fluens*, the now that flows or passes—an expression that is close to Haufniensis's reference to time as a "passing-by" (*Gaaen-forbi*)—whereas eternity is constituted by the *nunc stans*, a now that "stands."[123] In contrast to a conception of eternal life as a life that, despite its everlasting duration, is nevertheless still spread out through time, the *nunc stans* proposes a conception of eternity in which all of life is gathered in a single now. This divine now is strictly atemporal: in contrast to the now that belongs to finite temporal existence, it does not pass. Only such a now, in which the whole of temporal existence is gathered, would do right to divine *perfectio*, which would be irreconcilable with the necessarily fragmented, divided character of temporal existence. This is captured in the following passage from the *Consolation of Philosophy*:

> For whatever lives in time proceeds as something present from the past into the future, and there is nothing placed in time that can embrace the whole extent [*spatium*] of its life equally. Indeed, it does not yet apprehend tomorrow but it has already lost yesterday, and even in the life of today you live no more fully than in a mobile, transitory moment. [. . .] Whatever includes and possesses the whole fullness of illimitable life [*interminabilis vitae plenitudinem*] at once, and is such that nothing future is absent from it and nothing past has flowed away, only this is rightly judged to be eternal, and of this it is necessary both that being in full possession of itself be always present to itself and that it have the infinity of mobile time present [to it] [*infinitatem mobilis temporis habere praesentem*].[124]

Haufniensis's account of time and eternity draws directly on Boethius's doctrine of the *nunc stans*. If passing time is to enter into a relation to another time in order for history to "begin," this other time, the time of eternity, is defined as a "present" (*Nærværende*)—but one that must be distinguished rigorously from any temporal present. "The eternal is the present and the present is fullness [*Fylde*]," Haufniensis writes. "It was in this sense that the Latinist said of the deity that he is *praesens* (*praesentes dii*)."[125] The present of eternity has no past or future because it gathers all of time within itself and restores the unity of what was scattered in time: "The instant signifies the present as a something that has no past [*Forbigangent*] and no future [*Tilkommende*], for it is just in this that the imperfection of the sensuous life lies. The eternal, too, signifies the present, which has no past and no future, and this is the perfection of the eternal [*Eviges Fuldkommenhed*]."[126] The conception of eternity that Haufniensis introduces is thus, on the one hand, strictly distinguished from time: eternity is defined not as everlasting duration within time but rather as the relief of temporal existence from that which determines it as temporal in the first place, namely its successive character. Haufniensis will indeed refer to eternity as "the present in terms of sublated succession" (*ophœvede Succession*).[127] At the same time as the two are strictly distinguished, they are, however, placed in a definite relation: eternity is nothing but time brought to its *Fuldkommenhed*, a state of perfection and completion in which time is released from the successive order. "The concept on which everything turns in Christianity, that which made all things new, is the fullness of time [*Tidens Fylde*]."[128] Eternity is, in other words, not a negative abstraction of time, nontime; it is a plenitude that never ceases to be divided and torn apart as long as time passes.[129]

Just as Kierkegaard, in his early writings, attempts to expose the structural "deficiency" that stamps human language and turns every word into a call for the retrieval of a lost and inaccessible state of perfection, so the distinction between time and eternity in *The Concept of Anxiety* is an attempt to draw out a deficiency that would make every passing moment call for the recovery of a presence it had always already lost. What Haufniensis calls "temporality" (*Timelighed*)—the differentiation of past and future with which history "begins"—could only emerge out of the relation between "time" conceived in terms of the imperfection of inexorable succession and "eternity" conceived in terms of the perfection of a restored plenitude. Haufniensis will emphasize this doubled character of historical time when he refers to the instant in terms that recall the distinction between the *nunc fluens* and *nunc stans*: as the relation between the "atom of time" (*Tidens Atom*) and the "atom of eternity" (*Evighedens Atom*).[130] Temporality emerges not as the relation between different but commensurable "atoms of time," the comparison of at least two nowpoints whose sublation into a universal now was presented in Hegel's account of the development of time consciousness in the *Phenomenology*. If temporality emerges out of a relation between two atoms, it is the relation between the atom of time and an atom that is incommensurable to it and that does not lend itself to comparison and sublation. Before the passing moment is brought into a relation to another, every atom of time has already entered into a relation to that atom in which all of time would be gathered and released from the order of succession. Every passing moment would refer negatively to this state, would express this need through its sheer imperfection, the *Mangelfuldhed* or "fullness of lack" that Kierkegaard sought to lay bare in human language. But every atom of time would also—comically, accidentally—harbor a positive reference to the atom of eternity: the structure of the *nunc fluens*, which "has no past or future" in the sense that it is separated and divided from every other moment,

Once here in Copenhagen there were two actors who probably never thought that their performance could have a deeper significance. They stepped forth onto the stage, placed themselves opposite each other, and then began the mimical representation of one or another passionate conflict. When the mimical development [*Udvikling*] was fully taking its course [*i fuld Gang*] and the spectators' eyes [*Øie*] followed the story [*Historien*] while awaiting what was to follow, they suddenly stopped [*brøde de pludseligen af*] and now remained motionless as though petrified [*forbleve nu urokkeligen forstenede*] in the mimical expression of the instant. The effect of this can be exceedingly comical, for the instant in an accidental way becomes commensurable with the eternal.[137]

Haufniensis's choice of words in the description of this scene is important to note. What is interrupted here is a "history" (*Historien*), an unfolding narrative described as a "development" (*Udvikling*) that "takes its course" (*Gang*)— all concepts that not only echo the interruption of the "course of history" described in the early fragment but also tie this representation of history to the introduction to Hegel's *Lectures on the Philosophy of History*, which deploys exactly these terms.[138] Returning to the motif of conversation that had played an important role in the early writings, the two actors who "place themselves opposite one another" and engage in "one or another passionate conflict" perform the dialectic that drives this development. The continuous character of this "development" is emphasized in Haufniensis's description of the spectators' eyes (*Tilskuerens Øie*) as eyes that "follow" (*fulgte*) the history unfolding on the stage, and do so while constantly "awaiting what was to follow [*ventede det Følgende*]."[139] The view of history that is captured in the scene evoked here is thus one where the spectators' attentive inspection of the development unfolding before their eyes is accompanied by a constant expectation of what is yet to come, joining together what has just happened and what is about to happen. As Kierkegaard's rendering of this constant anticipation as an "awaiting of what follows" (*ventede det Følgende*) suggests, the future anticipated here is already preformed: before it has happened, what is yet to come is already construed as something that follows on—and follows from—the immanent development that is playing out before the eyes of the spectators. If there is a future here, it is one that is not conceived as *det Følgende*, that which merely follows from that which it follows on, as if it were the necessary next stage in a logical sequence.[140]

The instant when the actors "suddenly stopped" (*brøde de pludseligen af*)— the word Haufniensis uses, *afbrøde*, literally means to "break off"—is precisely the instant in which this temporal continuity is shattered.[141] What interrupts the continuity staged here is not some other, unexpected occurrence; it is the occurrence of the interruption itself. The arrest of time to which Hauf-niensis refers in his definition of the instant as eternity's "first attempt, as it were, to bring time to a halt" is here enacted literally in the sudden interrup-tion of the actors' movement.[142] But the real drama of this interruption does not take place on the stage; it happens on the side of the spectators. The sud-den interruption of the movement on the stage is accompanied by an inter-ruption of the continuous movement of the spectators' eyes, their attentive following of the development on the stage as the activity that guarantees the continuity between what has passed and what is yet to come. What is inter-rupted in Haufniensis's anecdote is therefore not merely the movement of the actors, but above all the representational activity of the spectator. In the in-stant of a sudden interruption, an interruption that could not have been fore-seen, the representation of time breaks down: in this interruption, it is first of all the represented "future" that shatters—that is to say, the future insofar as it is anticipated and foreseen by the spectators as *det Følgende*, that which is ex-pected to follow from what has passed. But if the anticipation of what follows has shattered in this sudden interruption, the ground that was supposed to sus-tain this anticipation loses its validity as well: with the entrance of the "sud-den" (*pludselige*) interruption, the "development" that was taking its course only shortly before can no longer maintain its purchase on the future; the past can no longer form the basis for a representation of this future as a time that can be conceived as a mere extension of the time that has passed. Together with the anticipated future, the representation of time in general breaks down in this interruption. Haufniensis can write that time is "as it were, brought to a halt" in this instant of interruption because, in this moment of interruption, there is no longer a "future" that could be extrapolated from the past, nor a "past" insofar as it provided the ground for the expectation of a future con-tinuous with it.[143] Not only the past and the future, but also the present found-ers in this instant, at least insofar as it is comprehended as—to use the expression that Haufniensis uses elsewhere in the same chapter—the "intermediary [*Mellemliggende*] of the past and the future" conceived in their continuity.[144] Haufniensis's spectator thus not only loses the determinate content of recol-lection and of expectation, a particular past and a particular future, but also, in the moment of interruption, is deprived of the possibility of establishing a continuity between the past and future as such. Together with this possibility, the representation of time as an endless sequence of now-points, strung to-gether into a continuous flow, is destined to founder as well.

In the shattering of the continuum, time suddenly manifests itself in a dif-ferent way; in the instant of interruption, time no longer manifests itself as a homogeneous flow but as the disjunction between the two absolutely heterogeneous times that Haufniensis had described earlier in the section. When the movement of the actors comes to a sudden halt, the past loses its purchase on the future; what is about to happen is suddenly permeated by indeterminacy. Conversely, without the anticipation of a foreseeable future, time manifests itself as a pure passing, where every moment vanishes into nothingness rather than contribute to a cumulative development. The special significance of even the most mundane interruption, of which the comic scene evoked by Haufniensis is nothing but an exemplary instance, is that it offers a glimpse of these two dimensions of time that collide in the "instant" and reveals them in their absolute disjunction and pure polarity. Passing time manifests itself here as pure vanishing; the time that is yet to come manifests itself in a pure indeterminacy—an indeterminacy that is concentrated only by the need that springs from time in its passing dimension, the need for a recovery of every passing moment. Every interruption thus has the character of a revelation, insofar as it lays bare a structure of time that precedes and exceeds every representation of time—a conflict of two heterogeneous times that could never be integrated into a continuum.

If the interruption can have an "exceedingly comical effect," as Haufniensis writes in his account of the stage play, and if this comical effect derives from the fact that "the instant becomes commensurable with the eternal in an accidental way," this is because the destruction of the future and past is analogous to the eternal conceived as a *nunc stans*—and in this sense it is a "reflection [*Reflex*] of eternity" in time.[145] But this "reflection" of eternity, this duplication of it is not identical to the eternity attributed to divine existence: even though it has a structural resemblance to divine eternity, this "first reflection" of eternity in time could not be further removed from the divine *praesens*. This is not a now of pleromatic presence, but rather a now that is marked by its specific relation to nothingness, or what Kierkegaard calls in a footnote *to kenon*—the empty.[146] The sudden interruption of the comic play is a figure of a shattered representation of time in which future, past, and present all perish and the subject is—at least for an instant—left with nothing. It is this perishing that Kierkegaard has in mind when he juxtaposes, in the same footnote, his account of this scene from a stage play with a citation from an ancient text:

> In the New Testament there is a poetic paraphrase of the instant. Paul says that the world will perish *en atomō kai en ripē ophthalmoū* (in a moment and the glance of an eye). By this he also expresses that the instant is commensurable with eternity, precisely because the instant of perishing [*Undergangs-Øieblikket*] expresses eternity at the same instant.[147]

The instant, here rendered as *Undergangs-Øieblikket,* is, then, an instant in which the "world perishes" in the sense that the representations of the future and past break down, alongside the experience of the present that serves as their intermediary: it is the instant in which it has even become impossible to represent time as a continuous flow—if only for an instant. But this instant is not just "empty" in the sense of a deprivation, an instant in which one is left with nothing; in contrast to the "infinite contentlessness" of represented time, Kierkegaard conceives of this *Undergang* of the temporal continuum as an emptiness that harbors the promise of another time—an experience of time that has nothing to do with the one that corresponds to the "course of history" that Kierkegaard references in his early journal or the "development" of the play evoked in *The Concept of Anxiety.* "Only now [*først nu*]," Haufniensis writes, "does the aforementioned division [*Inddeling*] acquire its significance: the present time, the past time, the future time [*den tilkommende Tid*]."[148] Only now, *først nu,* only in *this* now when the continuous flow of time is arrested, can the division between these categories first assume their significance; that is to say, only now can it be an *Inddeling* that does not merely divide up a homogeneous, uniform time but acts as a division in the emphatic sense, namely a division between absolutely different, heterogeneous, and incommensurable times. In the breakdown of the representation of time, a different experience of temporality opens up, namely an experience of temporality as the conflict between the time that passes and a time with a wholly different structure, a time that is yet to come.

In the temporalization to which Haufniensis refers here, a privileged role is reserved for this time of what is yet to come, the future as *det Tilkommende.* This is hardly surprising, given that the sudden arrest of time captured in Haufniensis's story of the interrupted stage play manifested itself first of all as the shattering of the future insofar as it was foreseen by the spectators. It is in this shattering of a future conceived as something that follows from what has preceded it, the future as *det Følgende,* that the possibility of another future opens up. This other future could not be conceived as one that is defined by the same structure of anticipation and merely directed toward a different object: it would rather be an attempt to think a *tilkommende Tid* in the strict sense of the word, a time that comes from the future rather than flowing into it, a time that arrives *ex futuro* rather than being constituted as an extension of the past *in futuro.* Such a future would exceed any attempt to reduce what is yet to come to what has already been. "In this division," Haufniensis therefore continues to write, "attention is at once drawn to the fact that, in a sense, the future means more than the present and the past, because the future is in a sense the whole of which the past is a part, and the future can in a sense signify the whole."

And he adds: "This is because the eternal means first the future, or because the future is the incognito in which the eternal, though incommensurable with time, wants nevertheless to maintain its commerce [*Omgængelse*] with time."[149] The "commerce" between the eternal and the temporal—between the "full" time of the *nunc stans* and the time that merely passes—is mediated by the category of the future. This future is nothing but the medium in which the eternal allows itself to be imparted to the temporal, an oblique and indirect medium that Haufniensis describes as "incognito" (*det Incognito*). The future is an "incognito of the eternal" principally in the sense that the eternal, as the fulfillment of time and therefore its end, can enter temporal existence only as a possibility that is yet to be realized—once it is conceived as the "fullness of time," the eternal can only ever lie in the future.[150] It is for this reason that Haufniensis will contrast the ancient concept of eternity, which conceives of the eternal as a past that is recollected, with the Christian concept of the fullness of time—a concept that, according to Haufniensis, "made all things new"—which must manifest itself as a fulfillment that is yet to come.[151] This future must, however, manifest itself as an "incognito" in the literal sense: That is to say, the possibility of fulfilled time manifests itself in the future only as a future that must remain unknown. In both *The Concept of Anxiety* and *Philosophical Fragments*, Kierkegaard will insist on the impossibility of reducing the future to a time that could ever be foreseen or known in advance: the futurity of *det Tilkommende*, what is yet to come, lies precisely in its withdrawal from all seeing and knowing. The future is thus marked by an indeterminate determinacy: it is the outstanding promise of the fullness of time, of the fulfillment of all time that passes, and yet it could promise this fulfillment only as an incognito—as a future that, even if it must remain unknowable and unforeseeable, makes an all the more forceful claim on every passing moment. A time that could be called historical—a time in which, as Haufniensis writes, history "begins"—would have to be thought as the ever-renewed relation between these two, entirely differently structured times: a time that passes and a time that is yet to come.

The Polemicist

The structure of time that is captured in the concept of the instant is anticipated in a figure that already appears in Kierkegaard's early writings: the polemicist. This figure does not just mark the point of view from which his newspaper articles of the 1930s are written; that Kierkegaard chose the name *Øieblikket* for the "paper" that served as the vehicle for his final polemic also suggests its close relation to Kierkegaard's later reflections on time. The relation between writing and time that the polemicist captures in the early writings is expressed first and foremost in an irresolvable restlessness. "The polemical striving [*polemiske Stræben*] never finds rest," Kierkegaard writes in a reflection on the polemic included in his dissertation—"rest is the very opposite of this kind of writing [*Ro er netop slig Digtens Modsætning*]."[152] In the figure of the polemicist, whose outlines can be constructed on the basis of fragmented remarks found throughout the early work, the discrepancy between the finite subject and its aspiration toward infinity is pushed to an extreme. Like the poetic ironist, the idea against which the polemicist measures the world exceeds every conceivable actuality and reduces it to nothingness. In the aspiration to rise above everything limited, however, the polemicist can no longer rely on the indifference of the poet; the given actuality renders it impossible to detach themselves.[153] For the polemicist, the given actuality has not just lost its validity; it has become a hindrance, something that holds back all aspirations toward infinity. In polemical irony—an irony that, in its extreme and uncompromised form, was what Kierkegaard called "humor"—the motto *nil admirari*, "admire nothing," is radicalized into a *foragtet Alt*, "despise everything."[154] This motto points to two crucial aspects of what Kierkegaard calls the "polemical striving": its purely "infinite" and "negative" character. First, the striving of the polemicist is infinite because it is not restricted to a determinate object: every polemic is ultimately a "polemic against the world" (*Polemik mod Verden*).[155] There is no doubt that the polemic tendency expresses itself in attacks on particular texts or opponents; but insofar as there is no conceivable actuality that could measure up to the idea, there is no determinate attack in which the polemic could find its fulfillment. The polemic is therefore also infinite, *uendelig* in the sense that it cannot come to an end; it could only find its fulfillment in the annihilation of a world that is perceived as an imperfect form, a hindrance to every aspiration to the eternal. Kierkegaard therefore distinguishes the polemical striving in the strict sense from what he calls the "positive polemic" (*positiv Polemik*)—a polemic that is undertaken from an already established standpoint that the polemicist aims to secure through his attacks. The polemical striving in the strict sense, however, has no positive content to communicate: because it has no access to the idea, it is not in the position to "thunder at teachers of false doctrines with the pathos of seriousness."[156] Every polemic in the strict sense of the word must be a "negative polemic" (*negativ Polemik*): it does not attack in order to affirm a certain position; rather, it merely and purely undermines the statements of its contemporaries to "calmly and inflexibly watch them sink down into absolutely nothing."[157] The polemicist annihilates every given actuality with no intent to put anything in its place. Only in the moment of annihilation does the polemicist glimpse an infinite, albeit negative, freedom: only in the instant when actuality sinks down into nothingness can the polemicist "breathe lightly and freely, under the vast horizon intimated by the idea as boundary."[158] But also from this freedom the polemicist needs to part as soon as it has revealed itself, if only because the passing of time will have stamped it with finitude the moment after. The polemic must therefore be taken up again at every instant. "The polemic tendency never finds rest [*finder aldrig Hvile*]," Kierkegaard writes; "because [it] consists precisely in continually freeing itself by means of a new polemic [*bestandig at frigjøre sig ved en ny Polemik*]."[159]

The restlessness that characterizes the polemic does not just play out as a relation between an already constituted self and world, but is already at work within the writing of the polemicist. "Every polemical line [*polemisk Strøg*] continually holds within itself something more [*indeholder bestandig et Mere*], the possibility of rising out over itself [*at gaae ud over sig selv*]," Kierkegaard writes in the same passage.[160] The term that Kierkegaard uses here—*indeholder*—must be read in its distinct ambiguity. That every polemical line holds something more in itself must first of all be read as a failure: the polemical line might free itself from what it destroys, but it never fully achieves the freedom toward which it aspires. In striving for freedom, the polemicist must write; but because every polemical *Strøg*, every "strike" at the world, takes the form of a *Strøg* in the sense of a "line," that is to say, a sentence, it has already limited itself and taken a finite linguistic form from which the polemical striving will, again, need to free itself. It is now this line in its linguistic dimension that ties this striving down, that fails to live up to the "something more" that the polemicist aspires to; and yet it is this same linguistic dimension that makes this line contain something more than itself and thus intimates the possibility of rising above it. What this line fails to attain—the "more" it contains—manifests itself here in the tendency of every line to say more than what it was meant to say, in the possibility of every line to move out of itself. Polemical writing never finds rest because every polemical line harbors the possibility to say something other than itself, to turn into an *allēgoria* in the strict sense: "During all this the writer grants neither himself nor the reader any rest, inasmuch as rest is the very opposite of this kind of writing. The only rest he has is the [. . .] eternity in which he sees the ideal, but this eternity is a nonentity, since it has no time, and therefore the ideal becomes allegory the very next instant [*og derfor bliver Idealet i næste Øieblik Allegori*]."[161]

In its particular restlessness, the polemic harbors an experience of time and history that is profoundly at odds with the one that Kierkegaard understood to be represented by Hegel's philosophy—especially where it comes to its relation to the new. From the standpoint of the polemicist, any future that is conceived as the extension of the present, any announcement of a new world arising out of the old through a continuous development is still compromised by the imperfect forms of the present. But as Kierkegaard notes in his dissertation, this paradoxically forces the polemicist to turn away from the future; the polemical work is focused only on what is given in the present, but this is now experienced only as an obstacle to the arrival of the new. "The old must be displaced [*fortrænges*]; the old must be perceived in all its imperfection [*sin hele Ufuldkommenhed*]," Kierkegaard writes here; "the given actuality has lost its validity entirely; it has become for him an imperfect form that is a hindrance everywhere."[162] In contrast to the prophet, who Kierkegaard treats as a figure who faces the future out of the present, the polemicist "has stepped out of line with his age, has turned around and faced it"; although this figure is "continually pointing to something that is yet to come [*peger bestandig hen paa noget Tilkommende*] [. . .] that which is yet to come is hidden from him, lies behind his back. But the actuality he so antagonistically confronts is what he must annihilate [*tilintetgøre*]; upon this he focuses his all-consuming gaze [*hans fortærende Blik*]."[163] In these remarks we find the inverse image of the immanent development culminating in an *Aufgang* of the new that Hegel evoked in the preface to the *Phenomenology*. The condition under which the new arrives is not the completion of a preceding development but rather a "displacement" of the old that strives to maintain the future in its absolute discontinuity from the present. The elements of the theory of historical transition outlined in Kierkegaard's dissertation are already found in an earlier fragment on Hamann—perhaps one of the key models for his own concept of the polemic—that was written in the same period as his newspaper articles. In the concluding paragraph of the fragment, Kierkegaard writes:

> I hope that it will be abundantly evident that everyone who in the proper sense is to fulfil a period in history [*udfylde en Periode i Historien*] must always begin polemically [*begynde polemisk*], precisely because a subsequent stage [*følgende Stadium*] is not the pure and simple result of the preceding [*Foregaaende*]. [. . .] Isn't it the case that, just as with a procession [*Procession*]—which is precisely the new that is yet to come [*det Nye, der skal komme*]—there are first men with staffs who make room [*først Stokkemændene gjøre Plads*]?[164]

In its emphatic gesturing toward the "proper" (*egenlig*) fulfillment of a period in history, the first sentence is not without irony. For the "fulfilment" that is evoked here would not be a matter of bringing an existing development to completion; as it turns out at the end, it would involve driving it away like a crowd, displacing and deposing what exists in order to make room for the new. If it is nevertheless the fulfillment of a period in the "proper" sense, this is because the *periodos*, as the time in which a phenomenon takes its course or, literally "turns around its orbit," does not result in a completion that must be understood as a return to itself. Rather, this "period in history" in which the age takes its course may be understood in terms of the parodic repetition that Kierkegaard never ceases to evoke in the early writings: the repetition by which a phenomenon comes to an end that is no completion but an emptying-out of all substance or meaning. The new—here initially ironically indicated as the "subsequent stage" (*følgende Stadium*) in a development for which it is mistaken in the "period" that Kierkegaard tries to bring to its "fulfilment"—is not a "pure and simple result"; as it will turn out, it is not a "result" (*Resultat*) at all, if this term suggests precisely something that arises out of its premises. The new does not follow out of premises; it arrives as if it were a procession—not the forward march of spirit through time, but a *processio*, an emanation of the eternal that, in a shift in register at the end of the sentence, turns out to be awaited like a parade that is yet to arrive. The image of the parade, playing on the double sense of the *Procession* evoked at the beginning of the sentence, implies a sudden inversion of the structure of historical transition that is suggested by the vocabulary of "stages," "results," and "premises." Rather than the outcome of a continuous development that drives itself forward, this transition must be understood as a collision between "what came before" (*det Foregaaende*) and "what is yet to come" (*det Tilkommende*); a transition in which the course of history does not produce the new but obstructs its arrival; a transition that does not involve the work of "concluding and introducing" that is reserved for the "absolute trumpeter," a figure that Kierkegaard will evoke elsewhere in his work.[165] Rather, the work involved in this transition is captured in the polemicist, here portrayed as a figure "with a stick" whose task is to make room, to displace the given actuality in order to prepare the way for the arrival of a future that cannot be known or foreseen. That such work may well never come to an end is suggested by the sentence that Kierkegaard appends to the end of the note: "Naturally, here things depend in turn upon how quickly that which is new follows upon the polemic [*hvor hurtigt det Nye følger ovenpaa Polemiken*]—whether it is the truth, which must be defended for years and years, or merely one or another insignificant modification."[166]

2

Idolatry of Facts

Nietzsche

Hegel and the newspapers—like opponents [*so wie die Gegner*].
    —NIETZSCHE, NOTE FOR THE *UNTIMELY MEDITATIONS*[1]

"What is precisely most valuable about philosophy," Nietzsche writes in one of his early notebooks, "is to constantly teach the counter-doctrine to everything journalistic [*die Gegenlehre alles journalistischen zu lehren*]."[2] This hyperbolic remark may serve as a point of departure for an examination of the peculiar preoccupation with journalism that runs throughout Nietzsche's work. Especially in the writings of the early 1870s, when Nietzsche was working on the *Untimely Meditations* and his unpublished *Philosophenbuch*, this preoccupation will surface time and again: passages on journalism—consistently written in a hyperbolic register—are scattered throughout Nietzsche's early notebooks, the manuscripts for his Basel lectures and, most notably, the planned series of thirteen *Untimely Meditations*, which Nietzsche intended to conclude with an installment on "newspaper slavery."[3] But references to journalists, newspapers, and the press continue to make their appearance in his writings well into the following decade—especially in *Also Sprach Zarathustra*, where acerbic caricatures of the language of the newspapers occur alongside images of another kind of news, of unheard-of messages and rumors of an unknown future.[4]

If Nietzsche's juxtaposition of philosophy and journalism—and their seeming opposition in the definition of philosophy as *Gegenlehre alles journalistischen*—may serve as a point of departure for this chapter, this is first of all because journalism is introduced here emphatically as a *philosophical* theme. Not only does the counterposition of philosophy and journalism suggest that Nietzsche's critical engagement with journalism has a philosophical character, but philosophy itself, insofar as it is conceived as a *Gegenlehre*, is defined here in terms of its relation to "everything journalistic." Journalism is thus placed at the heart of Nietzsche's attempts to rethink philosophy—an attempt central to many of his unpublished writings of the time, in particular his work on the unfinished *Philosophenbuch*. To take the proposition of philosophy as a *Gegenlehre* of "everything journalistic" seriously, in all its hyperbole, suggests the possibility of a philosophical reading of the theme as it resurfaces throughout Nietzsche's work. Such a reading diverges from the typical interpretations of his preoccupation with journalism, which—in the rare cases where it is addressed at all—tends to be regarded as a concern that may be separated from his philosophy "proper."[5] Omissions of the theme are perhaps not surprising, given the tendency to maintain a crude division between Nietzsche's philosophical writings and his so-called "cultural criticism" or between the later and the earlier, supposedly immature work, of which the interest in journalism may all too easily be understood to be a mere residue.[6] Even in the more careful readings of his work it is only rarely recognized that Nietzsche's continuous engagement with the theme of "journalism" can only be adequately grasped if it is, as one of his important interpreters puts it, "not understood disparagingly" (*nicht abschätzend verstanden*)—that is to say, if it is understood as an engagement that is inseparable from his philosophical thought and its most important rubrics.[7]

Such an interpretation of Nietzsche's fragmented notes and remarks on journalism would have to start from an attentiveness to the role of figures in his philosophical work.[8] As in the case of Kierkegaard, the journalists and newspaper readers that populate Nietzsche's writings make their appearance first and foremost as types; how these types are constituted and what role is reserved for them are, however, specific to Nietzsche's work. Throughout the writings of the 1870s, the journalist will consistently enter the stage as one amongst a crowd of philosophical "opponents" (*Gegner*).[9] Like the "historian," the "scholar," the "cultural philistine," the "teacher," the "servants of the state," or the "religious ones"—a list that could continue indefinitely—the journalist is a figure that is constituted in and through a relation of struggle and antagonism. Like his other philosophical opponents, Nietzsche consistently treats the journalist as a caricature of itself—a figure that is studied through deliberate exaggeration, that is never described in a disinterested manner but consistently perceived through the lens of a cultivated "hostility" (*Feindschaft*).[10] "I never attack people, I treat them as if they were high-intensity magnifying glasses that can illuminate a general, though insidious and barely noticeable, predicament," Nietzsche writes in a later reflection on his *Untimely Meditations*—

and the attacks on journalists scattered through the early writings may be understood precisely as an example of this treatment.[11]

But when Nietzsche conceives of philosophy as a *Gegenlehre* of everything journalistic, this is not just an expression of a general philosophical antagonism. The journalist is presented not merely as one amongst a crowd of opponents, an enemy like any other: for Nietzsche, it is that *Gegner* in relation to which philosophy defines *itself*. To consider the journalist as an enemy in the emphatic sense of the word means that its relation to philosophy cannot be reduced to an opposition: *Feindschaft* is the name that Nietzsche reserves for a relation of antagonism that can only assume its characteristic intensity on the condition of a kinship or affinity that is already at work in it. In the third of the *Untimely Meditations*, Nietzsche indeed speaks of the *Feindschaft* of Schopenhauer toward his time—that thinker who is treated here as a figure of philosophical thought and who, not accidentally, took what he called *Zeitungsschreiben* to be one of the crucial signs of his time—as "a hostility that is at bottom directed against that which, though he finds it in himself, is not truly himself."[12] Nietzsche's ambivalence toward his own practice of reading the newspapers may be understood in this light. If the reports of an ascetic abstinence from newspapers in his correspondence—"I no longer read newspapers," Nietzsche writes to a friend in 1875;[13] "I pursue my thoughts without thinking of the date and the newspapers," he reports in a letter of 1880;[14] "I am not aware of the most well-known events and haven't read the newspapers even once," we read in his correspondence of 1882[15]—alternate with references to the latest news, ranging from newspaper clippings to weather reports,[16] this could be read not as evidence of hypocrisy or inconsistency but, rather, as the sign of an affinity between his philosophical work and the journalism from which it never ceases to distance itself.

The question that is raised by Nietzsche's counterposition of philosophy and journalism may thus be formulated in the following manner: what makes it possible in the first place to present philosophy as a *Gegenlehre* of everything journalistic? What is the affinity between philosophy and journalism that would render this relation of enmity possible? The thought that will guide this chapter is that Nietzsche's preoccupation with journalism is to be understood in light of a question that can be traced back to Kant and Hegel—a question that we have already seen to surface in the writings of Kierkegaard, but that arguably takes on its full force only in the work of Nietzsche. It is a question that one of Nietzsche's more recent readers has referred to as the "question of today" (*la question de l'aujourd'hui*): "What is happening today? What is happening to us right now? What is this 'now' in which we all live and which is the site, the point from which I am writing?"[17] It is the fundamental importance of this question in Nietzsche's philosophy that has made it possible to characterize Nietzsche as "philosopher-journalist" (*philosophe-journaliste*): "The first philosopher-journalist was Nietzsche. He has introduced the 'today' into the field of philosophy. Before him, philosophy knew only of time and eternity. But Nietzsche had an obsession for actuality [*l'actualité*]."[18] This characterization of Nietzsche as a philosopher-journalist may be accepted only if the conjunction of these two figures is taken to refer not to a harmonious synthesis but to a problem. Nietzsche's counterposition of philosophy and journalism must then be understood not as a refutation of this characterization but as an elaboration of it. If philosophy must now define itself in the face of journalism, this is because the philosopher and journalist have come to be concerned with one and the same question. If philosophy is to be understood as a *Gegenlehre* of everything journalistic, this is because it will treat this question in a manner that is fundamentally at odds with the modes of thought and experience, of reading and writing, which are, for Nietzsche, exemplified by the journalist and newspaper reader. The polemic between philosophy and journalism as it is staged by Nietzsche will therefore not play out around an opposition between the eternal and the temporal: as we will see, the philosopher and the journalist are conceived rather as the exemplary protagonists of a struggle between what is "timely" (*zeitgemäß*) and "untimely" (*unzeitgemäß*).

Unzeitungsgemäß

The concept of untimeliness plays an important role throughout Nietzsche's philosophical work, especially in his attempts to rethink the relation between thought and its time. Even if this role is most conspicuous in the writings of the 1870s, where the concept is programmatically introduced in the title of the *Untimely Meditations*—the series of essays that runs as a connecting thread through his early work—it continues to resurface well into his later writings, in particular those of the late 1880s. Rather than merely describing a vague "unfashionable" or "unseasonable" character of his early writing, the concept of untimeliness has a precise philosophical significance: it is, as Nietzsche puts it himself, a word that is to be "understood in the most profound way" (*im tiefsten Verstande genommen*).[19] It makes its first appearance as early as 1869 in a letter to Erwin Rohde, where Nietzsche uses the word with reference to Wagner—a figure who would later serve as one of the "untimely types par excellence" (*unzeitgemässe Typen par excellence*) that would be portrayed in the last two *Untimely Meditations*.[20] "He stands there," Nietzsche writes, "rooted firmly through his own force, with his gaze always over and beyond everything ephemeral, untimely in the most beautiful sense [*unzeitgemäß im schönsten Sinne*]."[21] The concept returns several years later, after the publication of *The Birth of Tragedy* and its implicit break with Schopenhauerian metaphysics, in the period when Nietzsche began working on his *Philosophenbuch*, the unfinished work that was concerned with, amongst other things, the question of whether philosophy was still possible in his time.[22] The significance of the concept of untimeliness may be understood in relation to this question. For Nietzsche, untimeliness is not an accidental attribute of thought, not a characteristic that may or may not be attributed to it: in a yet to be determined sense, untimeliness is one of its constitutive elements. "I do not know," Nietzsche writes in one of the *Untimely Meditations*, "what sense there would be to philology in our time, if not for the untimeliness that is at work in it"—and the same holds true for philosophy itself.[23]

This is thematized in the writings of the late 1880s, where Nietzsche returns to the concept on several occasions. In the retrospective on his work in *Ecce Homo*, the section titled "Why I Write Such Good Books," Nietzsche no longer refers to the *Untimely Meditations* but simply to his "untimelies" (*Unzeitgemässen*).[24] Perhaps leaving out that second word in their initial title— *Betrachtungen*—is an attempt to remove all traces of a conception of thinking as distanced and disinterested contemplation or reflection—a conception with which his planned project of thirteen periodical essays emphatically sought to break. But another way to interpret this consistent abbreviation of the title to a single word, the *Unzeitgemässen*, would be that the second word of the title could be omitted by Nietzsche because it was simply superfluous. If it is possible for Nietzsche to refer to his "untimelies," this is perhaps because there was already something tautological about their initial title: that is to say, if untimeliness is always already at the heart of any thinking in the strict sense of the word. A comparable gesture, including the transformation of "untimely" from an adjective to a noun, is found in the concluding section of his *Twilight of the Idols*, published as late as 1889 and titled "Wanderings of an Untimely."[25] "An untimely" (*ein Unzeitgemässen*): here this single word is used to characterize the thinker, the writer of this text. What is initially used as an adjective in the title of the *Untimely Meditations* turns into a substantive, no longer naming an attribute of thought but, as it were, the thinker qua thinker. It is untimeliness that constitutes thought in the first place, in particular that thought which can be called philosophical—the "philosophizing" (*philosophieren*) to which he refers in the subtitle of the same book.[26]

If "untimeliness" names a relation between thought and its time, it already presents this relation as an exit from another relation with which it is entangled. For thought to be "un-timely" (*un-zeitgemäß*) it needs to extract itself from a relation that is "timely" (*zeitgemäß*)—a word that Nietzsche uses rarely, but with the same precision as its counterpart. The concept is to be read literally: un-timeliness as an undoing, an extricating, a breaking away from timeliness. This relation to what is timely (*das Zeitgemässe*), already implied in the concept of the untimely itself, tends to be overlooked in most commentaries, even in those rare cases when untimeliness is taken seriously as a philosophical concept.[27] What risks being missed or obfuscated by considering the concept of untimeliness in isolation is precisely that untimeliness, for Nietzsche, is a movement rather than a stable feature, a struggle rather a fixed attribute. Untimeliness, one could say, is the movement by which thought struggles to extract itself from its condition of timeliness. In the occasional reflections on the concept that punctuate the *Untimely Meditations*, Nietzsche elaborates this understanding of thought as a struggle out of its own timeliness. In the third installment of the series, the essay on Schopenhauer, who figures here as the ideal type of the philosopher, the conception of untimeliness is polemically formulated around the image of the thinker as a "child of his time"—perhaps not accidentally a phrase that had already made its appearance in Hegel's portrayal of the relation between philosophy and its time in the preface to his *Philosophy of Right*.[28] In the vocabulary characteristic of the early writings, Nietzsche writes:

> If it is commonly accepted that every great human being would like to be seen as the true child of its age [*das ächte Kind seiner Zeit*], [. . .] then a struggle by such a great one *against* his age seems to be only a senseless and destructive attack *on himself*. But this is only seemingly the case: for what he is struggling against in his time is that which prevents him from being great, which means, in his case, being free and entirely himself. From this it follows that his hostility [*seine Feindschaft*] is at bottom directed against [. . .] the soldering of what is timely to what is untimely in him [*des Zeitgemässen an sein Unzeitgemässes*]; and in the end the supposed child of his time proves to be only its *stepchild* [*als Stiefkind derselben*]. Thus Schopenhauer strove from his early youth against that false, idle and unworthy mother: his time.[29]

Perhaps the project of the *Untimely Meditations* itself may be understood in analogy to this portrayal of Schopenhauer as a figure in which the struggle of thought out of a condition of timeliness manifests itself in an exemplary manner. What is presented to the reader here are not so much the meditations of a thinker who believes himself to already be untimely, a thinker of thoughts whose untimeliness would have already been established: it is, rather, a series of writings in and through which thought can first become untimely. Untimeliness, as an exit from a *zeitgemässe* relation to one's time that is in some sense prior to it, is for Nietzsche always already involved in this struggle, this "striving against" (*streben entgegen*) everything in its own thinking that obeys the laws of its time. That untimeliness is in this sense always already a "striving against" means not only that thought is conceived as a struggle from the very moment it comes into being, but also that it is always at risk of slipping back into the condition from which it attempts to extricate itself. That thought is only thought insofar as it is untimely means not only that it comes into being through a struggle with its own timeliness but also that it is always exposed to the threat of being drawn back into this timeliness.

If the philosopher is, for Nietzsche, a figure of thought in its untimeliness, an untimeliness embodied in the description of the philosopher as an "untimely one," the journalist appears in the early writings as a representative of thought in its most extreme condition of timeliness. In one of his early notes, Nietzsche alludes to this relation through a play on words, pointing out that philosophy can never be *zeitungsgemäß*, can never be commensurable with the newspaper.[30] In his correspondence from the period after the publication of the first of his *Untimely Meditations*, Nietzsche refers multiple times to the subsequent installment as *meine zweite "Zeitungemässheit"*—another play of words in which the *Zeit* in "untimeliness" blends into the *Zeitung*.[31] If untimeliness implies an exit from what is timely, *zeitgemäß*, the newspaper would thus seem to figure as a concrete model of this timeliness. The significance that Nietzsche attributed to journalism—and the particular intensity of the poignant attacks that he directed against it—may be understood in this light. The enmity that defines the relation of philosophy toward "everything journalistic" is the same *Feindschaft* of which Nietzsche speaks in the passage on Schopenhauer: it is an enmity that philosophy, to paraphrase Nietzsche's formulation, directs against all elements within itself that tie it to its time. Before philosophy is philosophy, it is journalism—thought tied to its time, thought that is constrained by the laws of its time. As his pun on what is *zeitgemäß* and what is *zeitungsgemäß* suggests, journalism is, for Nietzsche, a concrete figure of that relation to its time from which thought is to extract itself if it is to deserve its name at all. Perhaps this also motivates the various images of the journalist as a figure of bondage in the early writings, which are punctuated by references to the journalist as a "slave of the day" (*Sklave des Tages*), a "the servant of the moment" (*der Diener des Augenblicks*), and as a "paper slave" (*papierne Sklave*) who is "ruled by the moment" (*vom Augenblick beherrscht*) or "put on the chain of the moment" (*an die Kette des Augenblicks gelegt*).[32] A similar image returns in Nietzsche's outlines for the complete series of *Un-*

timely Meditations, where it appears as the main subject of its concluding book on "newspaper slavery" (*Zeitungs-Sklaverei*).[33] This is not the place for a more extensive discussion of the figure of the slave in Nietzsche's earlier writings or his account of the place of slavery in ancient Greece, which plays an important role in his unpublished 1972 essay on the Greek state; nor will we dwell on the relation of this figure to Nietzsche's comments on modern slavery and colonialism or the violence of metaphors of this kind.[34] In the context of his polemic against journalism, it may suffice to say that these hyperbolic references to journalism are not to be mistaken for simple mockery or derision but have a more specific significance. What these images show is Nietzsche's attempt to conceive of "timeliness" as a relation of force and present the journalist as a figure in which this relation takes on a form of the most extreme dissymmetry; the journalist, in Nietzsche's hyperbole, becomes the emblem of a complete subjugation and conformity to the demands of its time. These images must be read as the complements to the passage on Schopenhauer as an ideal type of an untimely, where the struggle of thought out of its condition of timeliness is compared to a struggle for freedom, a struggle of thought against the forces that constrain it.

What is at stake in Nietzsche's depiction of the journalist as a "servant of the moment" is thus not an attempt to contrast the eternal and the temporal, the permanent and the fleeting, between thought that is defined by its relation to its time and thought that has cut off all relations to the temporal and historical. This much is already suggested by the form of Nietzsche's *Untimely Meditations*, which were not published as books, the medium traditionally associated with timelessness, but conceived as a periodical publication. Nietzsche did not only plan the installments of his "untimelies" to be published with regular intervals, but also described them in terms that evoke a journalistic form: in his correspondence, he usually refers to them simply by their number or, as in a letter of 1873, as a *Heft*, a term that is used to refer to the issue of a journal, a *Zeitschrift*.[35] But if their form suggests that the *Untimely Meditations* have a journalistic character, that the writing they will accommodate is anything but timeless, their title announces that this writing is not simply determined by the relation to its time. If the writing undertaken in the issues of this strange periodical is *unzeitgemäß*, this untimeliness would have to be elaborated in and out of the relation to their own time that Nietzsche calls "journalistic."[36] This is undoubtedly why Nietzsche, in the same letter of 1873 where he reflects on the first *Heft* of his planned periodical publication, also emphasizes the "unusually hostile newspaper literature that emerged in response against it"—a claim that will return time and again in his correspondence.[37] The conflict staged here and in the *Untimely Mediations* is central to his early conception of philosophical thought as a play of forces that are understood in terms of two distinct relations between thought and its time. If the journalist is, for Nietzsche, the figure of a thought, language, and experience brought in conformity with their time, philosophy is understood as a work within, against, and out of this relation. When Nietzsche defines philosophy as the *Gegenlehre* of everything journalistic, it is perhaps what he has in mind: that philosophy exists only as a persistent struggle of thought against a timeliness that is always at work within it and always threatens to overpower it. Thought can never claim untimeliness as if it were a fixed property: if philosophy must, as Nietzsche writes in the same note, work "constantly" or "unceasingly" (*immerfort*) against the journalistic, this is because it is always pulled back into timeliness. It is timeliness understood in this sense, timeliness as a force that is constantly at work to bring thought in concord with its time, that Nietzsche will examine in the other polemical portrayals of the journalist and the newspaper in his early writings—portrayals in which this play of forces will be grasped first and foremost in terms of language, of reading and writing.

Legislation of Language

The struggle between what is *zeitgemäß* and *unzeitgemäß* plays an important role in Nietzsche's early reflections on the philosophy of language. In these reflections, Nietzsche reserves a special position for the "language of the newspaper" (*Zeitungssprache*).[38] In the language of the newspapers, Nietzsche detects one of the exemplary—and symptomatic—expressions of the predicament of language in his own time.

> The greater part [*Übergewicht*] of what the German person now reads every day undoubtedly comprises the newspapers [*Zeitungen*] together with the journals [*Zeitschriften*] that correspond to them: the language employed here, a ceaseless drip of the same tropes and the same words [*gleicher Wendungen und gleicher Wörter*], imprints itself on his ear, and since he usually does his reading in those hours when his wearied mind is in any case little capable of resistance, his ear for language [*Sprachgehör*] gradually comes to feel at home in this kind of everyday German and is pained when it notices its absence.[39]

Or in a note from the same year: "He speaks like a human being, who reads the newspapers every day [*er redet wie ein Mensch, der täglich die Zeitungen liest*]."[40] What Nietzsche calls *Zeitungssprache* is thus not limited to the pages of the newspaper itself, nor to the moment of reading; it is here presented as a language that imprints itself on the "ears" of the newspaper reader as well as his speech, on the senses of the contemporary and his ability to express himself. Throughout the early writings, assertions of its exemplary status of the language of the newspapers are indeed coupled with descriptions that allude to its ubiquitous, all-pervasive character. "The newspaper, this sticky stratum of communication [*klebrige Vermittlungsschicht*]," he writes in a lecture of 1872, "now cements the seams between all forms of life, all forms of life, all classes, all arts, and all sciences"—it is, in other words, the figure of a generalized state of language.[41] In attributing this privileged status to the language of the newspapers Nietzsche remains close to Schopenhauer, who already endowed the language of the newspapers with a special significance in the fragmented "physiognomy of the age" that he attempts to develop in his *Parerga and Paralipomena*.[42] For Schopenhauer, it is in *Zeitungslesen* and *Zeitungsschreiben* that the modes of reading and writing specific to our time are thrown into stark relief. Nietzsche will draw on certain elements from Schopenhauer's characterization of the language of the newspapers, in particular his emphasis on reading and writing—but not without rethinking them in relation to his own philosophy of language, in particular what he refers to in his notes for an unpublished *Untimely Meditation* on "Reading and Writing" as the "impoverishment and paling" (*Verarmung und Verblassung*) of language.[43]

What Nietzsche means when he speaks of this "impoverishment," or "paling," of language may be understood in the context of his reflections on language of the early 1870s, developed in conjunction with the *Untimely Meditations*. As is well known, Nietzsche in these years takes up the critique of conceptuality developed in *The Birth of Tragedy* but continues to elaborate this through a study of rhetoric.[44] Language, and conceptual language, is determined in these years as originarily figurative, as trope: its force resides not in the correspondence of words to things, but rather in what Nietzsche calls its force of "transposition" (*die Übertragung*)—that is, metaphor. A key passage from "On Truth and Lying in an Extra-Moral Sense" reads:

> To the creator of language [*Sprachbildner*], the "thing-in-itself" (which would be pure, disinterested truth) is absolutely incomprehensible and not worth seeking. He designates only the relations of things to men, and to express these relations he uses the boldest metaphors. First, he translates a nerve stimulus into an image! That is the first metaphor. Then, the image must be reshaped into a sound! The second metaphor. [. . .] When we speak of trees, colors, snow, and owers, we believe we know something about the things themselves, although what we have are just metaphors of things, which do not correspond at all to the original entities.[45]

The introduction of language—conceptual language in particular—is conceived as only one moment in the "metaphorical activity" that is constitutive of human experience. Experience, qua metaphorical activity, is thus considered by Nietzsche as a series of transpositions from one sphere of signs into another—an "overleaping [*Überspringen*] of spheres."[46] The description of this transposition as an "overleaping" points to its irreducibly discontinuous character: even if language enables different spheres of signs to relate to one another, it can never establish a direct communication. That conceptual language is the product of a metaphorical activity means, in other words, that it results from a transposition between spheres that remain absolutely heterogeneous, with no possibility of adequation.[47]

The introduction of conceptual language in this series of transpositions corresponds to a distinct moment in this metaphorical activity that Nietzsche describes as the "identification of the non-identical" (*Gleichsetzen des Nicht-Gleichen*). As the transposition of the image into the word, the concept marks the transition from the similar to the same, from analogy to unity. "Every word becomes a concept as soon as it is supposed to serve not merely as a reminder of the unique, absolutely individualized original experience to which it owes its origin," Nietzsche writes, "but at the same time to fit countless, more or less similar cases, which, strictly speaking, are never identical, and hence absolutely dissimilar. Every concept originates by the identification of what is non-identical."[48] The formation of the concept is thus for Nietzsche necessarily reductive: it is an abstraction that preserves only what is similar, at the cost of discarding individual differences between impressions. But the "poverty" of conceptual language resides not only in its identification of the non-identical; it is also at work in its designation of impressions that are held in common. For Nietzsche, the origin of conceptual language lies in a particular type of neediness: the need of the herd—not the individual—to communicate. Conceptual language develops under the pressure of these needs: it is linked to the urgency and dangers of action. It is the language of a herd that has no time to be interested in the differences between things or the differences traversing the unity of the herd itself. Under the pressure of neediness, conceptual language consigns to concepts average impressions and the evaluations of the greater number; it imposes as a norm the perspective of the herd. Insofar as language is conceptual, a structural uniformity is at work in it: in a note of the early 1870s, Nietzsche speaks of a "uniformity of word and trope" (*Gleichmässigkeit in Wort und Wendung*).[49] The same pressure of neediness in which conceptual language originates also demands for "the invention of a uniformly valid [*gleichmässig Gültig*] and binding designation of things."[50]

But even though the language of concepts originates in need, this is not the case for language as such. Conceptual language is for Nietzsche already a decadent language. In his early writings, Nietzsche contrasts the poverty of conceptual language to the richness of an "original language"—a language that "was poorer in words":[51]

> The more ancient languages were poorer in words, and general concepts were lacking; it was passions, needs, and feelings that were expressed in sonority. It could almost be argued that they were not so much languages of words as languages of feelings; at any rate the feelings formed the sonorities and the words [. . .] and the movement of feeling provided the rhythm. Gradually language became separated from the language of sonorities.[52]

This ancient "language of feelings" returns in the *Untimely Meditations*, where it is contrasted to a "language of thoughts": it is a language that prioritizes the tonality and rhythm of speech over words—"the most defective signs there are"—and prioritizes trope over proper meaning. This origin myth, and its corresponding story of a fall, illness, and impoverishment of language, is not to be mistaken for a historical account in the strict sense: its significance is first and foremost typological. As the description of this language as one that is "poor" in words—not devoid of words altogether—already suggests, the symbolic spheres presented here in succession are always at work in language at the same time. The inversion and revaluation that are implied in this myth serve a polemical purpose: by prioritizing the language of music and image, Nietzsche's origin story tries to dislodge the concept from its rule over "proper" meaning.[53]

Despite its "pale" and "impoverished" character, however, conceptual language unmistakably exerts a force: in the early writings, Nietzsche will consistently speak of the concept as an "invention" that now confronts humanity as an alien power. In "On Truth and Lying in an Extra-Moral Sense," he compares conceptual language to a *Zwingburg*, a prison fortress from where a city is commanded: "That drive toward the formation of metaphors, that fundamental drive of human beings, which cannot be discounted for one moment, because that would amount to ignoring man himself, is in truth not overcome and indeed hardly restrained by the fact that out of its diminished products, the concepts, a regular and rigid new world is built up for him as a prison fortress [*als eine Zwingburg*]."[54] Conceptual language is an artificial construct that comes to exert force over its inventor, a mighty architectural construct that comes to constrain its inhabitants. The complement to this image is found in Nietzsche's descriptions of the order of conceptual language as the most delicate of constructions: a "web of concepts," a building "light as gossamer, delicate enough to be carried along by the wave, strong enough not to be blown apart by the wind."[55] These two metaphorical architectures, a delicate, almost transparent web that at the same time acts as a powerful and oppressive force, converge in the passages on the impoverishment of language in the *Untimely Meditations*. "In our dimly perceived conditions language has everywhere become a power in itself [*eine Gewalt für sich*]," Nietzsche writes here—a power "which now seizes human beings, as if with ghostly arms [*Gespensterarmen*] and impels them to where they do not really want to go."[56]

If conceptual language can be conceived here as a "power in itself," then this may be because it implies the demand for all speech to conform to the "proper" meaning that is arbitrarily and artificially fixed in it. It represses the individual metaphor as dangerous for the life of the group and, in doing so, hides the metaphorical nature of the concept itself. What Nietzsche calls the "legislation of language" (*Gesetzgebung der Sprache*)[57] or the "compulsion of the correct and the conventional" (*die Zwänge des Correcten und Conventionellen*)[58] is the suppression of individual metaphor—that is, metaphors of impressions and experiences that resist the uniformity of the concept. This suppression is not the product of accidental historical circumstances: for Nietzsche it is structurally implied by conceptual language. The "legislation of language" is always already at work in language insofar as it has a conceptual character. "As soon as human beings seek to come to an understanding with one another," Nietzsche writes in one of the *Untimely Meditations*, "they are seized by the madness of general concepts [*der Wahnsinn der allgemeinen Begriffe*], indeed even by the mere sounds of words."[59] The origin of conceptuality in neediness continues to make itself in every word that is uttered: insofar as it is conceptual, language harbors an impulse to function ever more smoothly, more accurately, more efficiently. In order for conceptual language to fulfill its function, there must be a legislation of language, a demand that all speech conforms to its laws. Any divergence from these laws immediately threatens the securing of meaning; just as the imposition of the concept is accompanied by the suppression of individual differences, so the legislation of language is accompanied by a violent suppression of "forbidden metaphors [*verbotenen Metaphern*] and unheard-of conceptual compounds [*unerhörten Begriffsfügungen*]."[60]

When Nietzsche speaks of the "tyrannical preponderance [*tyrannisches Übergewicht*]" of words and concepts—the same word he uses to refer to the language of the newspaper—this is meant to emphasize at once the suppression at the heart of conceptual language and its intolerance toward all speech that diverges from the "proper" meaning it assigns to words. In the sphere of language, the *Zeitgemäßigkeit* from which thought needs to extricate itself in order to become thought in a more precise and fuller sense thus takes concrete form in the *Gleichmäßigkeit* of conceptual language and the structural demand for metaphors to conform themselves to it. Just as thinking requires a struggle against the forces that bring thought in conformity with its time, so language needs to struggle against the tendency toward uniformity that is always already at work in it. "Who wants to promise a future to the German language," Nietzsche writes, "must bring about a movement against our current German."[61] At its most fundamental level, the struggle of thought out of its condition of timeliness *is* this struggle out of a language that binds thought to its time and brings it in conformity to it.[62]

Zeitungssprache

Nowhere is the structural tendency of language toward *Zeitgemässigkeit* expressed more clearly than in the language of the newspapers—the "ceaseless drip of the same tropes and the same words" (*dem unaufhörlichen Tropfenfall gleicher Wendungen und gleicher Wörter*) that Nietzsche evoked in the first of the *Untimely Meditations*.[63] As this hyperbolic image suggests, what Nietzsche calls *Zeitungssprache* is to be understood first and foremost as a language in which the uniformity and regularity of conceptual language is driven to an extreme. Not only is the semantic dimension of speech reduced to a simple repetition of the same elements, the same tropes and words; also its musical dimensions, which manifest themselves in their most bare form as rhythm, is here reduced to the homogeneity of a *Tropfenfall*, the release of an excess through a regular dripping.[64] This homogeneity is also thematized in a note that stems from the same year, where Nietzsche writes, "To write like the entire world writes [*wie alle Welt schreibt*], that is to say, like the newspaper-writers [*die Zeitungsschreiber*]. [. . .] Who will ever write a positive linguistic doctrine of the entire-world-style [*eine positive Sprachlehre des Allerweltsstils*]?"[65] That this *Zeitungsschreiber* writes "like the entire world writes" does not mean that his language is what Nietzsche, in his notes for a planned *Untimely Meditation* on "Reading and Writing," calls a "common language" (*gemeinsame Sprache*).[66] Quite the contrary: that this is a language of *alle Welt* means precisely that it is a language that belongs to no one in particular. The language of the *Zeitungsschreiber* is a caricature of the language to which Nietzsche will refer as the expression of a "common and overflowing soul" (*gemeinsame und überströmende Seele*); it is a language that is valid only for an average, purely abstract speaker.[67] The question of whether a "positive doctrine" (*positive Sprachlehre*) of such a language will ever be written is thus not without irony:

for the dimension of conceptual language that is exemplified by the writing of the journalist would, insofar as it is a pure abstraction, have no positive reality. In this sense *Zeitungssprache* may be seen as the pendant of another such extreme: the supposedly "objective" language of science, which Nietzsche evokes throughout the early writings. If the language of science exemplifies the demand for "correctness" and "accuracy" inherent in conceptual language, the newspaper exemplifies its inherent tendency toward uniformity—its tendency to turn language into the carrier of average impressions and the evaluations of the greatest number.

Just as the conceptual dimension of language has its origin in a certain *Not*—the need of the herd to survive—so Nietzsche locates the origin of this extreme uniformity of *Zeitungssprache* in a hyperbolic version of this neediness. On the pages of the newspaper, language takes shape under the pressure of a perennial urgency that Nietzsche describes in terms of a demand for utility: "To make use of the moment [*den Augenblick benutzen*] and, to profit from it [*um von ihm Nutzen zu haben*], to judge it as quickly as possible [*so schnell wie möglich beurtheilen*]"—this is the demand under which the journalist writes.[68] The "judgment" of the moment at issue here must be taken in the strict epistemological sense: it means to subsume an impression as quickly as possible to a readily available concept. In another note from the early 1870s, Nietzsche writes that "the pernicious essence of the journalist" (*das verruchten Wesen des Journalisten*) consists precisely in the "hastiest cognition and exploitation of the ephemeral [*hastigste Erkenntnis und Ausnützung des Ephemeren*], yes of the momentary—and nothing but that!"[69] To make use of the fleeting, momentary impression in this sense thus means to reduce it to what is readily available and, in that sense, exhaust it; this *Benutzen* is also an *Ausnutzen*. The "haste" that drives this conceptual and linguistic operation, and of which the journalist is here presented as the exemplary figure, must not be understood as an accidental subjective disposition but, rather, as the expression of a neediness that Nietzsche thought to be at the origin of language insofar as it has a conceptual dimension. In the hyperbolic haste of the journalist, the writer whose words all stand under the pressure to subsume each moment under already available concepts, Nietzsche sees the caricatural exaggeration of a tendency that is at work in all conceptual language.[70]

That the journalist must complete this operation, this *Benutzen* and *Ausnutzen* of every passing moment, as quickly as possible means that the writing exemplified by this figure must always take recourse to already available words and concepts. That there is something mechanical about this writing is suggested by Nietzsche's descriptions of the journalist as a *Zeitungsfabrik-Arbeiter*—a "newspaper factory worker." This description may again be read as a caricatural image of the structure of conceptual language. When Nietzsche speaks in his Basel lectures of 1872 of "the style of our newspaper factory workers [. . .] the 'careful choice of words' [*gewählten Diktion*] of our writers," the reference to this *gewählte* diction must be understood in the literal sense: as indicating a speaking that is merely an activity of choosing, of picking words that are readily available.[71] The image also returns in a well-known passage in the second of the *Untimely Meditations*, where Nietzsche compares the modern subject to a "lifeless and yet uncannily mobile factory of concepts and words."[72] This factory-like character is, in this same passage, attributed precisely to a subject that "suffers from the malady of words and mistrusts every impression of one's own that has not yet been designated with words" (*die noch nicht mit Worten abgestempelt ist*).[73] The writing of the journalist is, for Nietzsche, the opposite of what is called *Sprachbildung* elsewhere in the early writings; it is a writing that mechanically subsumes every moment under already given concepts, that mistrusts every impression that has not yet been "stamped by words."

This same relation to language determined by choice and utility is already alluded to in Nietzsche's note on *Zeitungsschreiben*, which can now be cited in full: "To write like the whole world writes, that is to say, like the newspaper-writers do, who always take the first, most convenient word."[74] *Das erste bequemste Wort*—if Nietzsche can write that this word comes first, then this is because it is readily available, not formed anew while speaking. If this word is *bequem*, the reason for this may be that it requires no effort on behalf of the speaker: it is a language that is already given, where words would already have a clearly determined meaning. *Zeitungsschreiben* never loses time because it confines itself to the habitual meaning of metaphors. The writing of the journalist submits itself to the legislation of language and makes sure to subsume every impression under already available laws; it does not employ metaphors that are "unheard-of" (*unerhört*) or "forbidden" (*verboten*).[75] Because it always uses the first word, *Zeitungsschreiben* is a fluent writing, without pauses or interruptions. The journalist is always ready to give priority to the word that comes first and easiest over the word that expresses his experience more fully. Whatever seeks expression in language—whether it is "feeling" or "thought"— is here subjected to the demand not to lose time, to speak instantly and without interruption. Experience has to conform itself to readily available words and metaphors; anything that cannot be expressed in this language of "first words" is instantly excluded from it. In the *Untimely Meditations*, Nietzsche characterizes the language of the *Zeitungsschreiber* by evoking the image of "pens that never cease to flow."[76] This language is characterized by a peculiar virtuosity: there is no thought here that could interrupt the flowing of pens;

there is no occurrence that could render the journalist speechless. It is a language that can flow continuously because there is nothing that exceeds or disrupts the concepts whose meaning is already secured in it—a language that maintains its uninterrupted flow only insofar as it expels everything that it cannot directly absorb.

Besides standing in a close relation to Nietzsche's critique of conceptuality, the remarks on *Zeitungssprache* of the early 1870s also show the blurring of a distinction between two spheres whose opposition had still animated Nietzsche's first book: the sphere of speaking and hearing on the one hand, and that of writing and reading on the other.[77] In the passage from the first *Untimely Meditation* with which we started this section, Nietzsche begins to speak of the language of the newspapers—the "ceaseless drip of the same tropes and words"—as a written language that the contemporary "now reads every day" (*jetzt jeden Tag liest*) and then suddenly shifts to the sphere of spoken language, pointing out that this language now "imprints itself on his ear" (*prägt sich seinem Ohre ein*).[78] A similar transposition is found in another note of the same year, a note that consists only of a single sentence: "He speaks like a human being who reads the newspapers on a daily basis" (*Er redet wie ein Mensch, der täglich die Zeitungen liest*).[79] In these remarks, *Zeitungssprache* is portrayed as a language that belongs to the sphere of reading and writing and is subsequently transposed to that of speaking and hearing. There is a distinct ambiguity to these remarks and the transposition they stage. On the one hand, these remarks undoubtedly bear the traces of the prioritization of speech over writing—a prioritization that would still inform the interpretation of the appearance of *Leseliteratur* in ancient Greece as a "sign of degeneration," as it was developed in the course that Nietzsche gave at Basel in the following years. The language of the newspapers is treated as the emblem of a *Sprache* that is abstracted from the dimensions of voice and gesture—a language whose poverty would manifest itself precisely when this paled language is transposed once again into the sphere of speech. To "speak like someone who reads the newspapers on a daily basis" would mean to speak an impoverished language, a language that has been stripped of the pleromatic fullness that still seems to characterize speech at this point in Nietzsche's work. Yet at the same time as they bear the traces of the prioritization of speech, these notes unmistakably effect a reversal of this priority. *Zeitungssprache*, the language that more than any other exemplified the time in which Nietzsche understood himself to be writing, is here portrayed as a language that is written and read *before* it is spoken. It is, in other words, a *Sprache* that cannot be understood from the standpoint of speech, of voice and gesture; it is modeled not on the supposed fullness of the spoken word but rather on the written word—a word that "lies on the pages of newspapers" (*auf Seiten der Zeitungen liegt*) and that "stamps itself on the ear" (*sich einprägt*). It is in this sense that the remarks on *Zeitungssprache* anticipate the revaluation of reading and writing and the reconceptualization of speech and the figure of the speaker that will take on an ever more prominent role throughout Nietzsche's work.

Rumors

To the portrayals of the newspaper—and in particular its language, *Zeitungssprache*—as the figure of a certain timeliness, Nietzsche counterposes another image of language and thought: an image that is, not accidentally, compressed in the figure of a messenger who brings a different, untimely kind of news. Throughout Nietzsche's work we find various messengers of this kind, various images of an untimely tiding or *Zeitung* in the ancient sense of the word that serve as a counterpart to the philosophical caricatures of the journalist and the newspaper in the early writings. The exemplary instance of this untimely news is undoubtedly captured in the famous scene conjured up in *The Gay Science*: the scene where a messenger walks unto a town square, turns to his contemporaries and announces to them what is happening today, what is happening right now: the news of a "tremendous event" (*ungeheure Ereignis*) that, according to this messenger, defines his time, our time, the news that is compressed in the terse phrase "God is dead."[80]

Gott ist Tod—before being a sentence or a statement, a *Wort* or *Satz*—two terms that are customarily employed to describe the status of this phrase[81]—the death of God is presented in this scene as a *Nachricht*: that is to say, as a message or a piece of news. It is also this term that Nietzsche himself will use in the other aphorism of *The Gay Science* where he engages directly with the theme: the aphorism in the fifth book, added four years after the initial publication, that refers to "the message that the 'old God is dead'" (*die Nachricht, dass der 'alte Gott tod' ist*).[82] "Haven't you heard of that madman" (*habt ihr nicht von jenem tollen Menschen gehört*): if the death of God is announced as a message, a piece of news, then the figure who here makes his entrance into a town square must be understood first of all as a messenger. As a messenger, this *tolle Mensch* speaks without ever truly becoming a speaker: the message that is delivered here—the news of the death of God—comes from elsewhere. As the portrayal of the madman makes clear, this messenger is at no point to be mistaken for the stable origin of the words he speaks. Words pour out of the mouth of this wildly gesturing madman who "cries incessantly" (*unaufhörlich Schrie*): they are the words of a speaker who is not in control of his speech but rather possessed by it, the bearer of words that do not originate within himself. There is no speaker in this scene to which these words could be traced back: no identifiable origin that could guarantee their meaning. That the figure who walks unto a town square is designated as a "madman"—at least by the contemporaries who have supposedly related this story—must not be understood as a contradiction of its status as a messenger but rather its radicalization; the madman is here, before anything else, the figure of a speaker who could never lend authority to his utterances. Every word spoken by this speaker designated as a madman could be nonsense; it is not just that the contemporaries gathered on the town square may not understand his words—there is no guarantee that this messenger himself understands the words he speaks.[83] That not even the one who signs this aphorism, "Nietzsche," could be mistaken as occupying this position of authority is suggested by the phrase with which it begins. "Haven't you heard . . .": with this phrase, the possibility of referring to the signatory of this aphorism as its stable origin has also become problematic: the report of a madman who is delivering the news is, in turn, marked as a piece of hearsay.

As words spoken by a messenger who appears to his contemporaries as a madman, the news that God is dead does not just lack an identifiable sender; as the aphorism in the *Gay Science* makes clear, it also lacks an addressee. Even though this madman is unmistakably portrayed as a messenger who intends the message he bears to arrive, a speaker who goes to great lengths to make sure the words he speaks are heard, that is to say, who intends these words to be understood, this message remains without a final destination. The scene of a town square where a speaker addresses "his audience" (*seine Zuhörer*) is conjured up only in order to stage the breakdown of this familiar scene of speaking and listening, to perform the impossibility of this audience to hear this message and to fully understand it. After being initially greeted by "a great laughter" (*ein grosses Gelächter*), the audience "turns silent and looked at him in astonishment" (*sie schwiegen und blickten befremdet auf ihn*): but this is not the laughter of an audience that has understood what has been said but finds it ridiculous, just as the dumb silence that follows it is not the silence of an audience that has understood this message but chooses to ignore it. This laughter and this silence signal above all that this news is neither heard nor understood, that these words are spoken without an addressee who, despite the absence of a sender, is able to bestow on them their full signification. Just as this message has no speaker, so there is no addressee or destination—whether an earthly audience or a divine one—that could guarantee its meaning. Words are spoken, but they are fated to remain unheard.[84]

When the death of God is, once again, thematized in one of the aphorisms included in the fifth book of *The Gay Science*, which was added in 1886, four years after its initial publication, Nietzsche returns on two occasions to its status as a message or a piece of news. Not only does the last sentence of the aphorism refer to "the message that 'the old god is dead'" (*die Nachricht, dass der 'alte Gott tod' ist*), but this designation of the death of God as a *Nachricht* is already anticipated in the first sentence, which refers to "the greatest newer event—that 'God is dead' [*das größte neuere Ereignis—das 'Gott tot ist'*], that the belief in the Christian God has become unbelievable."[85] Even though the death of God is again characterized as an "event" (*Ereignis*), a term that reiterates the reference to the *ungeheure Ereignis* in the earlier aphorism, this "event" is once again presented only indirectly, as a message whose status is here marked by the recurrent use of quotation marks. When Nietzsche speaks of "the greater newer event—that 'God is dead,'" the inverted commas must be interpreted as quotation marks: it is as if the writer of these sentences refers to an event of which he has no direct knowledge, an event of which he has only heard reports. As in the case of the madman's announcement, this message does not seem to originate in the one who speaks these words or the one who signs these sentences: once more, the "death of God" is announced as if it were a piece of hearsay, a message that was overheard and passed on. When Nietzsche refers to this news, the news that "God is dead," he does so by reciting words that are not his own. These are words that are not imbued with a meaning by their writer; by placing them between inverted commas, their writer treats them as words that are as strange to him as they are to readers of this text. Once placed between inverted commas, these words are thereby also divorced from any concept that they may have been thought to communicate: they appear as bare words on the page, words that remain external and irreducible to any "proper meaning" that may be ascribed to them.

When Nietzsche repeats the initial reference to "the greatest new event—that 'God is dead'"—in the last sentence of the aphorism, which refers to "the message that "the old god is dead" (*dass der "alte Gott tod" ist*)," this effect is further emphasized though a shift in the position of the quotation marks. In an adjustment that remains untranslatable from the original German, in this second formulation the verb *ist* is excluded from this recited message, placed outside of the quotation marks. The message recited is thereby reduced to three words: *alte Gott tod*. "Old god dead": the message here confronts the reader as an opaque combination of words whose significance could never be fixed definitively or completely determined; a message of which it even has to remain uncertain whether it can be read as a *Satz*, a sentence or proposition. The message here appears as the ruin of a constative sentence: a ruin that is brought about, in particular, by the exclusion of the word that guaranteed the cohesive structure and function of the sentence, *ist*. It seems as if, in addition to the death of God, the possibility of saying *ist* has expired, too: as if the language in which the news of the death of God is to be communicated can no longer be a language that joins together subjects and predicates. The news of the death of God therefore bears the traces of the "tremendous event" that it announces: its language is stamped by that of which it speaks. This news takes the form of a message without a speaker or addressee, without intention or destination, without any guarantee of its proper signification. The news of the death of God is delivered as a message without truth, substance, or subject: a message that cannot even sustain its status as a constative sentence—*Gott ist Tod*—but must deteriorate into a combination of marks whose status as a sentence must remain uncertain: *alte Gott tod*. Perhaps it is possible to say that this errant, deteriorating message is not as much stamped by the event of which it speaks: perhaps the "tremendous event" of the death of God *is* nothing but the impossibility that is exposed in this errancy and deterioration—the impossibility of securing a stable referential ground.[86]

In the first part of *Thus Spoke Zarathustra*, which was published the year after *The Gay Science*, this impossibility is thematized once more. In the opening pages of the book, Zarathustra expresses his astonishment over the fact that the news of this death has not yet reached the first interlocutors he encounters on his wanderings. "How is it possible!" Zarathustra exclaims after his first conversation: "This old saint in his woods has not yet heard that God is dead [*hat noch Nichts davon gehört, dass Gott tod ist*]!"[87] The death of God is here treated as a rumor that does the rounds: a rumor that has already been circulating, perhaps since time immemorial. That the news of the death of God is here no longer proclaimed as an announcement but takes the form of a rumor is no accident: for it is the ancient form of the *Gerücht* that exemplifies the dimension of language in which God has always already died and must die again and again. The *Gerücht* is not just the exemplary instance of a message that is no longer tied to a speaker from which it originates, a message that shows itself to be irreducible to any given intention that would precede the act of speaking; nor does it just exemplify a message that is no longer tied to an addressee for whom it is destined, a message in which language shows itself to be always exposed to being heard and overheard by others. Besides this, the rumor also exemplifies a language that has ceased to be tied to a verifiable truth existing outside of it: it is language that shows itself to be irreducible to its reference to "things in themselves." The rumor of the death of God is like the other rumor that is evoked later in Zarathustra, not accidentally in the section "On Great Events," which relates in a digression how one day "the rumor circulated" (*lief das Gerücht umher*) that Zarathustra had disappeared—an unsubstantiated story that quickly spreads, transforming in an uncontrollable manner in the process, only to turn into the rumor that "the devil had fetched Zarathustra."[88] In the rumor, it has become impossible to secure the proper meaning of words—or rather, it becomes clear that this impossibility had been at work all along. But this impossibility is not merely a breakdown; it is also a liberation: language shows itself to be irreducible to the status of a means that serves an end outside of itself. Throughout his writings, Nietzsche will explore rumor as the figure of a language without a subject; rumors not only "circulate" (*laufen herum*) but also "spread themselves" (*verbreiten sich*) and "travel from door to door" (*ziehen von Haus zu Haus*).[89] When Nietzsche's messenger in a town square exclaims that the "tremendous event" of which he reports is "still underway and wandering" (*noch unterwegs und wandert*), these words echo the vocabulary of a wandering language that also characterizes his descriptions of rumors. The rumor would reveal that dimension of language that would resist any possible stable or definitive fixation of meaning.

"Rumor [*fama*]," Tertullian already wrote, "only lives on as long as it fails to prove itself. As soon as a rumor proves itself to be true, it expires: as if its task of reporting news were at an end, it quits its post. [. . .] Because a wise man puts no faith in an uncertainty, a rumor is believed by none but a fool [*stultus*]."[90] But for Nietzsche, there is a truth to this foolish belief in rumor: because this fool, this *tolle Mensch* knows that there is a sense in which all language, after the death of God, must have the instable character of a rumor. This instability must even affect the news of the tremendous event that God is dead. When Zarathustra sighs that his faithful interlocutor "has not yet heard" (*hat noch Nichts gehört*) of this tremendous event, this does more than just refer to the rumorous character of language after the death of God; it also characterizes this language as a language that is exposed to the possibility of remaining unheard, perhaps even fated to remain unheard entirely. It is certainly no coincidence that Nietzsche begins to stage the announcement of the death of God in *The Gay Science* with the same phrase, expressed once again in the negative mode. "Haven't you heard of that madman . . ."—who reads this aphorism is, each time again, addressed as a reader who may not have heard this news: it is as if the one who has heard this rumor, who has begun to think the breakdown of language that is imparted in this message without a speaker or addressee, has already begun to mishear it, to secure its proper meaning, to posit new origins and destinations. With each reading, the reader hears this news once again and forgets it once more. Perhaps this is why, with each reading, the messenger in the town square must reiterate that the "tremendous event" of which he conveys the news has not quite happened yet— that this news "has not yet reached the ears of men [*bis zu den Ohren der Menschen gedrungen*]."[91]

Idolatry of Facts

God may have died, but gods nevertheless continue to be worshipped—even by those who claim to have renounced all religion. As long as these gods are not deities of a genuinely new kind, as long as they are not the deities of the "new religion" that Nietzsche will proclaim in his later writings, these gods are mere reproductions of the old God in a different form—*Götzen*, not *Götter*.[92] One of the exemplary sites for this idol worship is, for Nietzsche, the newspaper. In the worship that is practiced here on a daily basis, the old God returns in a sphere that is claimed to be secular: the sphere of history. The second essay of Nietzsche's *Untimely Meditations*, "On the Uses and Disadvantages of History for Life," may be read as an attempt at exposing how the modern experience of history continues to harbor a concealed idolatry. This is programmatically announced toward the end of the essay, where Nietzsche exclaims, "What, there are no more living mythologies? What, the religions are dying out? Just behold the religion of the power of history!"[93] The old God lives on in the religion of history: not only in the form of lofty ideas of historical reason or progress, but also in the form of idols that are more difficult to recognize as such. Of the many idols that are attacked in the *Untimely Meditation* on history, the most pernicious would seem to be an idol that is claimed to have an utterly profane status: the "fact." "Every instant is turned into a bare admiration for success and leads to an idolatry of the factual [*Götzendienst des Tatsächlichen*]," Nietzsche writes; "an idolatry that is now generally described by the very mythical yet quite idiomatic expression "to take the facts into account [*den Tatsachen Rechnung tragen*]."[94] Toward the end of the same paragraph, these sentences are reiterated in summary form in a passage that suddenly turns to the reader, addressed directly as an *ihr*—you, the reader, you, the contemporary: "You make success, the factual [*den Erfolg, das Faktum*] into your idol, while in reality the factual is always stupid [*dumm*] and has at all times resembled a calf rather than a god."[95]

What is at stake in these two sentences is more than a commentary on the general reverence of facts that is characteristic of the modern study of history. The image of an "idolatry of the factual" captures a specific philosophical reflection on the constitution of the fact itself.[96] This is already suggested by Nietzsche's description of this *Götzendienst*, whose object is not *Tatsachen* but *das Tatsächliche*: not merely particular facts, but the factual as such—the fact considered in its facticity. Nietzsche's understanding of the basic structure of this facticity is suggested by the word with which he will replace *das Tatsächliche* in his second reference to an idolatry of the factual: *das Faktum*. Like the German *Tatsache*, the Latin *factum* refers to "something done"; but as a noun that is constructed out of a perfect participle of *facere,* it presents the fact emphatically as an act that has been completed. There is something ineluctable and irreversible about the fact considered in this sense: every fact would be the account of an occurrence that has already come to a conclusion, that has already been closed off, that is complete in itself. Read in this way, Nietzsche's reference to the *factum* would suggest that every fact has the structure of a *fait accompli*: just as the "accomplished fact" presents a history that has already completely transpired before it is imparted, so every fact claims to present a history that has taken place conclusively and definitively before it is recounted or interpreted. But Nietzsche's reference to the *Faktum* not only points to the complete, conclusive character of the fact that is here worshipped as an idol; it also points to the opposition that has traditionally sustained this determination of the factual—the opposition between *factum* and *fictum.* The fact is here strictly separated and opposed to everything that involves a *fingere*: a forming, molding, or, in the most general terms, a mere touching or handling. In its opposition to the *fictum,* the *factum* is conceived as that which has not formed, been touched: that which is directly and immediately given. The fact that emerges here is a positive fact: a fact that has an independent unity before it has been touched by any formative activity. *Factum* and *fictum* are therefore not merely opposed but also hierarchically ordered: the *fictum* is conceived as a representation that is always secondary to the factual—a representation that can, at best, stand in an adequate relation to the positive fact but is always susceptible to falsification. In the fact, historical reality is thought to present itself as a pure given that precedes any *fictum,* any account that is in turn conceived as a representation of an already established reality. Historical reality is conceived by this idolater as an aggregate of actual events: events that, in their independent unity as positive facts, would enjoy an existence that can be neatly separated from their writing or reading.

Only this pure *factum* conceived in a strict opposition to the *fictum,* only a conception of the fact as something that is directly and immediately given, could ever give reality the air of immutability and inevitability that lends full force to the demand to "take account of the facts."[97] *Den Tatsachen Rechnung tragen*—if this expression is "quite idiomatic," as Nietzsche writes, this is first of all because it implies that the fact renders the sphere of history comparable and therefore commensurable with the sphere of the *Rechnung,* that is to say, of counting and accounting. Who conceives of historical reality as an aggregate of facts, so it suggests, ultimately treats history in the same way that the accountant reckons with incomes and expenses: as facts that can be determined with absolute exactitude and without the least ambiguity, governed by the same rules of iron necessity that govern the balance sheet. When Nietzsche refers to this same expression—*den Tatsachen Rechnung tragen*—also as a "very mythological turn of phrase" (*sehr mythologische Wendung*), he may do so because it presents historical reality as if it were governed by iron necessity.[98] Insofar as the fact is believed to have a self-sufficient unity prior to all writing or reading, there is a sense in which every fact deprives historical reality of its plasticity and mutability.[99] Historical experience is thus denied the possibility of freedom implied in this mutability—but also sheltered from the groundlessness to which it opens up. The idolater of the factual may concede that every fact allows for multiple interpretations; but these interpretations are always opposed to a factual reality that is thought to be prior to it and thought of as secondary. In the demand to "take account of the facts," historical reality is presented as a mythical world that is not in any way made or shaped but can at best be responded to in an adequate manner. There is thus a relation between the fact and the category that Nietzsche understands to be central to myth: fate. Nietzsche will explicitly name this relation between *factum* and *fatum* in a later passage, contained in the third essay of the *Genealogy of Morality*, where he speaks of the "the *will* to stand still before the factual, the *factum brutum*, that fatalism of *petits faits* [*ce petit faitalisme*, as I call it]."[100] Such a small, petty fatalism would be the proper name for the pettiness of facts—a name that brings to the fore the fatalism that is at work in every fact. From the standpoint of such fatalism, historical reality is thought of as purely given, inevitable and ineluctable, predetermined by "actual events" that are supposed to be directly available to empirical consciousness. What claims itself to be an enlightened conception of history turns out to be stamped by the structure of fateful predetermination.

This "fatalism of *petits faits*" marks the point where the fact can turn into an idol. In the belief in the pure, positive fact, God lives on after his death—and it is in this sense that Nietzsche can write, elsewhere in the essay on history, that the idolater of the factual treats each fact as a manifestation of "God's sojourn on earth" (*das Wandeln Gottes auf der Erde*).[101] Only the belief in historical reality as an immutable given could ever provide the idolater with a stable referential ground after the old God has died. Only a *factum* that is strictly separated from the *fictum*, a fact that is denied its plasticity, could ever alleviate the burden of freedom inherent in the mutability of reality. That the fate to which the idolater submits is itself not a given is already suggested by Nietzsche's reference to "the *will* to stand before the factual."[102] The submission to a reality that is believed to be given and the imperative to take account of the facts imply a prior renunciation—a renunciation that Nietzsche, in the same passage from the *Genealogy*, describes as the "renunciation of any interpretation [*jenes Verzichtleisten auf Interpretation überhaupt*]: of forcing, adjust-

ing, shortening, omitting, filling-out, inventing, falsifying and everything else
essential to interpretation."[103] Nietzsche had already begun to problematize
the status of the fact as a pure given and pointed to this active renunciation
when he wrote that the idolatry of facts consists precisely in turning "the success, the fact" (*den Erfolg, das Faktum*) into an idol. These two words, *Faktum*
and *Erfolg*, juxtaposed to one another and only separated by a comma, are
here presented as if they are synonyms—two words that are purely tautological and potentially interchangeable. What is implied by the peculiar presentation of these two terms is not the general claim that history is written by the
victor, even if this thought surfaces on several occasions in Nietzsche's early
reflections on history, but a more specific claim with regards to the constitution of the fact itself. That every fact is an *Erfolg* suggests, first of all, that the
fact is not something given but always already an outcome or result, something
that follows from an activity. It is the translation of an *eventus* in the Latin
sense, an occurrence conceived as outcome. Moreover, that the fact is not
merely a *Folge* in the general sense of the word but an *Erfolg* would suggest
that this it is not merely an arbitrary outcome of an activity: the fact is that in
which a certain activity finds its final accomplishment. Every fact, so it
would seem, must be thought of as an accomplishment; the fact is not simply
given, but that which has achieved the status of facticity. Finally, the term
Erfolg in the sense of a success suggests that Nietzsche understands this process by which the fact claims its facticity—and can thus first come to count as
a fact—in terms of a relation of force. This relation of force is, at its most fundamental level, the force by which something that is an outcome of an activity—
the *Faktum* as *Erfolg*—comes to achieve the status of a reality that is thought
to be directly given.[104]

   If one reads the passage from the *Genealogy* from this perspective, this
means that it is not just other interpretations that must be renounced in order
to construct the positive fact in its independent unity: what is renounced is
"interpretation as such" (*Interpretation überhaupt*). In a note from 1875, which
once again takes up the theme of a worship of the factual, Nietzsche makes
this explicit when he writes: "Everything that is suppressed by success [*alles
durch den Erfolg Unterdrückte*] punts up gradually; history as scorn of the victor; servile disposition and devotion for the fact [*servile Gesinnung und Devotion vor dem Faktum*]."[105] If every fact is the outcome of a relation of force, this
relation is here construed in terms of suppression. What is suppressed in every
fact is left undetermined here because it is implied in the concept of the fact
as *Erfolg*, an outcome: before it can count as a fact, every fact has already suppressed that it is not a given but constituted. This repression is exactly what is
evoked in Nietzsche's claim that the idolatry of the factual emerges only out

of a "bare admiration of success" (*nackte Bewunderung des Erfolges*). This "bare admiration" would be an admiration that turns the accomplishment that is admired into a bare accomplishment, that is to say, an outcome divorced from the process through which it is constituted: to turn the fact into an idol, to take it as a pure given and posit it as a stable referential ground, entails forgetting the process through which "reality" is made—and it is only in this forgetfulness that the fact is constituted.

Echographies

Throughout his writings, Nietzsche will attempt to articulate an experience of history that does not lapse into an "idolatry of facts" and its representation of history as a sequential arrangement of what "actually happened." One of the principal directions that he will begin to explore in his early writings revolves around acoustic imagery and the concomitant attempt to rethink historical experience on the model of sound, resonance, and echo. The sound will serve here as a model for both a critique of the hypostasis of historical reality and the attempt to escape from it. An exemplary instance of this imagery is found in one of his notebooks of 1882, which includes the following brief note: "Now it is first through an echo that events acquire 'greatness' [*jetzt ist es erst der Widerhall, durch den die Ereignisse "Größe" bekommen*]—the echo of the newspapers [*der Widerhall der Zeitungen*]."[106] The image of the "echo of the newspapers" is here introduced in the context of a note whose premise is implied by its first word: *jetzt*. History, so it would seem, does not always take place in quite the same way. In our time—the "now" to which the writer and the reader must both relate themselves—"events" acquire their "greatness" in a way that is different from any other time. That this note is written in the same year that the *Gay Science* was published suggests that this now has a specific inflection: the *jetzt* in which "events acquire their 'greatness'" (*die Ereignisse "Größe" bekommen*) through an echo would be the same now in which the madman in the marketplace announces the "enormous event" (*ungeheure Ereignis*) that is the death of God. The note and its reference to the echo of the newspapers are thus stamped with a specific date: "now"—now that God has died—history can no longer take place as before, nor can it be spoken of in quite the same way. Even though the words that are employed in this note to refer to history—"event" and "greatness"—seem to have remained intact, their use is now punctuated by the same marks that appeared in the announcement of the death of God. Who stamps his notes with this date—"now"—could, so it seems, no longer use words such as "event" or "greatness" without placing them between quotation marks. Who attempts to live up to the demand implied in this date could only speak these words by citing them, passing them off as words that are not his own, marking them as words that can no longer lay claim to the meaning that once seemed proper to them.

In another note that is found on the same page, these quotation marks return, together with the categories of the "event" and "greatness." Here Nietzsche exclaims: "I do not believe in the greatness of all these 'great events' of which you speak [*ich glaube nicht an die Größe aller dieser "großen Ereignisse", von denen ihr sprecht*]."[107] Even now, precisely now, in a time when the news of the death of God spreads like a rumor, there is apparently talk of "great events": talk that is here, once more, attributed to the "you" in the plural—you the readers, you the contemporaries, but also a you that implicates and admonishes the writer of this note, who will reread it in his notebooks. Even though "great events" are still spoken of in this now—and it is words like these that above all characterize the *Zeitungssprache*—this writer who begins his sentences with the word "now" must call them into question, renounce them as words in which he does not "believe" (*glauben*), a word that Nietzsche uses as a term that has both an epistemic and a religious sense, suggesting that these categories must be rejected in the same way that one would reject a false God. But when Nietzsche claims that he does not believe in the "great events" that the newspapers never cease to talk about, this must not be mistaken for the claim that other "events" could unproblematically lay claim to this "greatness." What is denounced here is not merely the "greatness" of some occurrences, a denunciation that would correspond to the claim that this "greatness" could only be rightly attributed to others. Similarly, Nietzsche does not claim that a conception of "greatness" measured on the basis of mere effects is to be denounced in order to attend to the "event itself." What is called into question here is the category of "greatness" as such—and together with it the conception of the "event" that could ever "acquire greatness" (*Größe bekommen*), that is to say, the event that is hypostasized as an independent substance of which it becomes possible to predicate attributes such as "greatness."

This critique of the hypostasis of history that is implied in the category of the "great event" is already undertaken in Nietzsche's early writings. To better understand what is at stake in these notes from the 1880s, one could turn to a passage at the outset of the fourth of the *Untimely Meditations*—the essay on Wagner, which is the text where Nietzsche deals most extensively with questions of sound and music. "No event has greatness in itself [*an sich hat kein Ereignis Größe*]," Nietzsche writes in the first paragraphs of the essay, "even when whole constellations of stars disappear, entire peoples fall, expansive states are founded and wars are fought with tremendous forces and losses; the breath of history [*der Hauch der Geschichte*] has blown through many things of that kind as if through flakes of snow."[108] He then continues to elaborate this proposition in acoustic terms: "It can also happen that a powerful human being strikes a blow [*einen Streich führt*] that sinks down from a stone surface without having any effect [*wirkungslos niedersinkt*]: a brief, sharp echo, and all is over [*ein kurzer scharfer Wiederhall, und Alles ist vorbei*]." "History," he concludes, "has almost nothing to report of such as it were blunted events [*die Geschichte weiss auch von solchen gleichsam abgestumpften Ereignissen beinahe Nichts zu melden*]."[109] Even though Nietzsche is, in his writings of the time, himself still entangled in the talk of "great events" he will later emphatically denounce, it already shows the attempts to struggle to escape from such talk. The claim that "no event has greatness in itself" is such an attempt. What is problematized here through the category of greatness is the very separation between the "event" and its "effects" that first makes it possible to speak of "great events." When Nietzsche evokes occurrences on a world-historical and even a cosmic scale—from the disappearance of constellations of stars to wars in which tremendous force is expended—these exemplify not so much the most extreme asymmetry between an "event" with an independent unity and its effects but, rather, the complete dissolution of the category of the "event" into these effects. An occurrence without effects, an occurrence that is purely *wirkungslos*, would not have occurred at all; the "event" would be nothing but *Wirkung*. As long as the talk of "events" continues, this point can only be approximated, only gestured at by referring to those "truncated events" of which history has "almost nothing" (*beinahe Nichts*) to report.

But in this approximation, the passage from the *Untimely Meditations* already signals an attempt to think of an occurrence that is nothing but an occurring, an occurrence that is no longer ascribed to an "event" that can be separated from its "effects." Although the passage remains caught in the talk of "event" and its "effects" on a conceptual plane, the images introduced here further elude this distinction altogether. It is no accident that images of sounds, reverberations, and echoes return throughout the reflections on history in the *Untimely Meditations*. These images are not to be mistaken for mere illustrations: they are examples of imagery in and through which Nietzsche attempts to problematize how "history" is constituted. If the sound serves as a privileged image for the historical occurrence, this is because it problematizes any understanding of history as a sequence of "actual events" that may be isolated and described as a thing in itself. Every sound resists the possibility of being separated from its *Wirkung*: the sound is nothing but its sounding, its resonance and reverberation. This sounding is, in turn, always already marked as a resounding: there is no original sound that could ever be separated from its sounding as a cause that could be separated from its effects. A "blow" may be

struck—and Nietzsche tends to use the *Streich* not only as the most elementary of all sounds but also as the most elementary of all deeds—but it can take
place as a sound only insofar as it resounds. Only in and as this resounding
does the sound take place. When Nietzsche refers to the event as a *Widerhall*,
this must therefore be understood in the literal sense: as the *Wider-hallen*, the
resounding and resonating in which a sound is first constituted. If it is translated as "echo" then it must be understood as an originary echo, the sound
insofar as it is always already constituted as echo and cannot be traced back to
a sound that exists prior to it. To think history in terms of a sounding and resounding would therefore remove the possibility of ever tracing history back
to what "actually happened," of ever isolating a sequence of "actual events"
that can be neatly separated from their effects: the sound would be the model
of an occurrence that is nothing but an occurring—a resonating and reverberating, pulsating and echoing, fading away and dying out without a substantial subject.

The attempt that informs Nietzsche's use of acoustic imagery, the attempt
to speak of history without separating between "events" and their "effects," returns in his later recourse to the word *das Geschehen* in his reflections on
history. Nietzsche uses *Geschehen* as a reluctant noun, a noun that indicates
an occurrence that has almost managed to indicate nothing but its occurring,
its distinction from the verb *geschehen* reduced to the most minimal distinguishing mark of a capital letter. But precisely in the minimal difference between the two words, occurrence and occurring, it also testifies to the stubborn
tendency of language to separate and hypostasize a subject. It is no coincidence
that Nietzsche derives his images from the sphere of sound, which—like rhetoric, although the two models of language are ultimately irreconcilable—
indicates an aspect of language that is prior to its conceptual function. The
fate that is reserved for the *Geschehen* that Nietzsche captures in the image of
the sound, once it is transferred into language, is the same as that of the well-
known example of the flash of lightning in his later reflections on language
and grammar.[110] Just as language, in its grammatical structure, is there said
to "separate" (*trennen*) the "bolt of lightning" (*Blitz*) from its flash (*seinem
Leuchten*) and "takes the latter for a deed, an effect of a subject called lightning," so the *Geschehen* of history can only appear as doubled once it has entered language. The *Geschehen* is separated into the occurrence and its
occurring, into "effects" which are attributed to an "event" that is taken to be
their cause. In this separation, the "event" is taken to have a reality apart from
its effects; like the "subject called lightning," the "event" is taken to be a sub-
stratum independent of its effects, the doer of a deed. This separation is driven
to an extreme in the talk of the "great event," where the hypostasis of the "event"

culminates in its treatment as an object that could be placed in front of an observer—an object that could be inspected and measured just as one would ascertain the *Größe* of a stone on a table. What is forgotten in this talk of "great events" is the same as that which is forgotten by those who speak in sentences like *der Blitz leuchtet*: "There is no 'being' behind the doing, the effect, the becoming [*dem Tun, Wirken, Werden*]; the 'doer' is a mere fiction added to the doing [*der Täter ist zum Tun bloß hinzugedichtet*]—the doing is everything. People at bottom double the doing when they allow the lightning to flash. That is a doing-doing [*Tun-Tun*]: it posits the same occurrence [*dasselbe Geschehen*], once as cause and then again as its effect."[111]

Nietzsche's reference to the *Widerhall der Zeitungen* may be understood as an instance of such doubling. When he writes that "it is now first through an echo [*erst der Widerhall*] that events acquire 'greatness,'" the echo that captured the shift in the way in which history occurs "now," in a time when rumors of the death of God circulate everywhere, undergoes a strange reversal. The *erst* that is here pressed as closely as possible to the *wider-* seems to indicate not only a precedence in importance ("first and foremost") but perhaps also a precedence of a logical and temporal kind: the *Widerhall* that manifests itself in the newspapers is an echo that comes first, a resounding that occurs before the sound. Anticipating the "chronological reversal" (*chronologische Umdrehung*) between cause and effect that will become an important theme in Nietzsche's later writings, the *Widerhall* of the newspaper here signifies a writing that is only naïvely thought to be conditioned by the "actual events" of which it writes but is, instead, conditioned by this writing. Only afterwards, *nachträglich*, these "actual events" are projected as that which preceded this writing; the "actual event" is now posited as the cause of which the writing is a mere effect. Nowhere is this reversal expressed more clearly than in the category of the "great event," where the sheer volume of writing on an event that, in turn, first comes into being in this writing is mistaken for a property of an event that is thought to have caused it. What is considered to be a cause—the great event—is the effect of an effect, the echo of an echo.[112]

The schema of this reversal already appears on multiple occasions in Nietzsche's writings of the early 1870s. In the second of the *Untimely Meditations*, "On the Uses and Abuses of History," Nietzsche relates his attempts to understand history in terms of a sounding and resounding to a writing whose exemplary site is, again, the newspaper:

> The modern human being [. . .] has been brought to a condition that
> even great wars and great revolutions are able to alter for hardly more
> than an instant. The war has not even come to an end, and it has

already been transformed a hundred thousand times into printed
paper [*schon in bedrucktes Papier hunderttausendfach umgesetzt*], has
already been served up as the newest stimulant for the weary palates of
those greedy for history. It seems almost impossible to elicit a strong
and full sound [*starker und voller Ton*] even with the strongest sweeping of the strings [*Hineingreifen in die Saiten*]: immediately it fades
away [*sofort verhallt er*] and in the next instant it already dies out
[*klingt er ab*], historically subdued, evaporated, powerless.[113]

Before the war has come to an end, before this war has fully and completely
taken place, it has already been converted, *umgesetzt*, transposed into marks
printed on paper. This conversion into writing therefore does not take place
after the war, as a report that may be separated from that which it reports; this
war is already converted into writing before it has ended and takes place precisely at this writing. This conversion into writing is, moreover, not to be
thought of as a representation that could ever stand in a supposedly adequate
relation to the thing that is represented: it is an *Umsetzung*, a transposition
between spheres that could have no adequate relation to one another. As a
transposition in this sense—a transposition that has "already" (*schon*) occurred
and will have already occurred before any other "great war" or "great revolution" has taken place—the marks imprinted on paper would leave no possibility of gaining access to a history that has "actually happened." Shifting once
again to an acoustic register, Nietzsche compares this history that is inseparable from its writing to the sounding and resounding of a "sweeping of strings."
If history must be thought of in terms of such sounding and resounding, the
newspaper may be understood as an echo chamber that defines the conditions
and possibilities for its sounding and resounding—a chamber where sounds
resonate and reverberate in a manner that is characteristic of the time in which
Nietzsche is writing. The study of history would no longer be concerned with
what "actually happened"; rather, this passage suggests that it would have to
take the form of an echography. The study that Nietzsche begins to undertake here is a descriptive analysis of sounds that "fade away" or "die out," of
"brief" or "sharp" echoes, of sounds that are "cut off" or "evaporate." Such an
echography would seem to be concerned not only with the description of actual
sounds but also with a study of the echo chamber itself: a study of the conditions under which sounding and resounding becomes possible—a study of the
conditions under which sounds are muted and muffled, but also of possible
resonances and reverberations. This echography would start from a different
conception of what it means for history to occur, a different conception of the
Geschehen of *Geschichte*. The terms that Nietzsche uses in his initial attempts

at such an echography—*wiederhallen, verhallen, abklingen*—suggest that the
study of what "actually happened" would have given way to a study of history
understood as a sounding that is always already marked as a *wieder-, ver-, ab-*—
as a re-sounding and re-sonating that leaves no possibility of ever identifying
an original.

Prosopopoeia of History

In parallel to his attempts to conceive of history in acoustic terms, Nietzsche's
efforts to articulate an experience of history that does not fall prey to the posi-
tivism of facts will focus mainly on extending and reworking his early reflections on language. Even if rhetoric is no longer at the core of his philosophical
project after 1875, it will continue to play an important role in his reflections
on history.[114] This is suggested, for instance, by an important note from 1883,
the same year that Nietzsche published the first two parts of his *Zarathustra*.
The note reads as follows:

> A fact [*Faktum*] or a work is of a new eloquence [*von neuer Beredsam-
> keit*] for each time and for each new kind of human being. History
> speaks ever-new truths [*die Geschichte redet immer neue
> Wahrheiten*].[115]

The note foregrounds an important motif in Nietzsche's reflections on history:
a motif that might be referred to as the *prosopopoeia* of history, a presentation
of history as something that speaks. Throughout his writings, Nietzsche will
attribute speech not only to occurrences—the "facts and works" to which this
note makes reference—but also to the time of history, to the past and especially to the future, of which Nietzsche will write in a later note that it "speaks
even now in a hundred signs."[116] When this prosopopoeia is evoked in the note
on the "eloquence" of facts and works, it is easily mistaken for a mere extension of Nietzsche's perspectivism, applied and elaborated in relation to the experience of history. Understood in this way, the reference to the *Beredsamkeit*
of historical occurrences would be yet another reiteration of the thesis that
there is no fact without interpretation, that there is no such thing as an objective historical fact, only interpretations that are inseparable from the particular perspective from which they are undertaken.[117] But even though the
prosopopoeia of history that Nietzsche evokes in this fragment certainly stands
in a close relation to his doctrine of perspectivism, it is by no means exhausted
by it. The image of history presented here cannot be reduced to the status of
an illustration or application: it captures an experience of history—and its re-

lation to thought—whose implications are at once broader and more precise than concepts of "perspective" or "interpretation."

What does it mean, then, to think of historical experience in terms of a prosopopoeia? Besides implying that historical experience has a linguistic structure, the image of prosopopoeia first of all suggests that this linguality finds its model in speech. As such, it suggests that the object constituted in this experience—the "fact" and the "work" to which the note makes reference—is not understood as something passive in the way that a text is typically considered to be. Rather than being portrayed as a text that waits to be read, the historical occurrence is conceived as something that calls to be heard and understood, something that makes a demand upon the one who hears it. Moreover, that history not merely speaks but has an "eloquence" (*Beredsamkeit*) suggests that the speech and the language spoken here have an emphatically *rhetorical* character. The rhetoric of facts and works would be a rhetoric of a specific kind: it would be an *eloquentia*, a rhetoric of persuasion. What is the one who hears this speech of history persuaded of? What would be the effect of such persuasion? Before anything else the eloquent fact would persuade its audience that there is a speaker, that there is a "fact" or a "work" that speaks. In other words, the two types of occurrences that the note distinguishes between— the *Faktum* and *Werk*, the pure given and the pure intentional act—do not precede their speech: they are rather the effects of this speech, this eloquence that persuades the listener that they exist. The *Beredsamkeit* of history is not merely the eloquence of an already established speaker who proves his persuasive force by making what is said appear as the truth. More fundamentally, this eloquence once again follows the schema of metonymy: as in the case of the "echo of the newspapers," the real persuasive force of this eloquence is the substitutive reversal of an effect for a cause, of what comes first and what comes after.[118] That history "speaks ever-new truths" (*redet immer neue Wahrheiten*) must be understood both as a confirmation of this thesis and as a further elaboration. There is a notable dissonance here between the "truth" and the "speaking" to which Nietzsche refers here, which is not a *sprechen* but a *reden*. This is not a truth that has an existence prior to its own communication in a language of concepts and propositions—it is a truth that is produced by a language of persuasion.

Not only does Nietzsche's image of an "eloquence of facts" therefore undermine the notion that history consists of "actual events" that precede this eloquent speech; it also undermines the notion that these "actual events" could ever be organized into a linear sequence. That history "speaks ever-new truths" would not only mean that the same "fact"—if this can even be isolated—speaks to each epoch differently. Nor would it simply extend this claim by proposing that each fact not only has a different thing to say to each epoch, but has a different way of speaking, a different eloquence, a different *Beredsamkeit*: its persuasive force differs from one epoch to another, together with its possible effects. Insofar as that which speaks is constituted only in the speech itself, the thesis of an *Beredsamkeit* of history does not merely involve a claim that the same occurrences are seen in an ever-new light; it suggests precisely that these occurrences themselves—the facts and works of history—are constituted ever anew in this speech. Such truths would be "always new" (*immer neu*) in a specific sense: they would never persist through time but only persist in the form of their return and renewal.

In an aphorism that is included in *Daybreak*, which was published two years earlier, Nietzsche had already attempted to think a historiography that would no longer seek for a stable ground in "actual events." Returning to the question of factuality, he writes:

> *Facta!* Yes, *facta ficta!* A historian has to do not with what actually happened [*was wirklich geschehen ist*], but only with events supposed to have happened [*vermeintlichen Ereignissen*]: for only the latter have produced an effect [*haben gewirkt*]. Likewise he only has to do with supposed heroes. His theme, so-called world history, is opinions about supposed actions [*Meinungen über vermeintlichen Handlungen*] and their supposed motives, which in turn give rise to further opinions and actions, the reality of which is however at once vaporized again [*deren Realität aber sofort wieder verdampft*] and produces an *effect* only as vapor [*und nur als Dampf wirkt*]—a continual generation and pregnancy of phantoms [*Zeugen und Schwangerwerden von Phantomen*] over the impenetrable mist of unfathomable reality [*über den tiefen Nebeln der unergründlichen Wirklichkeit*]. All historians speak of things which have never existed except in their representation [*Vorstellung*].[119]

History, that with which the historian concerns himself—and for Nietzsche we are all historians of our own life—can be said to consist of "facts" only insofar as these facts are understood as *facta ficta*, facts that are made rather than given. The fact is here treated according to the schema of Nietzsche's theory of rhetoric. The distinction between *doxa* and *epistēmē* that Nietzsche elaborates in the notes for his lecture course of the early 1870s—a distinction summarized in the claim that "language is rhetoric because it desires to convey only a *doxa*, not an *episteme*"[120]—is applied here to the sphere of history and the opposition between *factum* and *fictum*. Just as concepts are not to be mistaken for the carriers of a proper meaning, so history is not to be mistaken for "what has actually happened": just as the concept of the "hero" hypostasizes a subject that precedes its actions, so the "fact" hypostasizes an "event" that precedes its effects. What "actually happened" only has "reality"—if it is still possible to use this word—insofar as it produces effects. If it is possible to speak of a reality, this is the reality of ever-renewed vaporization—a reality that exists only as its own aftereffect, an effect that has no reality in itself but only in producing other effects, in vaporizing yet again. History is not the stable account of "what has actually happened"; it is precisely the "continual generation and pregnancy of phantoms"—phantoms that can never be stabilized as a self-same phenomenon but always differ from themselves. There is no substantial ground to history conceived in this way: the reality with which the historian is concerned is *unergründlich* not only in the sense that it is unfathomable, that one has no access to "what actually happened," but also in the sense that there is no reality that could ever provide a stable ground for a complete and definitive account of history. The ever-renewed vaporization that constitutes historical reality does not consist of phantoms over an unfathomable but stable ground, but over a "deep mist" (*tiefen Nebeln*)—a groundless ground that is itself nothing of vapor.

The model for the conception of history outlined here by Nietzsche is not the "fact," but rather the linguistic form—if it can still be called a form—in and through which the news of the death of God will be imparted: the rumor. If "history speaks," as Nietzsche claims in his note of 1883, it speaks a rumorous speech that has no stable reference to a speaker, a "fact" or a "work" that could be established before their speech and identified as its origin. To conceive of history as a rumor would mean, first of all, that neither the question of who is speaking, nor that of what is spoken of, can ever be determined with any certainty. The rumorous speech of history is, for Nietzsche, not an aberration from factuality proper. Quite the contrary: what is called a "fact" is nothing but a rumor whose status has been forgotten and suppressed—a suppression that can only continue to exist on the condition that it persuades the listener through its eloquence that it hears what has "actually happened." This reversed relation between fact and rumor is thematized in a passage in one of Nietzsche's letters, also written in the early 1880s, where he provides his friend Heinrich Köselitz with a detailed description of his encounter with a rumor.

> Here, in the hermitage that lies alone in the woods and whose hermit I am, there is a great emergency [*große Noth*]. I actually do not know what has happened [*ich weiß eigentlich nicht, was geschehen ist*], but the shadow of a crime lies over the building. Someone has buried something, others have discovered it, one heard terrible whining, there

were many police officers, a house search took place, and at night
I heard someone sighing in heavy torment, so that I could no longer
sleep [der Schlaf floh]. Also there appeared to be digging in the woods
in the middle of the night, but something surprising took place, and
then there were tears and cries again. A civil servant told me that it was
a "story of bank notes" [Banknotengeschichte]—but I am not curious
enough to know as much as is probably known by the whole world
around me.[121]

In its density and specific choice of words, the passage stands out from the letter and reads almost like a philosophical aphorism. The "history" that Nietzsche relates here to his friend is a history that takes place in the medium of
rumor. Even though the author of the letter "does not know what has happened [was geschehen ist]," the signs that something is happening are unmistakable. Whatever is happening speaks to the author of this letter—and it does
so in the register of tears and cries, of a whining and sighing that wake him
from his slumber. What appears to the "civil servant" who enters the stage at
the end of this story as a Geschichte, a coherent story presented as a sequence
of actual events, is experienced by the author of the letter as a constellation
of dispersed occurrences—signs that resist being fixed definitively as a sequence of causes and effects. Rather than asking what has "actually" happened,
however, the experience of this history as rumor is deliberately maintained—at
least in the account that the author of the letter gives to his friend. Besides
the claimed indifference toward the question as to what has "actually" happened—an indifference that Nietzsche ascribes to his lack of "curiosity"
(Neugier)—there is an unmistakable pleasure in suspending the knowledge
of the "facts." Perhaps it is a pleasure that stems from the sense that there is
a different truth to the experience of this history as a rumor whose proper
meaning cannot be fixed conclusively—an experience that gives up on the
construction of a coherent history and suspends the search for an account of
what "actually happened."

Reading and Returning

When the preoccupation with journalism surfaces again in Thus Spoke Zarathustra and the work of the following years, its renewed emergence is closely
related to a problem that had already appeared in Nietzsche's early writings
but that would come to play an ever more important role in the later texts: the
problem of reading. The figure of the journalist, which still appeared in the
early lectures, has disappeared entirely from the later writings; not the language

of the newspapers, but *Zeitungslesen* and *Zeitungslektüre* will figure as a central trope in the texts of these years. "We despise every formation that has a tolerance for newspaper reading [*jeder Bildung, welche mit Zeitungslesen verträgt*]," Nietzsche writes in an exemplary note of 1885.[122] At the same time as it returns to the theme that was central to his Basel lectures of early 1872—*Bildung*, understood here in the sense of the formation of subjectivity—this note replaces the figure of the journalist, which served as a negative image of the formation that these lectures had sought to articulate, with the image of an activity, a certain mode of reading. The question of *Bildung*, which was already in the early lectures understood as a question concerning the future, is now framed as a question of reading, of a certain relation to text and meaning; and this question is, in turn, framed as a matter of extricating oneself from a specific mode of reading—the reading of the newspaper. An initial indication of how Nietzsche understood the specificity of this reading is suggested by another fragment that stems from a notebook of the same months, where *Zeitungslesen* is described through a series of adjectives:

> The coarsening of the European spirit, a certain plump directness
> [*ein gewissen täppisches Geradezu*] that likes to hear itself celebrated
> as rectitude, propriety or scientificity [*Geradheit, Redlichkeit, oder
> Wissenschaftlichkeit*] [. . .]—this is the effect of newspaper reading
> [*die Wirkung des Zeitungslesens*].[123]

Newspaper reading would thus be a reading that stands under a single imperative: *Geradezu*. This word captures two aspects of this reading: as an adverb, it evokes a certain literalness, a certain relation to meaning as something that is simply and directly given; and it presents the retrieval of this literal meaning—by way of an ironic metaphor—as a movement that follows a straight line, a movement that goes "straight towards" (*gerade zu*) its goal. The word that follows on from it, *Geradheit*, evokes the same directness—but here, like the English translation, "rectitude," it transposes this directness into a moral register, rendering the straight movement as a good movement. To read well means here: to move straight toward the meaning of the text, without detours— to read as one reads the newspapers.

To grasp the significance of this provisional characterization of *Zeitungslesen*, it is crucial to understand these remarks in relation to the analysis of reading that Nietzsche developed in the same period. Reading is here not conceived in terms of a direct, straightforward comprehension of the meaning of inscribed signs but, rather, as an activity that is modeled before anything else on a certain movement of turning or, more precisely, a movement of returning (*Wiederkehren*). Nowhere is this articulated in a more careful and

programmatic way than in a dense passage on reading found in the preface to
one of the texts of the late 1880s—a passage included in a *Vorwort*, the place
at the threshold of the text that Nietzsche already liked to use for the sparse
reflections on reading in the early writings. In this passage, itself introduced
as an aside, Nietzsche formulates a theory of reading that is organized around
a figure of return: "rumination" (*Wiederkäuen*):

> If anyone finds this writing [*diese Schrift*] incomprehensible and hard
> on the ears, I do not think the fault necessarily lies with me. [. . .] An
> aphorism, properly stamped and moulded, has not been "deciphered"
> ["*entziffert*"] just because it has been read out [*abgelesen*]; on the contrary,
> only now must its *interpretation* [*Auslegung*] first begin, and for this an
> art of interpretation [*Kunst der Auslegung*] is needed. [. . .] I admit that
> you need one thing above all in order to practise the requisite reading
> as *art* [*Lesen als Kunst zu üben*], a thing which today people have
> been so good at forgetting [*verlernen*]—and therefore the "readability"
> ["*Lesbarkeit*"] of my writings will take some time—and for which one
> must almost be a cow and certainly not a "modern human being":
> *rumination* [*das Wiederkäuen*] . . . [124]

In reading this passage, it is crucial to bear in mind that the word Nietzsche
used, *Wiederkäuen*, differs in a crucial way from every translation that has its
roots in the Latin *ruminari*—a word that has its root in the Latin *rumen*, the
throat or gullet. The English "rumination" not only lacks the element of return that is emphasized in the German, the *wieder-* that would come to assume such a specific significance in the writings after the summer of 1881 in
Sils-Maria,[125] but is also a term that, insofar as it derives from the *rumen*, lacks
the distinct emphasis on the materiality of the text that is evoked by the German *Wiederkäuen*—a term that maintains a certain resistance to a conception
of reading as a purely ideal process that takes place within an already constituted subject. What allows rumination in the sense of *Wiederkäuen* to serve as
a crucial image of reading for Nietzsche is not only its emphasis on the movement of a return, but also its reference to the irreducible externality and materiality of the text. This will play an important role in Nietzsche's understanding
of rumination as a reading that can only be thought of as a returning reading,
a reading that is always a once again and a once more.[126]

Rumination is a chewing that repeats another chewing; it is an eating of
what has already been eaten, a chewing over what has already been chewed—
it is, ultimately, a return of what has already returned before. The chewing to
which *Wiederkäuen* refers never takes place for the first time, nor for the last;
its *wieder-* suggests not only that it must be preceded by another chewing, but

also that it is bound to be repeated again: it is an eating without a definitive closure or reconciliation. For this reading there is no such thing as a reading that happens only once: reading only begins in the return to a text that had remained unread in a first reading that, in turn, only emerges in its repetition. It is no accident that Nietzsche begins this reflection on reading in the preface to a "book" of "essays" that are, in a sense, more like a collection of aphorisms—*The Genealogy of Morality*—for the aphorism is the form par excellence to illustrate this strange reading. There is no aphorism, in the specific sense in which Nietzsche uses the word, that could have ever been read on a first reading. The thought of a ruminating reading is thus advanced through a writing—"this writing" (*diese Schrift*)—that would itself only be read through such a repeated reading. What must be learned by any reader who "practices" (*üben*) such a repeated reading, by any reader who exercises this repeated reading again and again, is that any renewed reading displaces the reading that preceded it. That Nietzsche refers to "this" writing, points to a writing that is supposedly immediately present, is thus not without irony. Not only does "this writing" no longer quite mean what it seemed to mean before; that the reader of "this" writing now faces "another" writing also means that the words themselves appear in a different way in the movement of return. To the reader who ruminates, who returns to the text and consumes it yet another time, the word is no longer an unequivocal carrier of meaning; it comes to appear as a cipher, as something that needs to be *entziffert*, that withdraws from understanding. In this repeated reading, writing thus appears at the same time as that which makes reading possible and as that which resists its own comprehension or what Nietzsche here calls "readability" (*Lesbarkeit*)—a term that needs to be placed between quotation marks because it would precisely suspend the usual understanding of the word. In this repeated reading, words do not simply signify something different than in the "first reading" in which the reader took their significance to be self-evident. As ciphers, words come to signify in an altogether different way: their meaning is no longer thought to be stable or given.[127]

Reading conceived as rumination thus has a double structure, for which Nietzsche here reserves two words that, in their form, almost appear like displaced repetitions: *ablesen* and *auslegen*. Only in the repetition of *ablesen* as *auslegen* does it become possible to speak of reading in the strict sense: only when the initial reading (*ablesen*) has already transpired can the other reading (*auslegen*) begin. There is no such thing as a first reading, in the sense that any first reading could only manifest itself as a missed reading, a mere *ablesen*. Any reading that takes place only once would not have taken place at all. The thought of an a priori repetitive reading is contained in the phrase

Nietzsche uses—*nun erst hat dessen Auslegung zu beginnen*: in the "now" indicated here, reading begins for the first time, but already as a repetition of
another reading—a reading that was, in turn, not yet a reading. In this repetition, the initial reading is not just displaced by another one; it also opens itself
to be displaced yet again. This thought of the repetitive structure of reading is
not formulated for the first time in the later writings; when it makes its appearance here, it does so as the repetition of an earlier reflection on reading
that Nietzsche included in the preface to his lectures *On the Future of our Educational Institutions*—the same text in which journalism first appeared as an
important theme. This preface also reflects on the reading that is demanded
by the writing that it introduces, this *meditatio generis futuri*; and like the one
of 1887, this preface conjures up a reader who has not yet forgotten or "unlearned" (*verlernt*) a certain mode of reading:

> The reader, from whom I expect something [*etwas erwarte*]—such a
> human being has not yet unlearned to think while he reads [*zu
> denken, während er liest*], he still understands the secret of reading
> between the lines [*das Geheimniß zwischen den Zeilen zu lesen*], yet he
> has such a squandering disposition that he even thinks again about
> what has been read [*noch über das Gelesene nachdenkt*], maybe long
> after he has put a book away.[128]

The double structure of reading that Nietzsche describes in the *Genealogy* as
an *ablesen* and *auslegen* is here anticipated by the thought of a reading that is
split into a "thinking while reading" (*denken, während er liest*) and a thinking
that is deferred, a thinking that takes place after the initial reading, a *nach-
denken* that is at the same time a *noch denken*, a thinking that maintains itself
as a return. These two coincide in the image of a reading that is a "secret"
(*Geheimniß*) to the extent that it has been forgotten or unlearned, perhaps must
be forgotten each time such reading is undertaken: the secret of "reading between the lines." Such a reading would not exhaust itself in the "first reading"
that believes itself to restore the presence of the lines of text on the page; it
would also attend to the text that remained unread in this reading, the blank
space between these lines. This blank space between the lines would point to
the irreducible openness of any reading to another reading—an openness that
lies not in *Sätze*, sentences that would be able to present their significance in
its fullness, but in *Zeile*, lines on the page that retain an irreducible externality and meaninglessness. This other reading, as a reading between the lines,
would have to be understood as a parallel reading, which takes place at the
same time as the *lesen* that it accompanies but is always a deferred reading
(*nachlesen*) and a repeated reading (*noch lesen*). If the "first" reading of the

text is conceived as the transubstantiation of the meaning of what is written, this reading that takes place *nach* and *noch* would be conceived as a priori iterative, a reading that can only take place as a rewriting of what is written in the space between the marks on the page.

This same conception of reading as iteration also surfaces in the passage on rumination from the preface of 1887, which claims that the exemplary instance of the "art of rumination" can be found in the book that it prefaces and that the reader, in reading this preface, "this writing" (*diese Schrift*), has already begun to read. "In the third essay of this book I have given a specimen [*Muster*] of what I mean by 'interpretation' in such a case," Nietzsche writes. "This treatise is a commentary [*Commentar*] on the aphorism that precedes it."[129] The doubled reading of rumination that Nietzsche has described here as an *ablesen* and an *auslegen* thus corresponds to another double in the aphorism, the double of *Schrift* and *Commentar*, between "this writing" to which Nietzsche refers in the first sentence of the aphorism and another writing, a writing in the margins of a text that only "lays out" the writing it supplements by producing yet another text. If the reading that Nietzsche proposes to call *Wiederkäuen* is a priori repetitive, this is because it is a priori iterative.[130] Rumination would be an eating that is not only a repeated eating but also a repeated regurgitation of what is eaten. If reading is conceived in the familiar sense, as the rendering present of the signification of what was written, it always does so only as a repeated iteration of the marks on the page—a repetition that, because of the pure externality of these marks, never coincides with the signification it repeats but always has to remain separated from it. Reading is always a double of a reading that was missed at the moment of inscription; but it is also always a renewed inscription—a writing between the lines of the text—that has to remain unread at the moment of its inscription and is only read in its repetition.

In the early writings, this a priori repetitive reading is counterposed to another reading—a reading whose exemplary figure is the newspaper reader. In the drafts for his *Philosophenbuch*, Nietzsche claims that philosophical writing—here exemplified by the aphoristic style of Heraclitus—demands a reading that is incompatible with that of "readers who skim and race": *lesenden Schnellläufer* whose eyes move as smoothly over the page as the pen of the writer that never ceases to flow.[131] As in the case of the references to *Viellesen* that punctuate the early writings, what is at issue in *Schnelllesen* is not the pace or quantity of reading as such. It should go without saying that Nietzsche's reflections on reading do not dismiss a voracious reading and writing, an intense and excessive relation to the text. What is at issue is, rather, the calculating and controlled relationship to the text that is implied in both *Schnelllesen* and *Viellesen*. The image of the *Schnelläufer* captures this relationship as one of a runner who attempts to achieve an already given goal in the fastest possible way, that is to say, as effectively and efficiently as possible. It is no coincidence that the German term can also refer to a certain type of machine, which is characterized by the speed of its mechanical, purposeful movement. In contrast to the wanderer, another crucial figure throughout Nietzsche's writings, this reader has no time to return to the same text. Nor the need—for who reads like a *Schnellläufer* acts on the presupposition that the text only needs to be read once. Nowhere is this relation to the text exemplified more clearly than in the figure of the newspaper reader. Schopenhauer already counterposes newspaper reading to a practice of reading whose main principle is an ever-repeated but ever-displaced return to the text—a reading undertaken under the motto *repetitio est mater studiorum*.[132] Nothing could be more distant from the aphorism, the form of writing that demands to be read repeatedly if it is to be read at all, than the newspaper, whose writing is written to be read only once and that is supposed to release its meaning entirely in this single reading. The newspaper reader never returns to an article because it has already served its purpose: once it has been read a single time, it has communicated all it needed to communicate. To read the newspaper twice would be an absurdity: for this reader expects the meaning of the text to be fully present and available at every moment—at least in principle. *Zeitungslesen* is a reading that operates on the supposition that every word can be not only comprehended directly and immediately, but also completely and conclusively. Such a reading can only maintain its supposition of a simple readability if it never returns to the text: for every rereading of a text would have exposed the instability of the text, intimate the impossibility of a simple repetition and, like Nietzsche's *Wiederkäuen*, turned words into ciphers—ciphers that not only render reading possible but also resist and limit this possibility. The *lesende Schnellläufer* would, in other words, not be a figure of a hurried reading that fails to "properly" understand the text, quite the contrary: it would be the figure of a reading that is defined by a perennial flight from its own finitude.

Vomitus Matutinus

The relation of reading to its own finitude also determines the appearance of the theme of journalism in the later writings. The central figure of finitude in the writings of these years—"nausea" (*Ekel*)—is here never far away in Nietzsche's treatment of *Zeitungslesen*.[133] "How can a clean hand touch a newspaper without a convulsion of nausea [*eine Convulsion von Ekel*]?," it is asked in a note of the late 1880s.[134] Later in the same notebook, the relation between reading and nausea is condensed in a single phrase: *"vomitus matutinus* of the newspapers."[135] Yet it is in *Thus Spoke Zarathustra*—the text that is traversed by questions of finitude—that the association of the newspaper with nausea and its culmination, the act of vomiting, is elaborated in most detail. Whenever Zarathustra or his interlocutors make reference to the newspaper, this is always accompanied by imagery of throwing up and spewing out, of *erbrechen* and *herausbrechen*—of a return, in other words, which would seem incommensurable with that of rumination. An exemplary instance of this imagery appears in the first part of the book, in one of Zarathustra's speeches—a speech that deals with "new idols" of various kinds:

> Just look at these superfluous! They are always sick, they vomit up their bile [*erbrechen ihre Galle*] and call it the newspaper [*und nenne es Zeitung*]. They devour [*verschlingen*] one another and are not even able to digest themselves [*können sich nicht einmal verdauen*].[136]

The motif returns once more in the text, in the third part, where a foam-mouthed fool screams at Zarathustra, in a language that is itself tainted by the nausea of which it speaks:

> Oh Zarathustra, here is the big city. [. . .] Do you not hear how the spirit here turned into wordplay [*Wortspiel*]? It vomits a disgusting dishwater of words [*widriges Wort-Spülicht bricht er heraus*]! And they even make newspapers out of this dishwater.[137]

These passages, and the strange role that is reserved here for the newspaper, can only begin to be grasped if they are understood in their relation to the problem of reading. Like rumination, *Wiederkäuen*, the regurgitation that Nietzsche associates with the newspaper also expresses a certain relation to the text, to the written word. When the first of these passages compares the newspaper to the regurgitation of bile, this is not merely to be understood as a reference to a bitter language full of resentment. It must rather be read in the specific physiological sense: what is ejected here is precisely the fluid that aids digestion—*Galle* as the supplement without which the digestion of what is eaten would not have been possible. If reading may be likened to a process of consumption and digestion, a process by which meaning is extracted from the text, internalized and appropriated with no remainder, then the indigestible leftover that is spewed out here is exactly that which first rendered digestion possible: the supplement that is necessary if meaning is to be conveyed—the word as such, the word in its irreducible externality to the meaning it was supposed to help convey. This remainder is spewed out because it is disgusting, nauseating; it instills nausea because it is in the externality of the word—an externality that is exemplified above all by the written word—that reading confronts its own finitude. The word that is ejected here is not only the word that remains after meaning has supposedly been conveyed; it is above all else the word that reminds that another reading is still possible, that the reading that was supposed to be concluded is unfinished, incomplete—and that another reading would have already been possible.

This interpretation is confirmed by the second passage, where the imagery of nausea and vomiting accompanies an exclamation on the state of the spirit. As in the case of the previous passage, what is vomited up here is at once a supplement and a remainder: *Spülicht*, the water in which the indistinct leftovers of a meal are gathered—what could be consumed, what was uneatable, indigestible. These remainders, vomited up by the spirit, are here explicitly and precisely determined: what is ejected is a *Wort-Spülicht*, a dishwater full of words. If the movement of the *Geist* is understood as a self-externalization that is always followed by a reinternalization, a reappropriation that is supposed to be without remainder, then the *Wort-Spülicht* would contain that which cannot be transubstantiated, that which cannot be incorporated in the movement of spirit and must be excreted if it is to continue functioning properly. By a play of alliteration, the *Wort-Spülicht* would reveal itself to be the word in a specific sense; what is ejected by the spirit, what is vomited up here is the word insofar as it participates in *Wortspiel*—the word insofar as it is engaged in a play that has nothing to do with the immanent movement of the spirit. That this playful word is, with another alliteration, *widrig*—disgusting, at least for the spirit that ejects it—must again be understood in terms of the finitude that it keeps on recalling. The word that participates in wordplay is a word that knows no *telos*, that serves no end or purpose—and it is for this reason that the spirit must eject this nauseating remainder, excrete the word that threatens its purposeful movement.

The *vomitus matutinus* that is associated with the morning newspaper would then be the excretion of that which remains after every reading: the word in its irreducible externality. That the reading which Nietzsche thought to be exemplary, symptomatic of the time in which he was writing—*Zeitungslesen*—is characterized as a nauseous reading means that it has become aware of its finitude. But instead of confronting it, this reading ejects the remainder that it finds disgusting: it ejects and expels this remainder in order to ward off the threat that it poses.[138] Nothing could be more different from the reading of rumination, which begins from the word that is encountered in a repeated reading—a word that, as we have found Nietzsche to describe in one of his prefaces of those years, has already revealed itself as a cipher whose meaning is displaced at every repeated reading. *Zeitungslesen* is a reading that is nauseated by this displacement and the instability that it exemplifies—once the news has been taken in, the reader must rid himself of the newspaper, must throw away the text that risks inducing nausea. Yet at the same time as *Zeitungslesen* exemplifies a reading that is most nauseous at its own finitude, it is also on the pages of the newspaper that this finitude comes to be most pronounced: for it is in the newspaper that a writing that seemed to be full of meaning yesterday turns out to have lost this fullness the day after, that the same words have come to mean something else to this reader than they did only a day before. In contrast to the book that, with its implicit claim to timelessness, might still leave the semblance of an identical repetition intact, the newspaper must remind every reader who returns to it of the impossibility of such a repetition. It is perhaps for this reason—not for the sake of its content—that Nietzsche can claim, in yet another note of the same period, that every newspaper must present the text as a fabric of signs that must make every reader shudder: "Every newspaper provides the signs of the most horrible human perversity: *un tissu d'horreurs*. This *dégôutant apéritif* accompanies the morning meal of the civilized human being. *Tout, en ce monde, sue le crime*."[139]

The Last Human

Nietzsche reserves a specific name for the nauseous inhabitant of this city at the end of history that is described to Zarathustra by a foaming fool: the "last human" (*der letzte Mensch*).[140] When Zarathustra, at the start of the book, descends from the mountain and addresses the crowd of contemporaries whom he encounters there, he will conjure up this figure when concluding his speeches. "See!" he exclaims. "I show you the last humans [*ich zeige euch den letzten Menschen*]"—but the crowd fails to understand the words he utters.[141] "They stand there," Zarathustra sighs. "They stand there and laugh: they do not understand me, I am not the mouth for these ears."[142] If the crowd evoked here, like the crowd surrounding the messenger in *The Gay Science*, does not understand the news that is conveyed to them, then the reason for this may be that they do not understand that this last human is not a species that is yet to come, but that Zarathustra is pointing his contemporaries to themselves—and to himself—as exemplars of this last humanity. The name of the "last human" is reserved for a humanity that is defined by the paradoxical contemporaneity with a "monstrous event" that is still on its way, like a rumor doing the rounds: the death of God. That Zarathustra's speeches on the *letzte Mensch* cannot be understood is no accident, for the one who would have truly understood this news would have ceased to be a human in the sense in which the term is used here. The humanity that would have heard this news in the full sense—who would have *incorporated* it—would have become someone other, would have ceased being a human. In this sense, the last human is the figure of that humanity which is stamped by its contemporaneity to an event of which it has yet to become a contemporary in another, stricter sense of the word. In the attempts to speak of this last human, even Zarathustra himself has already conjured up new idols, has already lapsed into the same language of designation and presentation—"I show you," *ich zeige euch*—that has lost its legitimacy.[143]

The journalist and the newspaper reader, the *Zeitungsschreiber* of Nietzsche's early writings and the *Zeitungsleser* of the later work—are these not best understood as the exemplary specimens of this "last human" proclaimed in Zarathustra's prologue? To grasp the continuous preoccupation with journalism in this way means to reserve a decisive role for a question whose importance for Nietzsche's thought still remains to be fully gauged: the question of *language*. The language of the newspapers, *Zeitungssprache*, together with the modes of reading and writing that correspond to it, could only assume their exemplary significance for Nietzsche because the occurrence with which we have found them to be irreducibly bound up—the "death of God"—is already understood in linguistic terms. What Nietzsche's persistent preoccupation with journalism throws into relief is, in other words, his recurrent attempt to think this monstrous occurrence as a fact of language—a fact that, as the recurrent incomprehension of the news of this death attests, allows itself to be simply unveiled. If Nietzsche's hyperbolic portrayals of journalists and newspaper readers show anything, it is that the "dead" God survives his own death—that is, continues to inhabit the language that has "killed" him. Under the heading of *Zeitungssprache*, Nietzsche thus analyzes the duplicity of the language of the last human—a language that can no longer speak the truth but cannot help but believe that it does so.[144]

Precisely because it is inseparable from the problem of language, the continuous preoccupation with journalism that resurfaces throughout Nietzsche's work testifies to the inadequacy of any simple division between the early writings and the mature work. The remarks on journalism never cease to lay bare the breach that Nietzsche's early analysis of language already opened up in a certain metaphysics which still animated the work of that period. And it is precisely because of this breach that Nietzsche could already anticipate the death of God in the writings from the period of the *Philosophenbuch*—the years of his intensive engagement with rhetoric. A passage on journalism from the third of the *Untimely Meditations*, written in 1874, indeed already draws up the schematic outline of the condition that Zarathustra would later ascribe to the last human:

One no longer has the slightest notion how far the seriousness of philosophy is removed from the seriousness of a newspaper. Human beings have given up the last remnant not only of a philosophical but also of a religious disposition and have instead of all this [*statt alledem*] obtained not even optimism but journalism, the spirit and spiritlessness of our day and our daily papers [*den Geist und Ungeist des Tages un der Tageblätter*].[145]

The elements of Nietzsche's later treatment of the theme of journalism are already contained in this passage in summary form. Journalism—and the "seriousness" that corresponds to it—is associated with the collapse of a disposition that is as much philosophical as it is religious. The place that is occupied by journalism is one that is marked by a loss; human beings have had to "give up" (*einbüßen*) their philosophical and religious disposition entirely, up to its "last remnant" (*letzten Rest*). This is not to say that nothing remains; the place that was previously reserved for this lost philosophico-religious disposition is now occupied by journalism. The logic is one of exchange: human beings have had to give up the disposition that had oriented them since the beginning of their history, only to "obtain" (*einhandeln*) something else in its place. For it to be possible to speak of such an exchange there would have to be a semblance of equivalence; journalism would have to appear as the equivalent of religion and philosophy in the present. But even though journalism takes the exact place of the philosophico-religious disposition, it is at the same time at the furthest remove from it. That it is almost impossible to sense "how far removed" the seriousness of philosophy is from that of journalism may be read both in the historical and the logical sense. Philosophy and journalism would relate to one another as two extremes that are at one and the same time a beginning and an end; the historical process that Nietzsche sketches begins with philosophy and reaches its end in journalism. But even though they exist at the furthest remove, they are not simply opposed. If the *Gesinnung* of which Nietzsche speaks is at the same time philosophical and religious, and if it has always received its meaning and purpose, its *Sinn*, from a God which it has been forced to relinquish, then what is left in place of this God is not so much an absence as an ambiguity: a *Geist und Ungeist*, a spirit and non-spirit, a presence that is at the same time an absence. This ghostly apparition finds its peculiar embodiment in the daily papers, the *Tageblätter*: papers that, even though they serve as the ground on which new idols present themselves, cannot quite conceal that their sheets no longer have the weight and substance of the tablet; that they cannot lay claim to the permanence and immutability of the book; that every reader who returns to this text will find that every word on these pages has come to mean something else, has altered irreversibly in the repetition.

The exemplary species of the last human, the newspaper reader, would be the figure of that ghostly spirit—the *Geist und Ungeist des Tages*—that is confronted by its own finitude; unable to overcome its own finitude, the reading exemplified by this figure attempts to forget and expel everything that might remind of it. The "seriousness" (*Ernst*) that is ascribed to the newspapers would thus not simply be opposed to the religio-philosophical seriousness from which it is so far removed: if *Ernst* is understood in the strict sense of the word, as the disposition in which things are treated in accordance with their essential being, the possibility of such a disposition would have to perish together with the essence toward which it oriented itself. The seriousness to which the newspapers lay claim would be a seriousness that has outlived itself—a seriousness that must continuously erect new idols in the absence of the old God. It is in this sense that the theme also resurfaces in the last of the *Untimely Meditations*: "Now only one kind of seriousness is left over in the modern soul [*in der modernen Seele übrig geblieben*]: the seriousness that concerns the messages that are brought by the newspaper [*den Nachrichten welche die Zeitung bringt*]."[146] When the drafts for the *Philosophenbuch* that were written in the same period as these passages conjure up the figure of the "last philosopher" (*der letzte Philosoph*), this figure should perhaps be understood as the counterpart to this last human, the newspaper reader, and the seriousness to which it clings.[147] Even though this "last philosopher" would be a specimen of this humanity at the end of history, it would be an untimely specimen—one that would not only relinquish the old seriousness in the face of God, but also suspect every new seriousness of being mere idolatry. While distrusting this seriousness, this persistent desire to speak properly and conclusively, Nietzsche's *letzte Philosoph* nevertheless knows that there is no way to avoid falling prey to it. If this last philosophy is the "counter-doctrine of everything journalistic" of which Nietzsche speaks in a note of the same year, this *Gegenlehre* could never be conceived in a simple opposition to the seriousness of the last human—a seriousness that has outlived itself after every stable point of reference has been lost. The seriousness of journalism would find a counterpart in another seriousness: one that the 1873 draft for the preface to the *Philosophenbuch* describes as the most serious play—*ein Spielen mit dem Ernst*.[148]

3

Last Days

Benjamin

The opening sentences of Benjamin's last exposé of his *Passagen-Werk* are organized around an unlikely juxtaposition of two emblematic figures: those of Herodotus—who appears here as the first, ancient historian—and the modern newspaper. "The subject of this book," Benjamin writes, "is an illusion expressed by Schopenhauer in the following formula: for the one who wants to seize the essence of history [*wer das Wesen der Geschichte erfassen wolle*], it suffices to compare Herodotus and the morning newspaper [*für den genüge es, Herodot mit der Morgenzeitung zu vergleichen*]."[1] The exposé then continues: "This is the expression of a historical feeling of vertigo [*eines historischen Schwindelgefühls*] that is characteristic of the conception of history of the past century. It corresponds to a way of seeing [*Betrachtungsweise*] in which historical phenomena appear as wholly reified [*als gänzlich verdinglichte eingehen*]"—or what is described in the French version of the same text as "a point of view [*point de vue*] that composes the course of the world out of an unlimited series of facts congealed in the form of things [*une série illimitée de faits figés sous forme de choses*]."[2] With this announcement of the subject matter of his planned magnum opus, Benjamin places the preoccupation with journalism and its emblematic form—the newspaper—at the heart of his philosophical work. The newspaper is here introduced as the emblem of a *Betrachtungsweise*, a certain mode of observing and contemplating historical phenomena that is characteristic of the nineteenth century—the epoch that would be treated in the book outlined in this exposé as an *Urgeschichte* ("primal history") of his own time, of the moment in which he is writing. What would be at stake in this comparative analysis of the newspaper and its ancient counterpart is by no means a historical investigation in the traditional sense of the word, let alone a merely empirical study. Benjamin leaves no doubt that the newspaper and its counterpart assume their emblematic significance—the peculiar "sufficiency" to which the formula cited here alludes—only for those who would want to apprehend the "essence of history" (*das Wesen der Geschichte*). The newspaper would, in other words, take on its special significance precisely in a study of history that would not play out on an empirical level but, instead, concern itself with its "essence"—a study that would have a strictly *philosophical* character.[3]

But if the newspaper would have a special significance for the historico-philosophical inquiry par excellence, the inquiry into the "essence" of history itself, this significance is already presented in the form of a problem. The *Betrachtungsweise* that is captured in emblematic form by the *Morgenzeitung* is described here as one for which the course of history congeals and petrifies as soon as it comes into contact with it—a kind of Medusa's gaze. Historical phenomena, as soon as they enter the stage and are inspected from this *point de vue*, turn into an unlimited series of facts that confront the viewing subject as things. This congealing and petrification of phenomena seems to take place with no delay or remainder: in the same moment that phenomena "make their entrance" (*eingehen*) onto this stage, historical phenomena already appear as "wholly reified."[4] If a world that consists merely of things is a world without history, the newspaper, that same form that is to be studied by those who want to apprehend the essence of history, would also be the emblem of a *Betrachtungsweise* from which history in a stricter sense of the word seems to have vanished entirely.[5] That this formula is presented as a paraphrase of a remark of the philosopher of resignation *par excellence* is certainly no accident. Not only does history—in a sense that has yet to be fully determined—seem to have vanished from this world that takes its course as an unlimited series of facts passing in front of a viewer; this world would seem to have closed itself off entirely from the possibility for history to occur.

The ambiguity of the term that Benjamin uses to describe the feeling that corresponds to (*entspricht*) this way of seeing—*ein historisches Schwindelgefühl*— captures this sense of deprivation at the same time as it points to a possible renewal. Like the earlier reference to an "illusion" characteristic of the nineteenth century, this *Schwindelgefühl* would not only name a sense of being swindled, of being deceptively deprived of something; it would also, in the sense of the word that is carried over to the French translation, *une sensation de vertige*, refer to a feeling of vertigo that has a highly specific significance for Benjamin. This same term is employed in the concluding paragraph to another crucial text, the prologue to his first published book—here even more emphatically, as a "significant feeling of vertigo" (*bezeichnende Schwindelgefühl*)[6]—to describe the feeling that corresponds to the encounter with the whirling movement of what is here called an "originary phenomenon" (*Urphän-omen*): a phenomenon that occupies an intermediary status insofar as it is one in which the world of ideas confronts the historical world, intimating itself to philosophical interpretation at the same time as it withdraws from it.[7] Insofar as it arouses this feeling, the juxtaposition of the newspaper to the figure of the most ancient historian would, not unlike the comparison between trag-edy and *Trauerspiel*, yield the promise of grasping the originating rhythm of repetition and dislocation that, in his earlier book, Benjamin had ascribed to the historical articulation of the idea. But in this case, the feeling of vertigo would not concern one idea among others, if it is possible to speak of the world of ideas in this way—for it is the idea of history itself that would here confront the historical world.

This problem—the problem of the possibility of history as it crystallizes around the *Vergleich* between Herodotus and the morning newspaper—will guide the following study of Benjamin's engagement with the theme of jour-nalism. This chapter will touch on some of the numerous reflections and re-marks on journalism dispersed throughout his writings but concentrate on the reading of a single text: Benjamin's three-part essay on Karl Kraus that was published in four installments in the *Frankfurter Zeitung*, the newspaper for which Siegfried Kracauer was the literary editor.[8] The sprawling essay, which Benjamin described as his "nine-month baby," had been in preparation since at least 1928 but drew on reflections on Kraus that punctuate Benjamin's writ-ings since the early 1920s.[9] It is no coincidence that precisely this text serves as the place where Benjamin's ongoing reflections on language and history are tied together with his interest in journalism. Not only does Kraus's work, for Benjamin, provide an unparalleled dissection of journalism as a modern phe-nomenon, developed through his "fire-eating, sword-swallowing philology of the newspapers [*Philologie der Journale*]"—a phrase to which we will return later in greater detail.[10] Besides the insights offered by his polemic against jour-nalism, Kraus himself—the writer whose work appeared for the most part in *Die Fackel*, the journal of which he was not only the editor but also, for most of its existence, the sole author—is for Benjamin also an emblematic journal-ist in a peculiar, yet to be determined sense.[11] This is already suggested by one of Benjamin's plans for a lecture series in the early 1930s, where the figure of Kraus is coupled to "journalism" just as Kafka is coupled to the "novel," Brecht to "theatre," and Bloch to the "essay."[12] Each of these figures appears here as an exponent of a distinct literary form—but supposedly exponents of a dubious kind, insofar as their sensitivity to the origin of this form also requires an explo-sion of its given, empirical reality. If Kraus can be introduced as an exponent of journalism, this is, as will become clear, because his writing in every respect responds to the enigmatic "vocation" that is central to Benjamin's earliest reflection on journalism. In the 1921 announcement of his planned journal *Angelus Novus*—a text and a project that we will turn to in the last part of this chapter—Benjamin describes the essence of the *Zeitschrift* in terms of a demand "to proclaim the spirit of its epoch" (*den Geist ihrer Epoche zu bekunden*).[13] It is this demand, which revolves around the relation between time and writing already implied in the form on which Benjamin chooses to focus his reflections, the *Zeitschrift*, which would lie at the origin of journalism and determines the vocation of Kraus's work as a writer. Everything that Kraus has written, without exception, may well be thought of as journalism in this sense: not only his countless glosses and articles for *Die Fackel*, the journal for which he wrote almost 25,000 pages, but also his lectures and aphorisms, his poems and dramas such as *The Last Days of Mankind*. That the relation of this journalism to its time is, however, of a singular kind is suggested by a definition that Kraus provides of his own writing in a note that we will have to consider in closer detail: "May my style capture all the sounds of the time and its temporality [*alle Geräusche der Zeitlichkeit*]. This should make it an annoyance to the contemporaries. But later generations will be able to hold it to their ears like a seashell in which there is the music of an ocean of mud."[14]

Yet it is precisely the scrutiny of journalism itself—and, in particular, the language of newspapers—that will play a privileged role in Kraus's attempts to register the "sounds of his time." Like Kierkegaard and Nietzsche, who both play an important role in his work, Kraus treats the journalist as a type: in his case, one in which the *Geist* of the epoch takes on a distinct, sensible form. The crowd of figures that together play out the drama of contemporary historical life in his writings—"journalists, aesthetes, politicians, psychologists, stupid people, scientists," as they are listed in a section title of one of his collections of aphorisms—are described by Kraus as the "basic types of the spiritual misery" (*Grundtypen des geistigen Elends*) characteristic of his own time.[15] Kraus will, in other words, turn to the scrutiny of journalism at the exact point where his writing shows itself to be journalistic in the sense in which Benjamin understood the word, that is to say, where it responds to the vocation to "proclaim the spirit of its epoch." As Benjamin's portrait of Kraus will show in an unparalleled manner, his writing will be a *Bekundung* in a peculiar sense: not the heroic declaration of progress that his writings would never cease to mock, but a declaration for a court of law—one of which the prime exhibits will be the newspaper articles, headlines, and phrases meticulously scrutinized on the pages of his own journal.

The historical background against which Benjamin's and Kraus's preoccupation with journalism takes shape is well known. Both write in the wake of a long nineteenth century, which saw the emergence of the modern news industry, shaped by developments in printing and communication technologies, an unprecedented growth of literacy, the emergence of mass markets, increasing competition and rationalization, the growing role of advertisements, the differentiation of journalism as a profession, and the genesis of modern journalistic forms, such as information and opinion, report and feuilleton, headline and masthead.[16] Neither of them is, however, interested in a socio-historical analysis of journalism per se; as we will see, the interpretation of journalism that Benjamin develops through his study of Kraus can be understood only by remaining close to the stipulation that is provided by the opening lines of the 1939 exposé of the *Passagen-Werk*: that the newspaper reveals its emblematic significance only insofar as it is subjected to a historico-philosophical interpretation. What is at stake in Benjamin's reflections on journalism cannot be reduced to the analysis of a discrete historical phenomenon—whether this is situated in nineteenth-century Paris, the Vienna of the early twentieth century, or the Weimar Republic—just as their origin cannot be understood purely in biographical terms. The common biographical interpretation of Benjamin's relation to journalism, which tends to focus on his turn to *Publizistik* in the mid-1920s, runs the risk of obfuscating the profound philosophical significance that the forms of the *Zeitung* and *Zeitschrift* have for Benjamin. Although the beginning of Benjamin's own prolific writing for periodical publications coincides with the two occurrences whose impact has been well documented— the famous rejection of his *Habilitationsschrift* in 1925, following on the hyperinflation that had wiped out his family fortune in the preceding years[17]— it is important to note that his interest in journalism is not simply born out of external pressure. Benjamin's reflections on the phenomenon of journalism and theoretical interest in the *Zeitschrift* as a form predate the shattering of his academic prospects,[18] just as his own experiments with a writing that would work within and against the conventions of journalism began well before his later exclusion from German academia.[19] As we will see, the precise nexus of history, time, and language that Benjamin recognizes in journalism, together with the concept with which it is closely connected, *Aktualität*, can be traced back to the writings of his student days. Like the essay on Karl Kraus, with its dense web of motifs that often have their origins in his early work, unpacking Benjamin's reflections on journalism shows the inadequacy of any schema that would neatly divide his work in different parts; instead, it points to his persistent attempt to, as he phrases it in a letter to Gershom Scholem from 1924, develop the "actual and political moments" (*aktuale und politischen Momente*) of his earlier thought.[20]

Ur-journalist

"Journalism, in its most paradoxical form, is Kraus" (*Journalismus, in seiner paradoxesten Gestalt, ist Kraus*).[21] This note, included in the extensive paralipomena to Benjamin's 1931 essay on the Viennese writer, is key to understanding the figure of Kraus as it is presented in the latter text. Kraus serves here as a figure through which Benjamin can develop a critique of journalism that is, at the same time, a rescue operation: a critique that would involve the recovery of *another* journalism and another experience of time and history, wrested from his own reading of Kraus's writing.[22] It is in the first part of Benjamin's essay, published as a semi-autonomous piece in the *Frankfurter Zeitung*, Benjamin explicates the paradoxical character referred to in his notes. If Kraus is journalism "in its most paradoxical form," this is first of all because it is precisely this writer, who could refer to himself in the first issue of *Die Fackel* as a "journalist" and to his publication as "newspaper" (*Zeitung*), that expressed the most intense antagonism against journalism.[23] This tension animates Benjamin's descriptions of Kraus in the first part of his essay, in the paragraphs after his evocation of the image of an archaic messenger, which return on multiple occasions to his "hatred" for journalists—a hatred characterized at first as the one "hurled by an ancestor [*Urahn*] upon a race of degenerated, dwarfish rascals that have sprung from his seed."[24] Kraus's relentless attacks on his contemporaries are, in other words, the attacks of an archaic kind of journalist on the journalism of his time—they are the attacks of an Ur-journalist that Benjamin recognizes in the ancestral figure of Kraus himself. The theme of Kraus's hatred for journalists of his time returns once more later in the same section of the essay—but this time Benjamin uses it as a starting point for a characterization of the figure of the journalist itself, the journalist in its essential "being":

> A hatred such as that which Kraus has heaped on journalists can never be founded simply on what they do [*was sie tun*]—however obnoxious this may be, this hatred must have its reason in their very being [*dießer Haß muß Gründe in ihrem Sein haben*], whether it be opposed or akin [*entgegengesetzt oder verwandt*] to his own. In fact, both are the case.[25]

The figure of Kraus stands in a paradoxical relation to journalism insofar as it is at once akin to the figure of the journalist and set apart from it; its relation is both one of antagonism and of affinity. This antagonism is not based on what journalists do: it is, in other words, not occasioned by this or that text they happen to have written. Kraus's hatred has its grounds not in any accidental feature but in what Benjamin calls their *Sein*: that is to say, in the mode of being that characterizes them as journalist. To describe this characteristic being of the journalist, Benjamin cites a passage from a recent portrait of the "journalistic human being" (*der journalistische Mensch*) by Peter Suhrkamp—a portrayal that Benjamin also introduces in a radio broadcast of the same years as an exemplary study of the "human types" (*Menschentypen*) shaped and formed by their profession.[26] In the essay of 1931, this "most recent" portrayal is put to work for a different purpose, namely to juxtapose the figure of the modern journalist to that of Kraus, taken to represent a journalist of a different kind:

> The most recent presentation of the journalist characterizes him directly, in the first sentence, as "a human being who has little interest either in himself and his own existence, or in the mere existence of things, but who first registers things in their relationships, above all where these coincide in events—and who only in this moment becomes united, essential, and alive." What we have in this sentence is nothing other than the negative of an image of Kraus [*das Negativ des Bildes von Kraus*]. Indeed, who could have shown a more burning interest in himself and his own existence than he, who cannot leave this theme behind; who could have shown a more attentive interest for the mere existence of things, their origin [*die bloße Existenz der Dinge, ihren Ursprung*]; whom does that coincidence of the event with the date, the witness, or the camera cast into deeper despair than him?[27]

Benjamin's citation tears Suhrkamp's characterization of the *journalistische Mensch* away from the original text and inserts it into the context of Benjamin's writing. Just as the figure of Kraus can only be understood in relation to the figure of the journalist introduced here, so the latter takes on its specific significance only once it is juxtaposed to Kraus. That the two relate to one another as "negative images," or rather, that the image of Kraus is the negative of the image of the journalist evoked in the cited sentence, does not mean that the two are simply opposed: as in the case of the photographic *Negativ*, the two extremes are held together by a structural resemblance. The resemblance that plays a crucial role in this passage primarily concerns the relation of these two figures to history. If Kraus is akin to the journalist, it is because his writing is concerned first and foremost with history as it takes its course in the moment. But it is precisely in his conception of history that Kraus is most opposed to the journalist. The journalist "first registers things in their relationships, above all where these coincide in events" (*wo diese in Ereignisse aufeinandertreffen*):

in the context of Benjamin's text, this means firstly that the "things" with which the journalist is concerned are always already integrated into the concatenation of empirical events that together constitute the historical world. It is no accident that Benjamin uses the same word—*aufeinandertreffen*—again in the last sentence of the passage: for it is here that the relationship between things that underpins the journalist's conception of history is characterized concretely. The reference to "that coincidence of the event with the date [*jenes Aufeinandertreffen des Ereignisses mit dem Datum*], the witness, or the camera" evokes a specific conception of history and of historical time. That, for the journalist, the event coincides with the *Datum* may be read in relation to its original Latin sense: that the occurrence of history, the *Ereignis* of history as such, is taken to be a *datum*, something that is immediately given. It is this sense of the word that is emphasized in Benjamin's subsequent reference to the coincidence of the occurrence of history "with the eye witness or the camera" (*dem Augenzeugen oder der Kamera*): for the history registered by the journalist is taken to be the object of an empirical consciousness—one that could register history objectively and mechanically, whether it is through the account of the *Augenzeuge* or the continuous sequence of images of a camera. As such, Benjamin's paraphrase of the cited description of the *journalistische Mensch* also implies a certain conception of historical time that is already implied in the reference to the *Datum* in the sense of the "date": for history as a purely empirical given would be unproblematically datable; its occurrence could be assigned a determinate location in a linear time that could be ordered chronologically. History would be the coherent, unbroken concatenation of events narrated by the eyewitness, unfolding in a mechanical time that is not unlike the virtually continuous sequence of images produced by the camera—the "unlimited series of facts" that Benjamin associated with the morning newspaper in the exposé for his *Passagen-Werk*.[28]

Nothing could be more different from the experience of history that motivates the writings of Kraus. Like the journalist, Kraus has his eyes on the course of history—but the "things" with which he is preoccupied are, in the end, not reducible to events strung together into a continuous series. His "interest" (*Interesse*), Benjamin writes, does not concern the series of facts that appears in the pages of the newspaper but is ultimately directed toward "the mere existence of things, their origin."[29] The "mere existence of things" (*die bloße Existenz der Dinge*) may here be taken to refer to historical phenomena ripped out of the causal chain in which they are inserted in the empirical world, stripped from the web of relationships in which they appear in the writing of the journalist. The "origin" (*Ursprung*) on which Kraus's interest is focused cannot be reducible to the process of coming into being and passing away that defines the journalist's understanding of historical genesis; instead, it would point beyond the empirical world and the laws of causation that govern it. At this point, Benjamin does not elaborate what constitutes such an origin, but the tension that is introduced here—the tension between history as it is reported by the journalist and another experience of history, closely related and yet diametrically opposed, condensed in the figure of Kraus, the *Urahn* of journalism—will structure the entire essay. Benjamin's elaboration of this tension will work toward an account of the disposition that is described here as a *helle Verzweiflung*—a despair that is not only deep, piercing but also bright, illuminating. If this is the despair over the "complete coincidence" of the event with the empirical *Datum*, it would belong to the confrontation with a historical world constrained entirely by the horizon of a subjectively limited actuality—a world from which the possibility of history in the strict sense would seem to have vanished entirely. It is this despair that will be at the center of Benjamin's attempts to articulate the experience of history that animates Kraus's journalism.[30]

Archaic Messenger

If the image of Kraus as an *Urahn* suggests that Benjamin attempts to portray him as the protagonist of an archaic journalism, a journalism close to its own *Ursprung*, it comes as no surprise that the essay on Kraus begins by conjuring up the image of a messenger that seems to stem from times immemorial:

> In old engravings there is a messenger who rushes towards us crying aloud, his hair on end, brandishing a sheet of paper in his hands, a sheet full of war and pestilence, of cries of murder and pain, of danger from fire and flood, spreading everywhere the "latest news" [*die 'Neueste Zeitung'*]. A newspaper in this sense [*eine Zeitung in solchem Sinn*], with the meaning that the word has in Shakespeare, is *Die Fackel*. Full of betrayal, earthquakes, poison and fire from the *mundus intelligibilis*.[31]

Just as the delivery of the news depicted in such "old engravings" is said to return in a contemporary "newspaper," *Die Fackel*, so it is the figure of Kraus that may be recognized in this crying messenger. In the scene presented here, the two central themes of the essay—history and language—are already announced and interwoven: the story of war, pestilence, murder, and pain that is conjured up here is inextricably tied to the *Blatt*, the sheet of paper, and accompanied by the *schreien* of the messenger—an inarticulate crying that points to a distinct experience of the occurrences of which he bears the news.

There is a sense in which the scene evoked here seems to stem from an archaic past, a domain outside of history. The "old engravings" on which it is presented are barely dated, and the messenger itself, recalling the figure of an archaic town crier, seems to belong to a time long before historical life was even recorded on a "sheet of paper." But at the same time as this scene and the engravings on which it is evoked have an almost mythical character, it points to a specific historical moment. The reference to *alte Stichen* suggests that this depiction of a messenger stems from a time at the threshold of modernity—the same threshold that Benjamin, in his *Origin of the German Mourning Play*, recognized in the baroque, the period in which cupper engravings with scenes of this kind would flourish. These *alte Stichen* and the messenger depicted on them may indeed be those of the kind made during the religious wars of the seventeenth century, whose suffering was captured in engravings and etchings that documented a world full of "war and pestilence, fire and floods" in hair-raising detail.[32] Also, the *Blatt* brandished by this messenger from an ancient past seems to be associated with this epoch: just as the reference to the violence and suffering of the Thirty Years War, here mentioned in the same sentences as *Die Fackel*, anticipates the Great War in which Kraus found his true subject, so this "sheet of paper" turns out to be one of the various kinds of newspapers that proliferated during the wars that raged through Europe in the early modern period.[33] When Benjamin describes this *Blatt* as *die "Neueste Zeitung"*, the reference here is not just to "the latest news," to the *Zeitung* in the original sense of a "tiding," but to a specific journalistic form: the *Neue Zeitungen* of the early modern period. As was well documented at the time Benjamin was writing his essay, the early newspapers described with this name had begun to spread throughout Europe since the invention of the printing press but bloomed in particular during the periods of war and unrest of the sixteenth and seventeenth century. The *Neue Zeitungen* appear in this period as a counterpart to the modern newspaper proper, the periodical weekly that was invented at the start of the seventeenth century and had its root in the newsletters written by diplomats and merchants for a professional audience. In contrast to the modern newspaper, the *Neue Zeitungen* were not periodical but appeared only once: rather than being published according to a uniform temporal grid, they were prompted by the occasion and dedicated to the report of a single event. Unlike the weekly newspapers, they did not have their roots in the correspondence among a limited network of the privileged; they appealed to a general public and reached a social stratum for which the weekly newspapers were too expensive. Most importantly, their attitude toward the histories they described was not one of impartiality or dispassionate distance; while the periodical newspapers of the seventeenth century were characterized by a certain cautious reserve, the *Neue Zeitungen* bore titles such as *Erschreckliche Zeitung* ("terrifying news"), *Erbärmliche Zeitung* ("wretched news"), or, in a formulation that is, as we will see, particularly suggestive in the context of the essay on Kraus, *Klägliche Zeitung* ("lamentable news").[34] It is a *Zeitung*, a tiding and newspaper in this sense of the word that Benjamin associates with Shakespeare: the playwright whose name not only ties this messenger to the early modern period but also, as a figure who, as Benjamin writes later in the essay, citing Kraus, "has known everything in advance," evokes this period as a past that anticipates the present.[35] If Benjamin's image of Kraus, the *Urahn* of journalism, as a crying messenger brandishing a sheet of paper presents us with a genealogy of journalism, its origin does not lie in the Enlightenment or the awakening of a universal human consciousness in the bourgeois public sphere. The *Urphänomen* of the newspaper—or at least of Kraus's "newspaper"—is provided not by the periodical newspapers circulating at the end of the eighteenth century but rather found in these sheets, still bearing the traces of an old world, reporting the wars and suffering that accompany the birth pangs of modernity.

With this in mind, it is hardly surprising that Benjamin's rendering of the historical world of which this messenger brings the news has an affinity with the "presentation of historical life" that he had found to be characteristic of the baroque mourning play in his *Habilitationsschrift*. As is well known, the problem of history is central to Benjamin's study of the German *Trauerspiel*. Historical occurrences are not just the material of the mourning play, Benjamin points out in the first sections of his study; "historical life as that epoch presented it to itself [*das geschichtliche Leben wie es jene Epoche sich darstellte*] is its content, its true subject."[36] One important aspect of this presentation of historical life, which determines its relation to the journalism of Kraus, is suggested by the opening lines of the essay. Benjamin's description of the newspaper brought by this messenger as a sheet "full of war and pestilence, of cries of murder and pain, of danger from fire and floods" echoes a similar list in his *Origin of the German Mourning Play*, where Benjamin cites Martin Opitz to characterize the subject matter of the mourning play as dealing only with "killings, despair, infanticide and patricide, conflagrations, incest, war and commotion [. . .] and suchlike."[37] It is not just the content of this list that resembles the news brought by the messenger depicted on "old engravings," but also the form of presentation. Whether it is news of war, pestilence, killings, or conflagrations, both lists present historical life as a succession of the most miserable occurrences in which the occurrence of misery is treated as the rule. If these occurrences evoke *unglück*, misery or unhappiness—a word to which Benjamin attributed a special significance—they thus do so in a specific way, namely by presenting a world in which there is, as a rule, no place for "good news," a world from which the very possibility of happiness seems to have been expelled. Historical life is staged here as an endless inventory of misery—a list that can only conclude in the words "and suchlike" (*und dergleichen*).[38]

What is absent from both lists—and this will prove to be decisive for Benjamin's essay on Kraus—is both the religious promise of redemption and the enlightened assurance of progress. It is in this sense that the messenger depicted in these "old engravings" shows itself to be the figure of an experience of historical life that may be called *mythical* in the more precise sense in which Benjamin used the term.[39] In his writings from the previous decade, Benjamin had conceived of myth as a prereligious, protoethical domain governed by "fate" (*Schicksal*).[40] In the mythical nexus of fate, there is—as yet—no room for the capacity for freedom or self-determination: every difference is always already integrated into the perpetual concatenation of guilt and atonement.[41] In Benjamin's early writings, myth is thus described as the "natural condition of the living" in the sense that it designates a condition in which the possibility of history has not yet opened up.[42] Already in his writings from the student days—texts to which we will return later in more detail—Benjamin had emphasized that history is only possible in and through a relation to a "future" in the strict sense of the word: a future that remains absolutely irreducible to any given past or present.[43] The mythical world knows no history in this sense in that it is not exposed to a future—it only knows the past and a self-same present. If myth is "that which has always already been" (*das immer schon Dagewesenen*), as Benjamin writes in notes from the period in which he had begun preparing his essay on Kraus, the possibility of history presupposes an exposure to "that which has never been yet" (*das noch nie Dagewesene*).[44] The image of the *Bote* at the outset of Benjamin's essay on Kraus already hints at this mythical aspect of the world of which this messenger delivers the news by describing it as "a sheet full of war and pestilence, of cries of murder and pain"; but the complete extent to which historical life is here absorbed into myth is only brought out at the end of this passage, which repeats this same list in yet another variation, this time characterizing the *Zeitung* brought by this messenger as a sheet "full of betrayal, earthquakes, poison and fire from the *mundus intelligibilis*." For what is presented here is not just the report of a sensible world of endless suffering that may be contrasted with another, ideal world—for instance the intelligible world of Kantian philosophy that, in its discrepancy with the empirical world, would present the task and the possibility of its future realization with which the domain of history opens up. If the *Bote* evoked at the outset of the essay on Kraus presents us with a report of the *mundus intelligibilis*, of the forms and patterns that constitute the intelligible structure of the sensible world, then these ideal forms are as thoroughly absorbed in the history of perpetual misery as the *mundus sensibilis* itself. The intelligible world, whether it is grasped as the origin or destination of the sensible world, is here characterized not by the fulfillment of a promise but its constant betrayal, *Verrat*; not by the restoration of a paradisiacal nature but an *Erdbeben*, a nature that confronts the human being as alien and hostile; not by a purification of life but by its endless corruption, *Gift*; and not by eternal creation but by endless destruction, the *Weltbrand* that Benjamin will describe later in the essay on Kraus as the "last act of creation." Although the messenger bearing this news may be understood as a mythical figure, the world that he reports on does not precede history; it is, rather, a world from which history has vanished and the promise of a future other than the ever-same present is—and will continue to be—betrayed on a daily basis.

Natural History

If the "sheet of paper" brandished by the crying messenger evoked at the start of Benjamin's essay on Kraus offers a presentation of historical life, this is a life that remains, to use a formula from his earlier reflections on myth, "improperly" historical.[45] The structure of this—as yet—improperly historical life will be further elaborated in an important passage later in the essay, which returns not only to Kraus's mythical experience of history but also to the theme of the newspaper. This passage appears midway through the first section of the essay, where Benjamin writes:

> For him, Kraus, the horrible years of his life are not history, but nature: a river, condemned to meander through a landscape of hell [*ein Fluß, verurteilt durch eine Höllenlandschaft sich zu winden*]. It is a landscape in which every day 50,000 tree trunks are felled for 60 newspapers.[46]

Kraus's journalism and the experience of history that permeates it are here connected firmly to the sphere of myth—the "natural condition of the living."[47] Just as the reference to the "horrible years of his life" (*die Schreckensjahre seines Lebens*) evokes the absence of the possibility of happiness that characterizes the mythical world, so the fateful predetermination of this world is captured here in the image of the river "condemned to meander through a landscape of hell." The river—an image that Benjamin had already employed in his book on *Trauerspiel* as an emblem of historical life as a process of continuous becoming, the river or flow of becoming (*Fluß des Werdens*)[48]—here reappears as a feature of the world of myth. If there is a reference to the sphere of law in the image of this *verurteilten* river, this is only insofar as law may—in contrast to justice—be understood as an institution of myth. The river that is sentenced to take a predetermined course is a river that is subordinated to the law of necessity—or what appears in the world of myth as law of guilt and punishment that secures the persistence of the system of fate. The hellish character of this landscape would, then, have to be understood not in religious but in strictly mythical terms. It would point to the ancient image of hell that surfaced in Benjamin's notebooks of the same period: the hell that finds its exemplary expression in the eternally self-same present of Sisyphos—a figure whose suffering unfolds in a *Höllenlandschaft* that is nothing but an extreme instance of a mythical world from which the possibility of difference seems to have vanished entirely.[49]

But the river and the mythical world to which it belongs are, however, not presented as an image of antiquity; they are said to coincide with the *Schreckenjahre* of Kraus's own life, which are the same years in which Benjamin is now writing. This much is suggested not only by the particular description of this mythical landscape—"a landscape in which every day 50.000 tree trunks are felled for 60 newspapers"—but above all by the fact that this landscape is derived from a gloss that Kraus had written in 1913 and that Benjamin had presumably encountered himself as a young reader of the *Fackel*. This gloss consists of two components: a brief report, written by Kraus himself, carrying the headline "Every day 50,000 tree trunks for 60 newspapers," resembling an item from a newspaper both in its style and typography; and a brief commentary, which consists only of a few sentences and is appended to this item as a postscript. The report conveys the information of the erection of an industrial site in Newfoundland, where a British newspaper magnate conducts "the plundering of the vast woods and a part of its processing into pulp for the production of paper."[50] In minute detail, it describes the infrastructure set up for the large-scale felling of trees, their transport, processing into pulp, and transport across the Atlantic, where "every week 1000 tons of paper are produced, which is barely enough for the newspapers of Lord Northcliffe, which appear in an edition of 25 million."[51] When Benjamin, on the first pages of the essay on Kraus, speaks of the information of "hair-raising precision" (*haarstraubende Akribie*) and "blood-steeped novelties" for which the *Fackel* provides a model, this must be the meticulous factuality that he has in mind.[52] While the report is kept free from explanation or interpretation, the following postscript frames it in a particular way: "And the world is still in doubt whether it is at its end. Every publisher of some standing [*bessere Erpresser*] now has at least 1000 tree trunks per day at its disposal. Oh poor life! One can no longer see the forest because of all the papers [*Blätter*]."[53] The factual account of the construction of this industrial site for the production of newspapers is thus held up as evidence, as material proof to a world that has not yet realized it has come to its end. But the image conjured up by the gloss is not conceived as a moral appeal or a call to action. The postscript presents this information without the faintest hope of having any consequences. Despite the play of words (the *Erpresser* as publisher and extortioner, the *Blätter* as leaves and as papers) its message is a grim one: the world is at its end because it is on its fateful course toward it— and there is no doubt that the course of history is as unavoidable as it is unalterable.

The name that Benjamin reserves for this repetition of myth in the historical world and relapse of the historical world into a mythical order is "natural history" (*Naturgeschichte*). The term, which had played an important role in the analysis of the baroque, returns here in the description of Kraus as a writer for whom "the horrible years of his life" are "not history but nature" (*nicht Geschichte, sondern Natur*).[54] Just as Benjamin's concept of *Naturgeschichte* has little to do with the empirical science of *historia naturalis*, so his concept of "nature" is not to be misunderstood for physical nature as an object of natural science or mathematics. The nature that is at issue here is closer to what the early Lukács had referred to as "second nature" in *The Theory of the Novel*, a text that Benjamin was deeply familiar with.[55] What Lukács here calls "second nature" is a world that is created by humanity and yet lost to it, confronting the human being like the "first nature" of the natural sciences. Even if this world is historically produced, it is subordinated to the law of necessity and is knowable only as a system whose coherence is guaranteed by mechanical causation. In this history that has congealed into nature, Lukács writes in his later essay on reification, "the here and now acquires the patina of an eternal law of nature."[56] The resonance of these passages with Benjamin's articulation of the concept of natural history in the *Trauerspielbuch* is unmistakable. Benjamin argues here that the conception of history particular to the baroque— world history as a "constantly repeated drama" (*ständig wiederholte Schauspiel*)— appeared to the writers "as the natural aspect of the course of history, essential in its persistence" (*als die in ihrer Beharrlichkeit wesenhafte, als die naturgemäße Seite des Geschichtsverlaufs*).[57] The "natural aspect of the course of history" is that aspect of history that makes it possible to speak of history as something that takes its "course." To speak of the *Verlauf* of history already implies that history has a natural development, that it may be understood as a process that unfolds according to given rules and towards a predetermined goal. Benjamin's image of the river that is "condemned to meander" through a landscape offers before anything else an image of this conception of nature—and it is certainly no accident that this river, when it is traced back to Kraus's gloss, turns out to be a human artifice. In his description of the landscape "in which

every day 50.000 tree trunks are felled for 60 newspapers," Kraus makes reference to a river dug with the purpose of transporting the felt tree trunks from
the inland to the coast—a historical construct that appears as natural after the
fact.[58] If the "landscape of hell" and the river that is "condemned to meander"
are emblems of the natural condition of the human being, this natural condition does not simply precede history but manifests itself as a history that has
congealed into nature. This is why Benjamin can write in his *Trauerspiel* book
that fate, just as it is neither a purely natural nor a purely historical category,
is also a category that is, in the final analysis, not mythical but natural-historical:
for it is in the congealing of history into nature, in the repetition of the mythical order in the realm of history, that fate would fulfill itself in the sense that
it would exert its full force. Kraus is thus the figure of an experience of history
in which this "natural aspect" is pushed to an extreme, has come to overdetermine
historical life to the point where history becomes almost indistinguishable
from nature—almost, because it is precisely in this congealed human history
that the terrible opacity and indifference associated with nature become most
palpable.[59] In this sense, Benjamin's portrait of this archaic messenger echoes
Lukacs's claim, in his essays on reification, that the figure of the journalist is
comprehensible only as the "apogee of capitalist reification."[60] But if history
has turned into nature for Kraus, the journalist, this turns out to be a nature
of a particular kind: one that differs from the "natural condition" of myth insofar as it is given a theological dimension. Nature is here no longer prereligious,
as it was in the realm of myth; in the repetition of myth in the historical world,
nature reappears as *fallen*.

History of Creation

If Kraus experiences "the horrible years of his life" not as history but as nature, Benjamin shows that this apparently secular nature has a theological dimension: for the course of history whose natural course is chronicled in
Kraus's journalism is consistently grasped as the unfolding of a "history of creation" (*Schöpfungsgeschichte*).[61] Nature is conceived as created nature; its history is understood as the story of its fall. In this story there is no human subject
that could serve as its protagonist, only a fallen "creature" (*Kreatur*) deprived
of grace.[62] Hence, Benjamin can write of Kraus:

> The fact that humanity [*die Menschheit*] is losing the fight against the
> creature [*die Kreatur*] is to him just as certain as the fact that technol-
> ogy, once deployed against creation [*die Schöpfung*], will not stop short
> of his master, either. His defeatism is of a supranational—that is,

planetary—kind, and history is for him only the wasteland that
separates his generation [*sein Geschlecht*] from creation, a history
whose last act is world conflagration [*Weltbrand*].[63]

Also here, Kraus's journalism turns out to be not unlike the baroque mourning play, which dealt only with historical subject matter and nevertheless presented the historical life through the prism of the contemporary theological
situation.[64] The same thing that Benjamin writes of the playwrights of the baroque can be applied to the journalism of Kraus: what is at issue in his writing
is "a worldly exposition of history as the story of the world's suffering [*Leidensge-
schichte der Welt*]"—but one at whose core is a conception of the human being as a fallen creature.[65] What brings about the endless suffering staged in
the *Trauerspiel*—its presentation of historical life as typical catastrophe—is
grounded not in the ethical being of humanity but in its natural being: "not
moral decay, but the very estate of the creaturely human being [*der Stand des
kreatürlichen Menschen selber*] provides the reason for the catastrophe."[66] In
the mourning play, this is perhaps most evident in the portrayal of the figure
of the sovereign—identified by Benjamin as the "principal exponent of
history"—who appears here not as the moral subject of history but as a sinful
creature.[67]

Images of the human being as a fallen creature also permeate Kraus's writings and experience of history; but here the creaturely life is not captured in
the figure of the fallen sovereign but instead, above all, in that of the newspaper reader. An exemplary portrayal of this creature is provided in the first paragraph of his "Tourist Trips to Hell" of 1920, a gloss organized around the citation
of a complete newspaper advertisement for luxurious excursions to the Verdun
battlefield "especially recommended as an autumn trip."[68] In his commentary
of this article, Kraus writes:

> I have in my hands a document that surpasses and seals the shame of
> this age, and would warrant assigning a place of honor in a cosmic
> boneyard to this money-hungry mess that calls itself humanity. If ever
> a newspaper clipping meant a clipping of creation—here we face the
> utter certainty that a generation to which such solicitations could be
> directed no longer has any better instincts to be violated.[69]

It is no coincidence that the "document" Kraus is here said to hold in his
hands—this evidence that "seals the shame of this age"—is a newspaper. For
Kraus, the newspaper is not only the sheet of paper described in "The End,"
a sheet of paper in whose production planetary exhaustion manifests itself in
its most wasteful and perverted form; it is also the sheet of paper that conveys

the information of this exhaustion—and it is thus in reading the newspaper that the reader finds oneself to be complicit with it. This complicity is folded into the 1913 gloss on the newspaper production facility, where the material evidence for this exhaustion is presented in the form of a newspaper article—but it resurfaces throughout Kraus's work. In a poem titled "The Newspaper," Kraus writes:

> Weißt du, der du Zeitung liest,
> wie viele Bäume mußten bluten,
> damit geblendet von Valuten
> du dein Gesicht in diesem Spiegel siehst,
> um wieder dich an dein Geschäft zu sputen?
>
> Weißt du, der du die Zeitung liest,
> wie viele Menschen dafür sterben,
> daß wenige sich Lust erwerben
> und dafür, daß die Kreatur genießt,
> der Kreatur unsägliches Verderben?[70]

In the newspaper reader we thus recognize the exemplary instance of Kraus's understanding of the human being qua fallen creature—a creature that is as complicit in the exhaustion of nature as in that of himself. It is in reading the newspaper that the impoverished "subject" of natural history is confronted on a daily basis with the world's suffering and finds himself to be complicit in it. But whereas the *Trauerspiel* is chronologically contemporaneous with the res- toration philosophy of history that provides its model,[71] the conception of the "creature" that underpins Kraus's journalism, on first sight, appears as an anachronism. But even though Kraus's writing has an affinity with the theo- logical speculations of the baroque, these are not simply reproduced in his writing:

> His concept of creation [*Kreaturbegriff*] contains the theological
> inheritance of speculations that last possessed contemporary validity
> for the whole of Europe in the seventeenth century. At the theological
> core of this concept [. . .] a transformation has taken place that has
> caused it, quite without constraint, to coincide with the cosmopolitan
> [*allmenschlichen*] credo of Austrian worldliness [. . .].[72]

What separates the natural-historical transformation of history in the baroque from Kraus's experience of historical life as "a river condemned to meander through a landscape of hell" is, of course, the Enlightenment and its concep- tion of history based in progress. In contrast to the sovereign monarch in the mourning play, the Krausian creature is one that has unmistakably lived through the Enlightenment. If the "theological speculations" of the seventeenth century acquire a new actuality in Kraus, a new resonance in the moment in which both Kraus and Benjamin are writing, then the condition of possibility of this resonance is precisely the collapse of the conception of history based on progress. For Kraus, as for Benjamin, the untenability of this view of history is not only given by the experience of the exceptional violence of the Great War but also by the monstrous banalities of which the newspaper provides evidence on a daily basis.

End Time

In the natural-historical world that is presented by Kraus, history is thus construed as the story of a fallen creation. But insofar as the main protagonist of this story is a creature completely deprived of grace, this history is one from which every possibility of redemption has been removed. Or as Benjamin puts it in his 1931 essay:

> This insolently secularized thunder and lightning, storms, surf, and earthquakes—cosmic man has won them back for creation by making them its world-historical answer to the criminal existence of human beings. But the span between creation and the last judgment here finds no salvation-historical fulfillment [*heilsgeschichtliche Erfüllung*], let alone a historical overcoming [*geschichtliche überwindung*].[73]

History, the span between creation and the last judgment of which Kraus chronicles a handful of horrible years, takes its course without the prospect of fulfillment. The fallen creature that Kraus substitutes for the historical subject of the Enlightenment is stripped of not only the faith in a divine act of salvation but also the belief in historical progress. This is the historical life conveyed by the archaic messenger and the sheet that he brandishes in his hands: an ever-same present devoid of the possibility of fulfillment, redemption or renewal.[74] Here, again, a theme from Benjamin's *Trauerspiel* study returns in the characterization of Kraus's experience of history. A peculiar characteristic of the German mourning play that is highlighted by Benjamin and central to his study is its complete absence of eschatology. Whereas the Christian chronicle of the Middle Ages had "rendered the world-historical [*welthistorischen*] as salvation-historical [*heilsgeschichtlichen*]," the baroque is characterized by the dissolution of the claim that historical actions could contribute to "the process of salvation" (*Heilsprozess*).[75] To the baroque, Benjamin writes, "nothing was more distant [. . .] than the expectation of an end

time [*ein Endzeit*] or even of an overturning of times [*Zeitenumschwungs*]."[76]
The "total disappearance of eschatology" leaves its mark on the conception
of history as the story of a fallen creation. "Whereas the middle ages present
the futility of world events and the transience of the creature as stations on
the road to salvation," Benjamin writes, "the German mourning play is taken
up entirely with the hopelessness of the earthly condition."[77] In the mourning play, history seems to disappear entirely; in the absence of the destructive
gesture of divine justice that would accompany the *Weltgericht* there is only
an endless play of unstable orders that always leaves the setting intact.[78] History has turned into the story of a fall without the hope of redemption, its
protagonist a creature deprived of grace, predestined to perpetuate its suffering. In its place, Benjamin writes, something new arises: an "empty world"
(*eine leere Welt*) from which the possibility of fulfillment seems to have completely vanished.[79]

   This "empty world" does not just appear in the mourning play; it is also the
world that Kraus conjures up in his journalism. The main protagonist of
the poem "The Dying Human" (*Der Sterbende Mensch*), a human being at
the end of the history of the world, laments, "There is nothing I have fulfilled
and nothing I have promised [*ich habe nichts erfüllt und nichts versprochen*]."[80]
But whereas the expectation of an end seems to have vanished entirely from
the baroque mourning play, Kraus's work is suffused with imagery of a world
at its end. "The End," the gloss of 1913 from which Benjamin takes the image
of a landscape that has become barren due to the production of newspapers
is no exception: throughout his writings, Kraus consistently treats the present
as an end time—even though it is an end without eschatology. Nowhere is
this expressed more clearly than in Kraus's great drama, *The Last Days of
Mankind*, which is the result of a period of prolific writing following Kraus's
prolonged silence in the months after the outbreak of the war. Published in
special issues of the *Fackel*, the 209 scenes comprising the five main acts, the
prologue of ten scenes, and the epilogue of the drama are all written over the
span of two years, between July 1915 and July 1917. Rather than allowing for
a presumably more "objective" distance to contemporary events, Kraus
chronicles the present in a language that is inextricable from the moment
in which it is written.[81] The drama offers an eschatology in the sense that it
engages in a "gathering of last things," calling to the stage many hundreds
of characters, ranging from journalists to prostitutes, from politicians to
tradesmen, from emperors to newspaper boys, from fictitious to actual per-
sons; but the end time it portrays is devoid of eschatology in the sense of a
redemptive fulfillment.

The occurrence of the end of the world, which is staged in the final scene of the play, is as empty of significance as the endless play of the *Trauerspiel*. The *Last Days of Mankind* may end with divine destruction, but this destruction itself is not an act of divine will. "I have not willed this" (*ich habe es nicht gewollt*)—these are the last words of the drama, with which God's voice breaks the silence left after the complete destruction of the world.[82] These are the same words attributed to Kaiser Wilhelm II at the outbreak of the war—an outbreak of which the possibility was, in Kraus's understanding, predicated precisely on the feverish reports in newspapers.[83] The apocalypse itself is here absorbed into a conception of history as nature: the end of history is neither divine nor properly historical in itself. More important, this vacuous world destruction is presented as a deus ex machina, which intervenes into an end time that is, in principle, endless. The other two hundred odd scenes of *The Last Days of Mankind* do not read as a narrative unfolding toward its end but, rather, as a recurrence of ever-same phrases and deliberations, interrupted by an apocalypse, which offers cessation but no fulfillment. This temporality of ever-same recurrence is marked by the cries of newspaper boys, which permeate the drama. The voice of god, which the drama ends with, has its counterpoint in the cries of newspaper boys—"Extra-a-a! Extra-a-a-a! [*Extraausgabee!*]"— which mark its beginning and recur until the end of the penultimate scene.[84] This is not an end time of intense destruction, but one where an exhausted creature is helplessly ensnared in a constant and potentially endless process of devastation. Kraus's journalism is marked by this paradoxical experience of an end time: an end time that retains its affinity with the endless play of the *Trauerspiel* to the extent that it remains without eschatology, without possibility of fulfillment. This end time is permeated by the recurrence of ever-same novelties, scandals, and chatter. The dialogue presented in "The Dying Man" begins, significantly enough, with the declaration "Now it is enough. I have not enjoyed this. And there also won't be anything new [*und Neues wird es auch wohl nicht mehr geben*]."[85] The true horror of the end time depicted by Kraus is not divine destruction but, rather, its absence—the ahistorical temporality that Benjamin characterizes as the recurrence of ever-same sensations.

The cries of the newspaper boys that punctuate Kraus's *The Last Days of Mankind* thus determine the time of this final act of world history: they serve as temporal markers of an end time that takes its course without a possibility of relief or fulfillment. Here it is exactly the announcement of the latest news that, in its endless repetition, provides the emblem of a world that persistently remains the same. Benjamin takes up this interpretation of journalism in his essay of 1931, where it surfaces in the passage at the end of the first part. In these last sentences, at the furthest remove from the image of the archaic messenger introduced in the opening sentences, Benjamin returns once again to the figure of Kraus and writes:

> To the ever-same sensations [*die immer gleiche Sensationen*] with which the daily press serves its public he opposes the eternally new "tiding" [*die ewig neue 'Zeitung'*], which is to report of the history of creation: the eternally new, incessant lament.[86]

The formula that Benjamin uses to characterize the news of the daily press— "the ever-same sensations"—harbors an inner tension. The nature of this tension becomes evident if one takes into account that sensation is for Benjamin the name for an encounter with the new or, more precisely, the newest. If the messages served up by the newspaper are, in the later notes for the *Arcades Project*, claimed to satisfy an "enigmatic need for sensation," this sensation is to be understood first and foremost as "the sensation of the newest" (*die Sensation des Neuesten*).[87] The "ever-same sensations" of which Benjamin speaks in the essay on Kraus would thus belong to an experience of history in which newness and sameness, pushed to their extreme in the categories of the "newest" and the "ever-same," collapse into one another. It is certainly no accident that these two categories are central to Benjamin's reflections on temporality that were written around the same time as the essay on Kraus. In a note on the "time of hell" that is closely connected to the time of the "landscape of hell" to which he likens Kraus's experience of history, Benjamin writes:

> The punishments of hell are always the newest thing [*das Neueste*] that there is in this domain. What is at issue is not that "the same thing happens over and over" [*das "immer wieder dasselbe" geschieht*] [. . .] but rather that the face of the world, the colossal head, precisely in what is newest never alters [*gerade in dem, was das Neueste ist, sich nie verändert*]—that this "newest" remains, in every respect, the same [*das nämliche bleibt*].[88]

The "time of hell" thus revolves around a peculiar convergence of newness and sameness. This convergence is not construed along the lines of a distinction between a changing part and a whole that remains the same; rather, persistent sameness here manifests itself exactly in and as the new. The face of the world never changes—but if it remains the same as ever, it now does so in what presents itself as the new or newest. The lack of change that characterizes this time does not merely consist in a simple stasis; a sameness that is driven to its extreme is not an absence of newness, but rather a sameness that asserts itself over the new and manifests itself even in the newest. If the natural aspect of history is to be grasped as the overpowering of historical life by a certain persistence of sameness, this persistence is ultimately not to be understood as endurance of the old or a return of what has been, but rather as a sameness that manifests itself as a returning newness and a newness that is ever the same. In a note from the same period, Benjamin distinguishes these two forms of persistence—"the remaining of the old" (*Altes, das bleibt*) and "the returning of what has been" (*Gewesenes, das wiederkehrt*)—from another category, which characterizes the time proper to the landscape of hell chronicled by Kraus's journalism: "the always-again-new" (*das Immer-Wieder-Neue*).[89]

For Benjamin, it is this convergence of the newest and the ever-same that determines the affinity between the mythical depictions of hell and the modern newspaper. If myth returns in the modern, then it does so in the return of the *Höllenstraf* in a newness whose form is always already predetermined. When Benjamin returns to a discussion of this convergence in a later note for the *Arcades Project*, he will associate it directly with the birth of journalism. This note, included in the convolute on "newness," unmistakably models its reflections on a collective that "knows no history" (*kennt keine Geschichte*) on the newspaper reader.[90] That the newspaper reader *knows no history* has nothing to do with a lack of "historical consciousness" in the usual sense: it has nothing to do with a lack of factual knowledge of events past or present, nor does Benjamin refer here to the failure to understand the present "in the context of the past." What is at issue in this "knowing of history" is something fundamentally different from the familiar complaints of historicism: it is the name for a relation to historical life in which the possibility of history in the stricter sense would open up. The newspaper reader is presented with historical life, the life of history is staged again and again—but the reading exemplified by this figure fails to grasp its properly historical element. What corresponds to this failure is a certain "perception of time" (*Zeitwahrnehmung*)—a perception of time that "stood at the cradle of modern feuilletonism" and is characterized in terms of the same convergence that had already appeared in the characterization of the daily press in the essay on Kraus: "the course of historical occurrence [*der Verlauf des Geschehens*] flows by before it as always the same [*immer Nämliches*] and always new [*immer Neuestes*]."[91]

Weltgericht

Like the archaic messenger presented in the baroque engravings presented in the opening sentences of the essay, Kraus the journalist brings the news of a world whose historical life is mythical in its structure. History, as it emerges in the pages of his *Zeitschrift*, takes its course fatefully: it is a process of coming-into-being and passing away, which obeys the same law as the one governing the mythical schema of guilt and retribution. History here turns into nature in the sense that historical life lapses back into what Benjamin calls the "natural life" of the human being: a life that belongs to a sphere prior to the ethical and the religious, in which there is no possibility of self-determination, no relation to an other that is not already integrated into the endless concatenation of events of which this messenger brings the news. Just as the course of history that is chronicled by Kraus has an affinity with the world of myth, it stands in a close relation to the repetition of myth in Christianity and its doctrine of original sin. There is no human subject of this history, only a sinful creature that has called its suffering upon itself; there is no possibility of relief, no redemption to hope for—only a history of suffering that is fated to perpetuate itself without end. The affinity between the three constellations at play in Benjamin's portrayal of the peculiar journalism of Kraus—myth, Christianity and the "cult religion" of capitalism, which structures the world of which the Viennese writer brings the news—lies in the ultimate indissolubility of the guilt nexus that characterizes all three of them.[92]

What emerges from this is an experience of history that is entirely stripped of the conviction of progress. So-called progress appears to Kraus in a wholly different form: as a "chimera." When Benjamin speaks of the "chimeras of progress" (*Chimären des Fortschritts*) in his essay of 1931, this means not only that progress reveals itself as an illusion, but also that this illusion shows itself to have a mythical character. Progress is, for Kraus, nothing but the perpetuation of the guilt nexus. In this sense, the essay on Kraus—and the time of history of *The Last Days of Mankind* that is central to it—anticipates the important thesis that is articulated in the most compressed manner in his later writings: "The concept of progress is to be founded in the idea of catastrophe. That 'things go on like this' *is* the catastrophe [*daß es 'so weiter' geht, ist die Katastrophe*]."[93] It is no coincidence that the counterpart of this thesis is found exactly in his own first experiments with journalistic forms of writing during the 1920s, the unpublished "Descriptive Analysis of the German Decline" on which he began to work in 1923—a text that directs its attention on the moment in which it is written and organizes its description, in a way that recalls Kraus's journalism, around the analysis of the phrases structuring the "talk of the day." "Amongst the stock of phrases in which the mode of life of the German bourgeois, welded together out of stupidity and cowardice, betrays itself on a daily basis," Benjamin writes here, "the phrase which refers to the catastrophe that stands before us [*der bevorstehenden Katastrophe*]—that 'things can't go on like this' [*indem es ja nicht mehr so weitergehen könne*]—is particularly noteworthy."[94] It is the insight into the history denied and concealed by this phrase that Benjamin recognizes in the depictions of hell of the mythical world: that the catastrophe is precisely that the "history of the world" continues to take its course.[95] Hence Benjamin writes, in an important passage that once again plays out the relation between the world of the baroque and the world conjured up in the journalism of Kraus at the beginning of the twentieth century:

> Just as in the most opulent examples of baroque altar painting, saints hard-pressed against the frame extend their hands, spread out in aversion, toward the breathtaking abbreviations of the extremities floating before them—of the angels, the blessed, and the damned— so the whole of world history [*die ganze Weltgeschichte*] presses in on Kraus in the extremities of a single newspaper article [*in den Extremitäten einer einzigen Lokalnotiz*], a single phrase, a single advertisement.[96]

Under Kraus's gaze, a single newspaper article suddenly turns out to contain "the whole of world history." World history must here be taken in the specific sense in which Benjamin used the term: history insofar as it offers itself in its worldly aspect and is to be distinguished from divine history.[97] Such a history of the world is, for Kraus, nothing but the history of its suffering: just as every occurrence is, for the messenger on ancient engravings, always an exemplary instance of a "typical catastrophe," so Kraus reads the smallest *Lokalnotiz* as the news of a history of suffering from which there is no escape. In this movement, the experience of history of the journalist—the "unlimited series of facts" that corresponded to the figures of the date, the eye witness and the camera— is pushed to an extreme. In the course of history that is chronicled by Kraus's journalism there is no break with the mythical order; by grasping the endless concatenation of events as a single catastrophe, the mythical history of the world is rather driven to its final consequence. For the *Urahn* of journalism that Kraus, the *Lokalnotiz* no longer conveys the news of an isolated fact, but the entire series of events grasped in their catastrophic sameness.[98] But even if Benjamin makes reference to the "whole" of world history here, this whole is not to be mistaken for a totality: insofar as it is a whole of suffering and of misery, of *Unglück*, it is a whole that manifests itself as an insufficiency. With every piece of news, this history of the world not only extends itself and continues to take its course but also, once again, expresses the incompleteness that stamps it in its entirety.[99]

For the messenger who brings the news of this *Weltgeschichte* there is, however, no conceivable relief from its suffering. Just as it is futile to hope for

salvation, every attempt to escape it or even renounce it would be in vain.
Least of all would it be possible to posit another world and another history. It
is in this light that one must read the reflections on history in which the passage just cited is embedded:

> "When the age laid hands upon itself, he was the hands," Brecht said.
> Few insights can stand beside this, and certainly not the comment of
> his friend Adolf Loos. "Kraus," he declares, "stands on the threshold of
> a new age." Alas, by no means. [. . .] Kraus is no historic genius. He
> does not stand on the threshold of a new age. If he ever turns his back
> on creation, if he interrupts his lamentation [*bricht er ab mit klagen*], it
> is only to file a complaint at the Last Judgment [*um vor dem Weltgeri-
> cht anzuklagen*].[100]

At its extreme—the extreme that is marked by Kraus's journalism—this experience of history is deprived entirely of every possibility to positively represent
another world. In the journalism of Kraus, historical experience reaches its na-
dir: there is no history other than the *Weltgeschichte* that fatefully takes its
course. Kraus is a figure of the most extreme petrification of historical life, a
despair without relief—but for Benjamin it is precisely from here that another
experience of history must be won. However, such a retrieval could never be
modeled on the figure of the "historic genius" (*historischer Genius*): the despair over the endless suffering that is world history is driven to an extreme in
Kraus, but his experience of history precludes every attempt to begin another
history through an act of creative positing. If there is a properly historical dimension to Kraus's journalism, it is not to be understood in a creative or even
constructive sense. As Brecht's description of Kraus suggests, it could only be
characterized as purely destructive: this historical dimension of his writing
would have to be thought in relation to a movement by which the *Zeitalter*
deprives itself of its own life. If Kraus's writing is relentlessly focused on his
own time, the purpose of his "burning interest" is ultimately destructive—the
Zeitschrift is to serve as the medium in which the epoch brings itself to an end.

In Benjamin's essay on Kraus, this crystallizes around a specific impulse
that emerges out of the experience of history as a continuous catastrophe, an
impulse out of which the possibility of another history could be retrieved: the
will to interrupt the course of the world.[101] This will may be understood as the
counterpart to the Kantian translation of a wishful longing for the "kingdom
of God on earth," the world in which the realm of nature exists in harmony
with the realm of morals, into the endless progression of ethical work. In his
Religion, Kant asks, "The wish of all the well-disposed is thus: 'that the king-

dom of God come, that his will be done on earth [*auf Erden geschehe*]'; but what preparations must they make in order that this wish come to pass among them [*mit ihnen geschehe*]?"[102] For the Kraus portrayed by Benjamin, the archaic journalist who experiences the history of the world as a continuous catastrophe, the answer to this latter question cannot have a positive character; if the realization of this wish demands for work to be done, this work can never have the structure of an eternal progression through time; the preparations that this "wish" call for can intend only the interruption of this progression and the time in which it unfolds. "Let time stand still! Sun, come to completion! / Make the end great! Announce eternity!" so Benjamin cites Kraus. "You golden bell, melt in your own heat, become a cannon against the cosmic foe! Shoot firebrands in his face! If only I had Joshua's power, I tell you, Gibeon would be again!"[103] To better understand the nature of this interruption—which coincides with the movement described by Benjamin as a turning (*kehren*), the turning with which Kraus was said to "interrupt his lament" in the face of the world's suffering—it is important to consider a crucial component in Benjamin's consideration of Kraus's journalism, namely its treatment of language.

Philology of the Newspapers

If the vocation of Kraus's journalism is to "proclaim the spirit of the epoch," then this proclamation unfolds before anything else through a study of its *language*. The newspaper takes up a privileged role in this study: for Kraus, it is the language of journalism in which the spirit of the epoch imparts itself. It is in this light that one must understand Benjamin's characterization of Kraus's work as a "philology of the newspapers" (*Philologie der Journale*).[104] A philology of the newspapers: that is to say, Kraus's writing is, above all, a matter of reading—a reading that treats the newspapers as a text whose language calls for the same meticulous scrutiny as an ancient scroll. Indeed, the *Zeitschrift* to which Kraus devoted himself would be nothing without this scrutiny: most of its glosses are constructed as meticulous studies of the language of newspaper articles, documents that Kraus either reproduces in their entirety or dissects into pieces, framing them by a commentary that analyzes their linguistic elements in the closest detail—an approach perhaps expressed most dramatically by his glosses dedicated entirely to a single phrase, word, or punctuation mark.[105] The same tension that marked Benjamin's description of the experience of history found in Kraus's writings also appears in his characterization of his mode of reading the newspapers: the language of the newspapers, if the latter are to be studied as ancient texts, would need to have a certain affinity with the order of myth and its collapse of nature and history in the endless concatenation of guilt and retribution.[106]

What is at stake in this *Philologie der Journale* becomes clear if it is read alongside another crucial proposition, introduced in the first section of the essay: that "journalism [. . .] is through and through the expression of the changed function of language in the world of high capitalism [*der veränderten Funktion der Sprache in der hochkapitalistischen Welt*]."[107] With this sentence, Benjamin ties Kraus's critique of the language of the newspaper to his own philosophy of history and the theory of language that underpins it. For Benjamin, the moment in which he is writing, the epoch that finds its expression in the language of journalism is—at least since his unpublished fragment of 1921—determined by the "cult religion" that bears the name of capitalism.[108] In the context of the theory of capitalism sketched out there, the adjective *hochkapitalistisch* also takes on a more precise meaning: it recalls the culmination, the extreme point of a movement that Benjamin described in his fragment as a "complete indebtedness" (*völlige Verschuldung*) that would even include God. God, Benjamin writes in this fragment, is not dead; also he has fallen, been "pulled into the fate of human beings" (*ins Menschenschicksal einbezogen*).[109] In the essay on Kraus, this complete indebtedness, which had already been anticipated by a messenger bearing the news of a *mundus intelligibilis* in the grips of the same endlessly perpetuated catastrophe as the sensible world, is now explicated in a linguistic register: the extreme point marked by the "world of high capitalism" is now grasped in terms of the "function" it attributes to language—the medium in which, as Benjamin had claimed in the preface to his book on the *Trauerspiel*, the promise of an intelligible world first manifests itself within the sensible world.[110] This proposition not only ties the historico-philosophical interpretation of capitalism to Benjamin's theory of language but also points to the place where it is closest to that of Kraus: in its critique of the reduction of language to its semantic or referential function.

Like Benjamin's own theory of language, Kraus's *Sprachlehre* is interwoven with a critique of instrumentalist understandings of language.[111] Kraus develops this critique, in particular, in his bundles of aphorisms initially published in *Die Fackel*, where it plays an important role in his reflections on the relation between thought and language. Throughout these aphorisms, Kraus seeks to dismantle the conception of language as an instrument that is, in principle, disposable—a means that could be utilized by a speaker to communicate already formed thoughts. Just as we "have" no language that could be used as an instrument, so we have no thoughts before there is language. Or, as Kraus writes in *Pro Domo*, a collection of aphorisms that Benjamin was undoubtedly

familiar with, in an aphorism hat may serve as a summary of this aspect of his
Sprachlehre and *Sprachkritik*: "The thoughtless person thinks that one can only
have a thought if one has it and covers it in words [*in Worte kleidet*]. He does
not understand that, in truth, the only one who has a thought is he who has
the word that a thought grows into [*das Wort in das der Gedanke hinein-
wächst*]."[112] Language does not cover a thought that precedes it; it is not external to the thought, added on to it only after it has already been thought.
Language does not relate to the thought as clothes do to a body. There is no
body that has already grown, no figure that has already taken on its shape and
that could subsequently be dressed, just as there is no possible adequacy between the two that could be compared to the relation between a body and the
clothes that cover it. The relation of thought to language is, rather, a "growing
into" (*hineinwachsen*): if the thought grows, this growth is indissoluble from
the language in which it takes place. Kraus's remark that "in truth, the only
one who has a thought is he who has the word that a thought grows into" is,
of course, not without irony. For the one who truly "has" a thought does not
have it at all, at least not in the sense of a stable possession—but neither does
this speaker "have" a word, insofar as there is no thinking subject yet to relate
to this word as if it were an object that could be possessed. If this aphorism
exposes a "truth," as it suggests, it is that there is no speaker that has a thought,
nor a thinker that has a word—that we are only that which has been spoken.[113]

Benjamin had been familiar with Kraus's writings since his student years.
Scholem locates his friend's first encounter with Kraus in 1916 and writes that,
during their period in Switzerland, they read *Die Fackel* "almost regularly."[114]
The theory of language that Benjamin had begun to systematically articulate
in a series of texts written in this same period—most notably the essay "On
Language as Such and on the Language of Man" of 1916, but also a corpus of
unpublished fragments from the following years—has remarkable affinities
with Kraus's *Sprachlehre*, especially its critique of instrumentalist understandings of language.[115] In this essay, which cannot be considered in detail here,
Benjamin seeks to articulate an alternative to what is here referred to as the
"bourgeois conception of language" (*die bürgerliche Auffassung der Sprache*)
as it is defined by three mutually related claims: "the means of imparting is
the word [*das Mittel der Mitteilung ist das Wort*], its object the thing [*ihr
Gegenstand die Sache*], its addressee a human [*ihr Adressat ein Mensch*]."[116]
Insofar as such a conception of language reduces the medium that it claims to
comprehend to a mere means to a given end, it denies language any existence
in itself. Language has no reality as such: it is turned into a disposable means
that is supposed to dissolve when its object is rendered present. If the theory
of language that Benjamin attempts to formulate in his early essay is supposed

to dismantle the instrumentalist understanding of language, it must not only break with the reduction of the word as a means of reference or signification, but also leave behind the schema of already established speakers and addressees, employing words to convey a meaning or to refer to things that are assumed to be extralinguistic. This "other" theory of language would be one that "knows no means, no object and no addressee of communication": it would be a theory of language for which communication *through* words is only a particular case, a derived form that depends on a prior communication—on that which communicates itself *in* language.[117] This project—which leads Benjamin in the early essay to develop the thesis that "language has no content" but rather communicates "communicability pure and simple" (*Mitteilbarkeit schlechthin*),[118] an as yet unfulfilled possibility and demand for things to communicate themselves—is taken up again in the essay on Kraus.[119] As in the case of the 1916 essay, it will unfold here through a critique of instrumentalist conceptions of language: a critique that will develop through a commentary on Kraus's philology of the newspapers.

The Phrase

If Kraus's *Philologie der Journale* is primarily to be understood as a study of the "changed function" of language under capitalism, this function is, for Benjamin, exemplified by a linguistic form that is at the center of Kraus's studies of language: the "phrase" (*Phrase*). The scrutiny of the phrases that punctuate the talk of the day—and in particular those that characterize the language of journalism—plays an important role throughout Kraus's work. His writings in the *Fackel* are often presented as the examination of a particular phrase, as is suggested by the title of an important collection of glosses written between 1910 and 1918, his *Catastrophe of Phrases*. The form of the phrase is, moreover, given a programmatic significance in Kraus's announcement of the journal and characterization of the age in which it is published. "What is planned here," Kraus writes in the first issue of the *Fackel*, "is nothing but the reclamation of the vast morass of phrases [*eine Trockenlegung des weiten Phrasensumpfes*]."[120]

What Kraus means here by *Phrase* is not merely a mode of expression characteristic of a certain speaker or language—whether it is the language of journalism, juridical language, or the language of technology—nor is the phrase merely a stereotype or cliché in the familiar sense of the word. As becomes clear in the reflections on this form, whose theory is tentatively developed throughout his aphorisms, Kraus understands the phrase first and foremost as a particular configuration of language and thought. It is the phrase in this sense that Kraus describes in an aphorism that, not by chance, proposes a definition of the figure of the journalist itself. "A journalist," Kraus writes here, "is some-one who utters [*ausspricht*] what the reader has already thought [*was der Leser sich ohnehin schon gedacht hat*] in a form that not every salesman is capable of producing."[121] In the phrase, language is no longer a medium in which thought comes into being, but treated here as a form that envelopes and pack-ages a content that has been "already thought" (*schon gedacht*). Thoughts that have already been thought are communicated in a form that they bear no in-herent relation to. Thought and language are not only separated from one another here—in the phrase, this separation is driven to an extreme. But there is something deceptive about the phrase. A thought that has already been thought, and which for that reason does not deserve to be called a thought at all, is clothed in language in order to make it appear as a thought. The virtu-osity of the journalist to whom Kraus alludes is thus of a disingenuous and deceptive kind: the skill of making worn-out thoughts appear to be alive. Lan-guage serves as envelope, *Hülle*, which brings about the illusion of thought. But whereas genuine thought, for Kraus, shatters the familiar, language here only serves as a means of making the familiar appear extraordinary. This is why Benjamin, in a parallel reading of Kraus and Adolf Loos, compares the journalist to the ornamentalist. Like the ornament, the flowery language that Kraus despised endows the thought with *Liebhaberwert*, value for the connois-seur, by rendering it extraordinary. But, like the ornament, even the linguistic envelope of the phrase is only extraordinary in a manner that can always be readily assimilated into the familiar.

In the first section of the 1931 essay, Benjamin might draw on this apho-rism when he summarizes Kraus's concept of the phrase in a formulaic prop-osition. "The phrase of the kind so relentlessly prosecuted by Kraus," he writes, "is the seal that allows a thought to be circulated as a commodity [*das Waren-zeichen das ein Gedanken verkehrsfähig macht*]."[122] With this formula, Benja-min ties together Kraus's concept of the phrase with his own attempts to grasp the language of journalism as the "changed function of language in the world of high capitalism." In the beginning of the same paragraph, Benjamin had cited another passage from Peter Suhrkamp's article on the profession of the journalist, which had described the *Zeitungsapparat* as being modeled on the factory: "At certain times of day—twice, three times in the bigger newspa-pers—a particular quantity of work has to have been procured and prepared for the machine," the passage reads. "And not from just any material: every-thing that has happened in the meantime, anywhere, in any region of life—politics, economics, art, and so on—must now have been reached and journalistically processed."[123] But if the newspaper apparatus can be compared to a factory, the commodity produced here is not limited to the contents it processes on a daily basis; the language in which this factory processes its historical material is subjected to the same logic of commodity production. In his reflections on the phrase, as the *Warenzeichen* that guarantees that the thinking produced in this factory can circulate as a commodity, Benjamin will emphasize its petrified (*starren*) character: Kraus is portrayed as "traversing the sentence constructions of newspapers by night, and, behind the petrified façades of phrases, peers into their interior, where he discovers the violation, the martyrdom of words."[124] But the petrification that here affects thought and language is, for Kraus as for Benjamin, of a specific and paradoxical kind. In one of his aphorisms, Kraus writes, "The phrase is the starched false front for a normal disposition [*das gestärkte Vorhemd vor einer Normalgesinnung*] that is never changed."[125] The image of the phrase as a "starched false front" is crucial here, for it implies two distinct, separate temporalities. On the one hand, there is the front, which is renewed every day, ever-same but in its appearance ever-new and fresh. On the other hand, there is the *Normalgesinnung* underneath it, unchanged, ever more grubby and squalid, concealed and protected by the starched and stiffened front as if it were a shell. Benjamin cites Kraus, who writes in "splendid abbreviation": "One ought to throw light on the way in which technology, while unable to coin new platitudes, leaves the spirit of mankind in the state of being unable to do without the old ones. In this duality of a changed life and a form of life dragged along by it, the ailments of the world live and grow [*lebt und wächst das Weltübel*]."[126] But Benjamin is careful to point out that the real issue in Kraus's critique of language is not concerned with a "petty-bourgeois revolt against the enslavement of the 'free individual' by 'dead formulae.'"[127] The question posed by the phrase is one of a linguistic form that gives the semblance of thought, by renewing itself in a mechanical, ever-same manner, and, behind this, of a thought which, separated from its linguistic form, no longer incited or challenged, but concealed and preserved by it, turns languid and foul.

Chatter

The "true substance of journalism," so Benjamin writes in the essay on Kraus, is "chatter" (*Geschwätz*).[128] This thesis is advanced in a dense passage in the second section of the essay:

> Only Baudelaire hated the satiety of healthy human understanding
> [*die Saturiertheit des gesunden Menschenverstandes*] as Kraus did,
> along with the compromise that intellectuals [*die Geistigen*] made

with it in order to find shelter in journalism. Journalism is betrayal of the literary life, of the spirit, of the demon. Chatter is its true substance [*das Geschwätz ist seine wahre Substanz*] and every feuilleton poses anew the insoluble question of the relationship between the forces of stupidity [*Dummheit*] and malice [*Bosheit*], of which chatter is the expression [*deren Ausdruck es ist*].[129]

Just as Benjamin refers to Baudelaire as the only one who equaled Kraus in his hatred of the *Saturiertheit des gesunden Menschenverstandes*, so Benjamin will return to Kraus in his later Baudelaire essay precisely in a passage where he will point to *Verständlichkeit* as one of the principles governing the language of journalism. What Benjamin calls "chatter" in this passage seems to be, above all else, language subjected to the principle of "understandability" (*Verständlichkeit*)—an understandability whose measure is, in turn, a human understanding, *gesunden Menschenverstand*. The concept is used in a similar way in the earlier text that Benjamin, certainly not by accident, returns to in his later essay on Kraus: his unpublished reflections "On Language as Such and on the Language of Man". Here Benjamin already distinguishes the word from its common usage, pointing out that it is to be understood "in the profound sense, in the way Kierkegaard uses the word"—probably referring to its appearance in the section from Kierkegaard's 1846 book review *Two Ages*, which had recently been translated into German as *Kritik der Gegenwart*.[130] Like Kierkegaard's use of the word, Benjamin's concept of chatter is not only philosophically but also theologically charged. In the 1916 essay, Benjamin uses "chatter" with reference to human language after the fall: the fallen creature is here simply designated as "the chattering human being, the sinful one [*der geschwätzige Mensch, der Sündige*]."[131] Chatter is presented as an emblem of the "enslavement of language" (*Verknechtung der Sprache*)—a formula that recurs in the essay on Kraus—or its reduction to a mere means.[132] Benjamin here takes up a motif that is central in the work of Hamann, who, as we have seen, speaks of the *Knechtsgestalt* of words—of words shaped like servants, reduced to mere carriers of concepts to which they bear no inner relation.[133] What Benjamin calls chatter is thus precisely language that is subjected to the principles of the bourgeois conception of language—conception of language that, as Benjamin writes here, holds that "the means of imparting is the word, its object the thing [*ihr Gegenstand die Sache*], its addressee a human."[134] When Benjamin, in the essay on Kraus, defines "chatter" in terms of *Verständlichkeit*, he returns to this earlier conception while elaborating it further.

If chatter is language subjected to the principle of *Verständlichkeit*, then this is understandability of a specific kind. In chatter, language is limited by the

possibility of it being *readily* understandable—the understandability characteristic of journalism, namely an understandability that prescribes the possibility for words to be understood in the same moment in which they are uttered,
punctually and with no delay. Only what can be understood without delay,
without interrupting the continuous flow of the conversation, may be said—
for otherwise, it would cease to be chatter. In chatter, language serves as the
medium of the actualization of a set of possibilities that is infinite and yet, at
the same time, limited and predefined. This is not to say that there is no room
for "novelties": in fact, chatter thrives on them. It means that anything new is
readily subsumed under a pre-existing concept. Before novelties are imparted,
they are already potentially understood. They merely serve as the material
through which this potential is actualized in chatter. Chatter is not subjected
to the demand of *verstehbarkeit*—if this suffix indeed has a special significance
for Benjamin[135]—but that of *verständlichkeit*. If *verstehbarkeit* would suggest a
specific kind of potentiality, an excessive demand that exceeds precisely the
given conditions of possibility, the *verständlichkeit* and the *Menschenverstand*
to which this corresponds merely express a limitation. It is this limitation, not
the supposed triviality of its subject matter, that constitutes the particular *stupidity* (*Dummheit*) of chatter to which Benjamin refers in the essay on Kraus.
It is not a stupidity that arises from a lack of understanding; but the stupidity
of thought that limits its activity to what can be readily understood—the stupidity of a thought that is always busy actualizing possibilities of what was already possible before it was thought.

In all its busyness, fluidity, and swiftness, *Geschwätz* harbors a petrified
thought and experience. The language of chatter does not set thought in motion, does not incite or shock thought, but instead absorbs and muffles these
shocks whenever they occur. Chatter does not tolerate a silence; it maintains
its own continuity, propels the speaker to incessantly move forward, immediately leaving any moment of disruption or excess behind. Chatter never dwells
on a subject (*Gegenstand*), nor does it tolerate a return to something that was
said only moments earlier. Its impatience arises not from a lack of attention,
but from an intolerance toward the thought that may occur when one dwells
on a topic or a silence disrupts its continuity. Chatter cannot stand a questioning of what is considered to be *selbstverständlich*; it is intolerant toward a questioning that renders strange what is supposedly familiar. Yet it is Kraus who
articulates this intolerance in an unsurpassed manner when he writes, "The
bourgeois does not tolerate anything incomprehensible in his house" (*Der
Burger duldet nichts unverständliches in seinem Haus*).[136] It is this intolerance that constitutes the *malicious* character of chatter, the *Bosheit* to which
Benjamin refers in the essay on Kraus. This is not an intolerance against a

particular viewpoint or position; it is an intolerance against thought and experience that exceed the limits of what it already held to be possible. It is in this sense that the stupidity of chatter mocks the idea of progress: "Before its radiance," Benjamin writes in the essay on Kraus, "the chimeras of progress evaporate."[137]

Engelsprache

In his essay on Kraus, Benjamin's attempts to grasp this tension—the tension implied in the conception of journalism as the expression of the "end point" and "turning point" of fallen language—culminate in his theory of "citation" (*Zitieren*). That citation stands in a special relation to the language of the newspaper is already made clear in the first sentences of the section where Benjamin introduces the concept:

> Out of the linguistic sphere of the name [*aus dem Sprachkreis des Namens*], and only out of this sphere, does Kraus' basic polemical procedure open itself up: citation. To cite a word means to call it by its name [*ein Wort zitieren heißt es beim Namen rufen*]. So Kraus' achievement exhausts itself at its highest level by making even the newspaper citable [*selbst die Zeitung zitierbar zu machen*].[138]

What Benjamin calls "citation" thus plays out around the distinction that was central to his early essay on language: the distinction between "word" and "name." Citation emerges out of the "linguistic sphere of the name": that is to say, it emerges out of a sphere that is concerned only with what imparts itself "in" language—a *Sprachkreis* that is, like a self-enclosed circle turned inward, absolutely indifferent to what is imparted "through" language. Citation, in other words, belongs to the same "circle" as translation, that other *Grundverfahren*, that linguistic procedure which "can never signify something for the original."[139] Citing, insofar as it is one of these procedures gathered around the name, is thus not to be understood as the transposition of the meaning of an original text into a new context. On the contrary: if to cite is to "call the word by its name," citation would seem to involve an interruption of this context. To be called by one's name is to be interrupted in one's activities, to be torn away from the goals that one was acting toward: the moment in which one is called is the moment in which all intentions are suddenly suspended. To "call" the word is thus to tear it away from the purpose it was meant to serve, to suspend the task of signification that it was supposed to fulfill in the original text. To cite must therefore be a matter of removing the word out of the textual "coherence" (*Zusammenhang*) that was supposed to guarantee that every word remains firmly directed toward its purpose and to secure what Benjamin refers to elsewhere as its "uni-directionality" (*Einsinnigkeit*).[140]

If "calling the word by its name" can be characterized as a "polemical" procedure, this is because it revolves around a destructive gesture (in which the word is wrenched from its context) that takes the form of an interruption (the suspension of its semantic function). Yet at the same time, the formula Benjamin uses—to call the word by its name—also seems to imply a positive dimension. To "call" is also to appeal to something: it means to call on something that previously lay dormant, to put to work something that was previously idle. Citation calls on the word, suspends its work of signification, but does so precisely by appealing to it as the bearer of a name. To cite is to make an appeal on the name that lies dormant in the word—on that part of the word which is an *Erbteil*, a partial and fragmented inheritance of the paradisiacal language of names. What is at issue in citation is thus not merely to remove the word from the original text and to relieve it of the task it was supposed to fulfill in that context in order to allocate another semantic function to it in the text into which it is transposed. Benjamin may write that the cited word—the word called by its name—appears "in the order of a new text" (*in dem Gefüge eines neuen Textes*): but this text is one in which the word, as a name, "stands alone and expressionless [*einsam und ausdruckslos*]."[141] The citation, in the specific sense in which Benjamin understood the term, does not call the word away from one task in order to put it to work for another. What is decisive is that the word, in the gesture of citing, ceases to signify at the same time as it reveals itself as a name; that this word, in the gesture of naming, points toward that which is and must remain nameless—that which cannot be expressed through any word or proposition. When Benjamin returns to this characterization of citation later in the same paragraph, he thus only explicates what was already implied in the initial formulation: "The citation [. . .] calls the word by its name [*ruft das Wort beim Namen auf*], breaks it destructively out of its context [*aus dem Zusammenhang*], but precisely thereby calls it back to its origin [*ruft es dasselbe zurück an seinen Ursprung*]."[142]

The claim that citation "exhausts itself at its highest level by making even the newspaper citable [*selbst die Zeitung zitierbar zu machen*]" may be understood in this light.[143] Citation must exhaust itself in the confrontation with the newspaper because it is in journalism—characterized, once more, as the expression of the "changed function of language" in a world that is ensnared completely in the guilt nexus—that language finds itself at the furthest remove from paradise. It is in the language of journalism as it appears in Benjamin's essay on Kraus—whether it is in the utter petrification of the "phrase" or the complete subjection of language to the laws of the understanding exemplified by "chatter"—that the word is tied most firmly into the mythical *Zusammen-hang* of the text and subjected most completely to the demand for *Einsinnig-keit*. Such a language would be "uncitable" because its words seem to be reduced entirely to means of designation: it seems no longer possible to "call them by their name." That Benjamin refers here to the "citability" (*Zitier-barkeit*) of the newspaper must be understood in close relation to the possibil-ity of "impartibility" that played a decisive role in the early essay on language. Like its counterparts, such citability refers not to an empirical but to an *a priori* possibility.[144] That language is a priori citable means that it is a structural possibility to "call the word by its name"—even if this possibility cannot be actualized by finite subjects. If to call the word by its name means to appeal to it as a name, and if such an appeal means to expose its irreducible imparting of impartibility, it also becomes evident how citability differs from its counter-part. That language is a priori citable means that the possibility of impartibil-ity and the excessive demand entailed in this is never irretrievably lost, even on the pages of the newspaper. Citability is thus closely related to impartibility but nevertheless of a different order: insofar as it is concerned with the possibil-ity of possibility, it corresponds to the wish that we found to be central to Ben-jamin's portrayal of Kraus's experience of history—the wish to retrieve a lost sense of the possible. If *Mitteilbarkeit* is a structural possibility inhering in language that first opens up history as the realm of its realization, *Zitierbarkeit* is the structural possibility of *retrieving* this possibility and the demand it implies—even from a language whose inherent dynamic seems to have petri-fied entirely, a language whose emblem is provided by the *Zeitung*, the sheet of paper brandished by the archaic messenger in the opening lines of the essay. In the paragraph on citation, included in the third part of the essay, this ar-chaic crier suddenly returns in the shape of another messenger, when Benja-min counterposes the language of the newspaper to another language, which recalls the *ewig neue Zeitung* evoked at the end of the first section: "In the citation [*Zitat*] [. . .] there is a reflection of the language of angels [*die Engel-sprache*], in which all words, driven out of the idyllic coherence of sense [*aus dem idyllischen Zusammenhang des Sinnes aufgestört*], have become mottoes in the book of creation."[145]

Angelic Messenger

In the last sentences of the essay on Karl Kraus, at the furthest remove from the ancient messenger introduced in its opening lines, Benjamin introduces an-other figure: an angelic messenger. Like the *Bote* at the beginning of the essay, the messenger that makes an appearance at its end is presented as an image of

Kraus, the writer who embodies journalism in its "most paradoxical form." The
Urahn of journalism is here presented as a "new angel" (*ein neuer Engel*):

> A new angel [. . .]—perhaps one of those who, according to the Talmud,
> are created, new ones each instant in countless throngs, in order to
> cease and pass into nothingness after they have raised their voices
> before God. Lamenting, chastising, or rejoicing? No matter—on this
> evanescent voice the ephemeral work of Kraus is modeled. Angelus—
> that is the messenger in the old engravings.[146]

If Benjamin uses the Latin term *angelus* here, rather than the German *Engel*,
this is perhaps to emphasize its etymological roots in the ancient Greek word
for messenger, *angelos*, "the one that announces." The announcement that is
brought by this ancient *angelos* is of a specific kind: in ancient Greek, the word
can be used not only to describe the messenger of the latest news, the harbin-
ger of messages conveyed by envoys or beacons, but also to describe the announcement conveyed by the birds of augury, the *oiōnos angelos*. When
Benjamin conjures up the image of an *angelus*, he thus presents a figure that,
by virtue of its name, is simultaneously closely related to the archaic messenger and distinguished from it. If the *Bote* evoked in the opening paragraph of
the essay conveys the news of the ever-same present of world history, the angel conjured up in the closing sentences would, in the sense of the Greek *angelos*, serve as the figure that discloses a world that is yet to come. That this
messenger is not just an *angelos* but its religious counterpart, an *Engel*—one
that, in Benjamin's rendering, has its origins in the Talmud[147]—suggests that
the future it announces cannot be thought of as a mere extension of the present. In contrast to the archaic messenger, whose cries express the ever-same
suffering of the world of myth, this angelic messenger belongs to the domain
of religion in the specific sense in which Benjamin had conceived of it in his
early writings: as a domain that dispels myth by exposing its ever-same present to a future that is radically other to it. If this angel is thus to announce a
future that is a *novum*, a future irreducible to what has already been, and if it
is to do right to the unprecedented and singular character of this future, it could
never be announced by an already existing figure who speaks in an already
existing language; this angel itself would have to be not only an angel of the
new but also an *angelus novus*, an angel that is, each time, new.

The angel evoked by Benjamin is thus first and foremost an *angelus*, a messenger; but it is not the angelic messenger who brings the news from the heavens
to the world, who delivers a divine message to human beings. Quite the contrary:
if these angels are intermediary beings who "raise their voice before God," these
messengers would—like the archaic crier in the opening lines of the essay—

bring the news of the world and its history. In an earlier draft of the passage, Benjamin writes that these angels are created to "sing a hymn [*Hymnus*]" before they cease and pass into nothingness.[148] Such a hymn would, however, not be the formalized song of praise of Christianity: perhaps it is better understood as the Jewish hymn that, like the *hymnos* sung in the Greek tragedy, where the chorus raises its voice to the Gods in response to the tragic events unfolding on the stage, emerges in response to occurrences in the world and each time has an irreducibly singular character. This interpretation of the hymns of the angels is supported by the description of the angel in the essay on Kraus, which leaves open whether the quickly evanescent voices of these angels are "lamenting, chastising or rejoicing" (*klagend, bezichtigend oder jubelnd*) or, in an earlier draft, whether it is "a lament, a complaint, or a song of praise" (*Klage, Anklage oder Loblied*) that resounds in their voice[149]—all three modes of expression that correspond to the modes of historical experience that Benjamin uncovers in Kraus's journalism.

Just as the cries of the messenger in the opening sentences of the text, the songs of the angelic messenger thus speak of *Weltgeschichte*. But as an intermediary figure that hovers between the worldly and the divine, Benjamin's angel nonetheless captures a relation between the history of the world and another history, which is strictly demarcated from it: between the realm of history of which it sings and another realm, which is here designated by the figure of God. In both versions of the image, the angel sings its hymn or raises its voice "before God" (*vor Gott*).[150] This *vor* unmistakably locates this messenger at a specific place: a place which, if the angel is to appear before God, cannot be that of history itself but rather, like the earlier image of Kraus raising his voice at the "threshold" of the *Weltgericht*, must exist at the end of world history, at a limit where world history must turn into something other than itself. As is suggested by yet another version of the passage, where Benjamin writes that these angels sing their hymns "before his throne" (*vor seinem Thron*), these hymns would establish a relation between the history of which they sing and the divine realm—the *Reich Gottes*, the term that Kant had used in his *Religion* and that Benjamin, following Hermann Cohen, understood as the realm in which history would find its messianic fulfillment and completion.[151] The different modalities of the angel's song to which Benjamin refers in the essay of 1931—*Klage, Anklage, Loblied*—are not only the modalities in which Kraus speaks of history; they also exemplify the different modalities in which world history, as the endless perpetuation of guilt and retribution, is related to the possibility of its own redemption.

It is this relation between catastrophic history and its messianic completion—which has now only been characterized in the most schematic manner—that is described by a concept that may be understood as the focal point of Benjamin's preoccupation with journalism: the concept of "actuality" (*Aktualität*). That this concept plays a decisive role in the text where Benjamin first engages with the theme of journalism—the announcement of his planned *Zeitschrift* that was supposed to be published under the title *Angelus Novus*—is certainly no accident. Nor is it an accident that it is precisely in this text that the figure of a Talmudic angelic messenger is introduced for the first time. In a passage that will be repeated almost verbatim ten years later in the concluding passage of the essay on Kraus, Benjamin here introduces the angel as the emblematic figure of the "true actuality" to which every *Zeitschrift* must aspire: "According to a legend in the Talmud, the angels, new ones each instant in countless throngs, are created in order to cease and pass into nothingness after they have sung their hymn before God. That such actuality may fall to the journal—the only true kind—is indicated by its name."[152] "Such actuality" (*solche Aktualität*): in order to grasp the significance of the image of the angelic messenger, both in its appearance in the "Announcement" and in its juxtaposition to the archaic messenger in the essay on Kraus, it is necessary to first examine what is at issue in this concept, which is so closely related to Benjamin's critical engagement with journalism. Such an examination would not only have to move through Benjamin's reflection on the essence of the *Zeitschrift* of 1921, where it is bound up with his own project of starting a journal, but also extend its detour through the writings of the early 1910s in which the concept surfaces for the first time.

Aktualität

The concept of *Aktualität* makes its initial appearance in the reflections on historical time that stem from Benjamin's student days. The concept is introduced in a set of writings that revolve around a problem that Benjamin articulated most concisely in a reflection on a literary form that—like the *Zeitschrift* in his writings of the 1920s—represents an emblematic configuration of time and writing: the *Tagebuch*. In a section from the *Metaphysics of Youth*, written as early as 1913, Benjamin speaks of a question that the *Tagebuch* poses to the diarist before a single word has been written: "the question in what time the human being lives [*die Frage in welcher Zeit der Mensch lebt*]."[153] It is this same question that Benjamin will raise in his journalistic writing of the following decade—especially in texts that will take recourse to the diary form, such as the *Moskauer Tagebuch* and the *Pariser Tagebuch* or some of his shorter *Denkbilder*, concise texts published as newspaper articles that are often reworked versions of passages from Benjamin's diaries of that period. In a letter to Hugo von Hofmannsthal about the *Moskauer Tagebuch*, Benjamin writes that his planned newspaper article is an attempt to capture "the time in which human beings over there live [*an die Zeit, in der die Menschen dort leben*]."[154] That this question returns in this context points to the close affinity that Benjamin sees between journalistic writing—whether it is the *Zeitung* or *Zeitschrift*—and the writing of the diarist: both are, in their essence, concerned with the temporal structure that is specific to human life—or, to be precise, the "living" (*leben*) of human beings. In the *Metaphysics of Youth*, Benjamin provides a concise response to this question: "With hopeless seriousness, the diary asks the question in what time the human being lives. That the human being lives in no time [*daß er in keiner Zeit lebt*] has always been known to those who think."[155] The human being lives *in* no time: that is to say, this time cannot be understood as a form that is indifferent to the life that unfolds in it. Implied in this is a thinly veiled critique of the Kantian definition of time as a pure form of intuition. The time of human life is no immobile and unchanging form in which objects of experience come to pass; the insight that the diarist and the journalist share is that time as such is transient—it does not stand outside of history but emerges and comes to pass day after day. What Benjamin writes about the *Tagebuch* anticipates his later reflections on the *Zeitschrift*: "The diary does not occur *in* time [. . .]. It is rather a book *of* time [*es ist ein Buch* von *der Zeit*]."[156] The time with which the diarist and the journalist are concerned thus cannot be an empty form; but neither can it be a homogeneous continuum in which mechanical change unfolds. Such a conception of time fails to account for the fact that the time of human life—that is to say, historical time—can only be thought as the relation between a time that passes to a time that is structured wholly differently: a time for which Benjamin reserves the name *Zukunft*.

The concept of *Aktualität* makes its initial appearance in a number of early writings that each engage with the problem of historical time. Benjamin introduces the concept for the first time in a text written in 1913, the same year as his reflections on the *Tagebuch*, well before the announcement of his own journal: in a short article titled "Thoughts on Gerhart Hauptmann's Festival Play."[157] The article takes the play by Hauptmann as an occasion for a reflection on the concept of history (*Geschichte*) that unfolds in a language characterized by its specific relation to the moment. Benjamin's early article is written in brief sentences that often refuse conventional rules of grammar and clarity, alternating between fully elaborated passages and ones that read more like unfinished notes. The language of this article, which was written to be published in a *Zeitschrift*, a journal, anticipates his later interest in a "prompt language" that would be "able to cope with the instant."[158] It is at the point where this language, in the early article of 1913, touches on the question of historical time that the concept of *Aktualität* surfaces for the first time in Benjamin's work. In the vocabulary typical of his student days, which still bears the traces of his involvement in the youth movement, Benjamin writes:

> We feel a kinship with history: not with a history of the past [*der vergangenen*], but one that is yet to come [*der kommenden*]. We will never understand the past, without wanting the future [*Zukunft*]. School makes us indifferent [*indifferent*], it wants to tell us that history is a struggle between good and evil. And sooner or later the good will succeed. From that standpoint there is no urgency [*Eile*] in acting. The present is, so to say, not actual [*die Gegenwart, sozusagen, ist nicht aktuell*]—time is infinite.[159]

"Actuality" is here treated as a predicate of the present: it is the *Gegenwart* that can be actual—or not. But at the same time as it allows for a possible convergence of the present and the actual, this last sentence also introduces a split between the two categories and thereby implicitly defines the concept of actuality over and against that of the mere present: if it is possible for a present *not* to be actual, as Benjamin claims here, then the concept of actuality would have to be more than an indifferent container—it would have to be something more than a mere designation of everything that is supposedly given in any present whatsoever. To say that something is *aktuell*—even if this is only said "so to speak" (*sozusagen*)—would not merely be the same as saying that it is merely *gegenwärtig*. What underpins the split between the two, the mere present and its actuality, is located in the experience of time that corresponds to the conception of history that Benjamin outlined before: the mere present that lacks actuality is a present in which "time is infinite." This infinite time is here characterized in terms of a lack of *Eile*: a lack of urgency or, literally, "haste." This time would be *unendlich* in the sense that it never runs out; it would correspond to a conception of history in which possibilities never expire, in which there is never a critical point, never a decisive moment in the course of history that may be seized or missed irrevocably. This time is thus not only infinite but also characterized by a uniformity and homogeneity. From the standpoint of this "indifferent" experience of time, every present is the same: it is, in other words, a time that is, like the "improper temporality" of which Benjamin speaks in a later note, barred from the differentiation of past, present and future.[160]

The conception of history that remains based on a representation of time as an infinite, uniform continuum is here presented as one that puts its trust in a certain idea of progress: it is a conception of history as a struggle between two already established categories, the good and the bad, in which the good will eventually come out as the victor—"sooner or later" (*früher oder später*), for such a conception of history is ultimately indifferent as to when this struggle is decided. Benjamin only draws the tentative outlines of another experience of history in which the present would not be deprived of its actuality. In the face of the complacent struggle with an already given outcome, history would have to be conceived as a "more severe and terrible struggle" (*strengerer und grausamerer Kampf*). Benjamin describes this struggle as one that does not play out between categories that are already given and known but precisely between two different histories, the *vergangenen* and the *kommenden*: history would be a "struggle between [. . .] those of the future [*Zukünftigen*] and those of the past [*Vergangenen*]." This future is not understood in terms of the past; it is an "unknown future" (*ein unbekannte Zukunft*), a future that is, in other words, not just unknown but also unknowable. Both of these histories would have a fundamentally different structure: while one corresponds to the sense for *das Gegebene*, what is given as a fact, the other corresponds to the sense for *das Aufgegebene*, a task that is irreducible to anything given and, for that reason, cannot manifest as an conscious intention towards an already known future; this task cannot be "captured in a reform program" because it could itself never be fully known; it would have to intimate itself as a "feeling for a task of the future [*einer zukünftigen Aufgabe*]."[161] The time that Benjamin attempts to articulate over and against the "infinite time" of progress is a time where the past and the future, what has been and what is yet to come, no longer exist in a uniform continuum, but are rigorously differentiated from one another. The present would be the point of collision between these two different histories, these two different structures of historical time. Rather than a progression toward a telos that can be fully known, a progression that is eternal in the sense that it is infinite, this would be a present that Benjamin describes in this early article as one in "eternal crisis" (*ewiger Krisis*), a present in which the very possibility of an unknown future is "steadily threatened" (*ständig bedroht*) by the passing of time. "With every present [. . .] what used to be spring turns into slowness [*was Schwungkraft war wird Trägheit*], spirit turns into stupidity. And through this the one, great historical good is lost: freedom."[162] It would seem that only such a present, a present in which the possibility of history itself exists under constant threat, could ever be called *aktuell*.

This same schema, of which Benjamin only draws the provisional outlines in his text of 1913, returns in the historico-philosophical reflections in the *Life of Students*—an important text that was written a year later, again for publication in a journal.[163] Although Benjamin makes no explicit reference to the concept of actuality in this text, its whole opening paragraph may be read as an attempt to elaborate his prior reference to the concept, together with the conception of history that is organized around it. As in the earlier article, Benjamin will set out his thoughts on time and history against a conception of history based on progress; and as in the earlier article, this conception of history is said to rely on a conception of time that, in its reliance on its infinity, fails to make a claim on the present.

> There is a conception of history [*Geschichtsauffassung*] that, trusting
> in the infinity of time, distinguishes only the tempo, rapid or slow,
> with which human beings and epochs advance along the path of
> progress [*auf der Bahn des Fortschrittes dahinrollen*]. Corresponding to
> this is the incoherence, the lack of precision and rigor in the demand
> [*Forderung*] such a conception makes on the present.[164]

Just as in his earlier article, Benjamin's outlines of an alternative conception of history here revolve around a strict conception of *Zukunft*, a future that is irreducible to what has already been and thus ultimately unknowable and unforeseeable; in contrast to his earlier reflections on history, however, Benjamin will further specify and radicalize the demand made by such a conception on the present in a now famous passage:

> The following remarks, in contrast, concern a particular condition
> [*einen bestimmten Zustand*] in which history [*Historie*] is gathered as
> in a focal point, something seen from time immemorial in the utopian
> images of thinkers. The elements of the final condition [*Endzustandes*]
> do not lie at the surface [*zutage liegen*] as a formless tendency towards
> progress [*gestaltlose Fortschritttendenz*], but are deeply embedded in every
> present as the most endangered, excoriated, and ridiculed creations
> and ideas. To give shape to this immanent state of perfection and to
> make it absolute, to make it visible and ascendant in the present—that
> is the historical task [*geschichtliche Aufgabe*].[165]

Benjamin specifies this formulation of the "historical task" in the last sentence of the paragraph: "To liberate what is yet to come [*das Künftige zu befreien*], through cognition, out of its misshapen form in the present [*aus seiner verbildeten Form im Gegenwärtigen*]—this is the sole aim of criticism."[166] History is not to be conceived as a steady advancement across the path of progress, a movement guided by an immanent *Fortschritttendenz* toward an end that—even if it can never be reached—can be known and represented. History can take place only as the "liberation" of a future that is to be strictly distinguished from any empirical present—Benjamin will write elsewhere in the same paragraph that any present can at most be a *Gleichnis* or *Abbild* of a final condition, an approximation of an idea that is strictly unrepresentable in any given present—but that is nevertheless embedded in the present "in misshapen form." The *Endzustand* is not located in a distant future that can be reached only through incremental advancement along a linear path—Benjamin describes this movement as a placid "rolling towards" (*dahinrollen*) an already given goal—but is both immanent and imminent in every present. Only a future that is unforeseeable and nevertheless imminent could make a "demand" (*Forderung*) on the present that is rigorous enough to open up the domain of history in the sense in which Benjamin had defined this in his earlier article—as a domain in which the history becomes perceptible only in its relation to a *künftige* history, a time that is yet to come. Actuality would be the name for this "determinate condition" (*bestimmte Zustand*)—a condition in which the demand of this future presses in on the present with the utmost intensity.

Announcement of a Journal

After it is introduced at a key position in his writings of the early 1910s, the concept of actuality seems to disappear entirely from Benjamin's work for the remainder of the decade. It suddenly resurfaces in 1921, in the text that begins by presenting itself as the "announcement" (*Ankündigung*) of Benjamin's planned journal, *Angelus Novus*, and ends by evoking the same image of the angelic messenger that will return at the end of the essay on Kraus. The story of Benjamin's attempts and ultimate failure to found this journal are by now well documented: the offer extended by Richard Weissbach, the publisher of his Baudelaire translations, to edit his journal, *Die Argonauten*; Benjamin's refusal to take up this offer, which led Weissbach to propose the possibility of founding a journal under his own editorial control; his attempts to define the place of his *Zeitschrift* in the context of a proliferation of small magazines in the early 1920s; Benjamin's endless conversations with and about possible contributors; the feud with one of his main collaborators, Ernst Lewy; the growing difficulties with his publisher, who ended up withdrawing support for the project in 1922.[167] The text that resulted from these endeavors—the "Announcement of the Journal: *Angelus Novus*," which remained unpublished in his lifetime—is, however, less concerned with an empirical description of this new journal than with a philosophical reflection on what Benjamin refers to as the "essence of the journal" (*das Wesen einer Zeitschrift*).[168] In turning to the *Zeitschrift* as a literary form, the text also returns to the question that had already been touched upon in Benjamin's early reflections on the *Tagebuch*: just as that other compound, the word *Zeitschrift* suggests that anyone who would attempt to reflect on its "essence" would have to start by considering the relation between time and writing that is named by it. Benjamin's text of 1921 may indeed be understood to return to the question that his early reflections had recognized in the *Tagebuch*, the question "in what time the human being lives"; and like the earlier texts, it attempts to think this time in terms of a tension between a time that passes and a time that is yet to come. This tension is already introduced obliquely in the prefatory sentences of the announcement, before the text has properly begun, in a brief reflection on the term *Ankündigung* that appeared in the title of the text, which announced the announcement of a journal called *angelus*, "the one who announces." In these opening sentences, Benjamin makes explicit what this play of announcements had already anticipated: that the "announcement" is the only form of speaking about a journal that would do justice to its essence. When Benjamin, in the first paragraph of the text, empathically distinguishes the "announcement" that is about to be undertaken from a "program," he has, in effect, already begun his reflections on the essence of the *Zeitschrift*. The opening sentences of the text read:

> The journal whose plan is presented here hopes to create confidence in its content by giving account of its form. This form arises from a meditation on the essence of a journal [*das Wesen einer Zeitschrift*]. Even if it does not make a program wholly superfluous, a journal should avoid it as an incitement to deceptive productivity. Programs are only valid for work of individuals and associations that is conscious of its goal [*zielbewußtes Wirken*]. A journal, as the expression of life [*Lebensäußerung*] of a certain kind of spirit [*Geistesart*], is always much more incalculable and unconscious [*unberechenbarer und unbewußter*], but also fuller of the future and richer in its unfolding [*zukunftsvoller und entfaltungsreicher*] than any expression of the will [*Willensäußerung*].[169]

The "program" is not an adequate form of announcing a journal—let alone a journal that bears the name *angelus*—because it betrays its relation to a time that is yet to come. The configuration of time and writing that is constitutive of the journal, conceived as *Lebensäußerung*—an "expression" or, literally, "utterance" of life—is distinguished here first of all from a *Willensäußerung*. In contrast to the *Lebensäußerung*, this expression, or "utterance" of the will, is characterized by a certain relation to a *Ziel*, an end conceived as an aim that can be posited and realized through purposeful activity. Such an expression of the will implies a certain configuration of time, a certain relation between the time of the journal and a time that is yet to come. In contrast to an announcement, the program treats the future as an end to be pursued, thus predetermining this future by subjecting it to the requirement that this future be representable and its realization calculable. To present a journal through a program would mean to mistake it for a *Willensäußerung*—an utterance of which the drafting of programs would be the exemplary form—and thus to relate it to a future that is thought to be realizable through intentional activity.[170] By contrast, Benjamin characterizes the *Lebenäußerung*, of which the journal is the proper medium, as "incalculable and unconscious": it does not hold up a future in front of itself as an end that may be intentionally pursued through conscious activity. But exactly for that reason it is *zukunftsvoller*, fuller of a future that is conceived as a time that is yet to come, as well as *entfaltungsreicher*, richer not in its possibilities for "development," as it is usually translated, but for a sudden unfolding of a state that is already immanent in the present but remains concealed. The *Zeitschrift* would thus seem to be concerned precisely with a future that, on the one hand, resists all conscious representation and calculable realization but that is, on the other hand, to use the expression from Benjamin's writings of the previous decade, "embedded deeply in the present."[171]

Before having properly started its reflections on the essence of the *Zeitschrift*, Benjamin's announcement has already anticipated one of the decisive claims it will make: if the journal announced here cannot be described in the form of a program, this is because its only true measure lies in its relation to a *Zukunft*, a time that is yet to come, which escapes all programmatic statements. Only in this light does it become possible to read the sentences with which Benjamin, once more, begins his reflections on the essence of the journal:

> The true vocation of a journal [*die wahre Bestimmung einer Zeitschrift*]
> is to declare the spirit of its epoch [*den Geist ihrer Epoche zu bekun-*
> *den*]. Its actuality [*dessen Aktualität*] is more binding to it [*gilt ihr mehr*]
> than even its unity or clarity and therefore it would—like the newspa-
> pers—be sentenced to inessentiality [*zur Wesenlosigkeit verurteilt*]
> if a life did not take shape in it that is powerful enough to save even
> what is questionable [*auch das Fragwürdige zu retten*], because this
> is affirmed by it. Indeed, a journal, whose actuality is without a
> historical claim [*historische Anspruch*], has no right to exist [*besteht*
> *zu Unrecht*].[172]

Even though its only measure is its relation to a time that is yet to come, the journal is directed toward its own time: the vocation of a journal is to "declare the spirit of its epoch." At first sight, there is something strangely pompous about this proposition, which may seem to recall the proud proclamations of the spirit of an epoch that propels the forward progression of history toward

an immanent telos. But as Benjamin's prior dismissal of any programmatic announcement of the journal as a *zielbewußtes Wirken* suggests, something else
is at stake here. The key to the interpretation of this proposition lies in its last
word, *bekunden*, the act of declaration that here replaces and specifies the *Lebenäußerung* of a *Geistesart* to which Benjamin had made reference in the first
paragraph. As the terminology of the passage and the rest of the "Announcement" suggest—throughout the text there will be talk of "claims," of "dictums"
and "verdicts," of "confessions" and "justifications"—the *bekunden* must be
read in the technical, legal sense of the word: as a declaration for a court of
law. The declaration of the "spirit of the epoch" has little to do with a proclamation, as the common English translation of Benjamin's announcement suggests; if the *Zeitschrift* declares the spirit of the age, it does so in the context of
a courtroom.[173]

If it is read in this way, the proximity of the "Announcement"—Benjamin's
first reflection on journalism—to the later essay on Kraus suddenly comes into
view: for it is here that he writes that the *Gerichtssaal*, the court of law, is, for
the Viennese writer, the forum that it has always been for "great journalists"
(*großen Journalisten*).[174] But in the essay on Kraus, this *Gerichtssaal* is never
merely a space in which a dispute is analyzed and judged according to a given
legal and juridical framework. If Kraus is, in Benjamin's essay, rendered as a
prosecutor, he never simply makes his accusations in the name of law; his *Anklage* is here always one in which law (*Recht*) itself stands accused.[175] What is
at stake here is, as in the 1921 "Announcement," the relation between the jurido-
political orders of the historical world and a coming justice. Significantly,
Benjamin employs the same term that he used in his earlier reflections on the
Zeitschrift when he writes in his essay on Kraus that the phrases and scandals
of the day with which this "great journalist" never ceased to occupy himself
turn into a "declaration" (*Bekundung*)—but one where "it no longer suffices
to call on the world as witness to the demeanors of a cashier; it must summon
the dead from their graves."[176] If the "declaration of the spirit of the epoch"
involves its presentation in a courtroom, this courtroom would no longer be a
worldly court of law but the *Weltgericht* to which Benjamin will make repeated
reference in the essay on Kraus—that is to say, the site where the entirety of
history lays claim to its messianic completion.

This is also implied in the term that Benjamin uses toward the end of the
passage, where he speaks of the "declaration of the spirit of the epoch" that
every *Zeitschrift* is destined to undertake as a declaration that has to involve a
"historical claim" (*historische Anspruch*). The reference to this "claim" may
be read in light of the reference to a "demand" (*Forderung*) of which Benjamin had spoken in the texts of the early 1910s, where it was closely tied to the

concept of actuality. The *Forderung* of which Benjamin speaks in these texts is a demand that emerges out of *Historie* taken in its totality—"gathered together"—and presses in on the present.[177] As we have seen, it is in this demand that history first enters into a relation to the condition that Benjamin describes as both an "end state" (*Endzustand*) and a "state of perfection" (*Zustand der Vollkommenheit*).[178] When Benjamin refers to a "historical claim" in his reflections on the essence of the journal, this claim occupies a comparable position. In the "Announcement," Benjamin speaks of this demand as a claim that has no determinate subject or object. The reference to a *historische Anspruch* does not present a subject that raises this claim or an object that is claimed; at most it suggests that, inasmuch as this claim is historical, it is a claim that emerges out of history itself. The *historische Anspruch* is not a historical claim made by an already established subject: it is a claim *of* history. Benjamin does not stipulate that the *Zeitschrift* has a right to exist only if it makes a claim on behalf of history: in its declaration of the spirit of the epoch, history itself must come to speak, must raise a claim that is immanent to it. The nature of this claim is suggested by the term *Anspruch*, which has a specific juridical meaning. To raise a claim (*ein Anspruch erheben*) does not just mean, in the general sense of the word, to assert one's right to something; insofar as it translates the Roman *vindicia*, it does not just evoke the claim over something as one's rightful property; in its more precise sense, it involves the claim for the restoration of something to a free condition.[179] The "historical claim" without which it is not possible to speak of actuality at all may perhaps be understood in this more fundamental sense: as a claim to a restoration that, in combining the demand for justice and freedom, recalls the references in Benjamin's writings of the previous decade to "the messianic kingdom or the idea of the French revolution."[180]

Like the "demand on the present" of these earlier texts, the "historical claim" articulated in the 1921 "Announcement" marks the site where history first enters into a relation with the messianic. This *Anspruch* would at the same time be a demand for a restoration, a return of all historical occurrences to their origin, and a demand that, as a still outstanding claim, opens up history as the domain of its fulfillment. It is this claim that plays a decisive role in the determination of the concept of *Aktualität*, which had already slipped into the text at the beginning of the passage without, at first, being defined. That Benjamin introduces what is arguably the key concept of the text by referring simply to "its actuality" (*dessen Aktualität*) suggests that an initial, provisional definition of this actuality has already been given in the preceding sentence. The pronoun that Benjamin uses—*dessen*—does not refer to the *Zeitschrift* but to the nominalized verb *bekunden*. Actuality is introduced as another name for what Benjamin describes as the *Bestimmung* of the journal, its "vocation" or "destination" to declare the spirit of the epoch. This is confirmed by the last paragraph of the text, where Benjamin refers to the vocation of the journal as a "striving for actuality" (*werben um Aktualität*).[181] If the actuality for which this journal strives is to be an actuality of the true kind, that is to say, if this journal is to have a right to exist, then it must involve the historical claim in the precise sense in which Benjamin uses this term: a claim of history to its messianic completion. What is here called "actuality" is thus not the state in which this claim is redeemed: *Aktualität* is rather the name for the state in which this claim makes itself heard in its full intensity. That the vocation of the *Zeitschrift* is also a "striving for actuality" means that it must set up a court of law in which the *Geistesleben* of this time can express the demand for its messianic completion in another time, a time that is yet to come.[182]

First Days

In his reflections on the essence of the *Zeitschrift*, Benjamin returns to this "claim" and the relation between *Historie* and *Zukunft* that it implies in the same passage where the concept of actuality also resurfaces for a second time in the text. After stating that the journal must prove its "sense for true actuality" through an elaboration of its "philosophical universality," this universality is now described in a passage in which the *Anspruch* resurfaces:

> For this journal, the universal validity of expressions of spiritual life [*geistigen Lebensäußerungen*] must be bound up with the question of whether they are able to raise a claim [*Anspruch zu erheben vermögen*] to a place in religious orders that are still coming into being [*einen Ort in werdenden religiösen Ordnungen*]. Not as if such orders were foreseeable [*absehbar wären*]. What is foreseeable is that, without them, what struggles for life in these days as the first days of an age [*was in den diesen Tagen als den ersten eines Zeitalters nach Leben ringt*] cannot make its appearance.[183]

The "historical claim" that no journal would have a right to exist without is here further specified: the *Anspruch* to restoration is now explicitly rendered as a claim that is related to the future—"the claim to a place in religious orders that are still coming into being." The reference to "religious orders that are still coming into being" must be understood in the precise historico-philosophical sense in which Benjamin had conceived of religion in the early writings: as the sphere in which myth opens up to the idea of a "kingdom of God on earth" as the realization of the idea of freedom in the empirical world. That the claim for a place in such religious orders must have a "universal validity" must also be understood as a specification of both the history and the fulfillment that is at stake here: the *Anspruch* that is raised here cannot be restricted to a particular language or polis; the demand for liberation must have a universal character, must concern all of history if it is to be a *historische Anspruch* in the emphatic sense. If Benjamin sticks to the terminology of "religious orders," this is not only to evoke this divine order in which history is first fulfilled, but also to reiterate the strict separation of this order from the *Historie* from which this claim arises: the order in which every historical phenomenon must be able to claim a place is an order that can never be posited from within history itself.

This strict separation of historical existence and *Zukunft* is further elaborated in Benjamin's stipulation that the "true actuality" described in this passage would involve a claim to a place in orders that are not "foreseeable" (*absehbar*).[184] This characterization must be understood as a specification and radicalization of the reference to an "unknown future" (*unbekannte Zukunft*) in his historico-philosophical reflections of the early 1910s.[185] That the future is not just unknown but *unabsehbar* means that what is yet to come is unknown, that it cannot be seen or represented from the perspective of what is given or conceivable within the categories of the present.[186] The term implies a specific temporal dimension: not only is the *Zukunft* unforeseeable in the sense that it is impossible to see what is yet to come, but also that it is impossible to ascertain when it is coming—and ultimately even that it has to remain uncertain *if* this future is ever to arrive. As a claim that relates itself to an unforeseeable order, the *historische Anspruch* must therefore remain radically indeterminate—at least from the perspective of the present. The claim to a place in an order where all of history finds its completion is a claim to a place in an order that can only be known once it has arrived, but which might never arrive at all. Because of this indeterminacy, the claim that is raised by historical phenomena could never be realized from within history itself: for it is only in the orders that are yet to come that such a claim could ever be understood or granted. What is only foreseeable—and this is the paradox of the claim that history is to raise in the courtroom of the *Zeitschrift*—is the impossibility that the claim of history for its salvation would ever be granted without these orders that are yet to come. Before such an order is realized—and whether it will ever be realized is uncertain—any claim for historical phenomena to their salvation cannot be heard completely. Only in the unforeseeable future would it first become possible to see, retrospectively, how this future was already called for in the present; only from the standpoint of this future order would it be fully apparent what it is that is still struggling for life "in these days" (*diese*

Tagen) but will allow to recognize them "as the first days of an age" (*als den ersten eines Zeitalters*).[187]

At this point it becomes possible to return to Benjamin's stipulation that, in order for any journal to gain actuality, a "life would have to take shape in it that is powerful enough to save also what is questionable [*auch das Fragwürdige zu retten*]."[188] What is meant here is not that such a life would be powerful enough to save historical phenomena, to bring history to its messianic fulfillment. What the life in this *Zeitschrift* must be able to save, if it is ever to gain actuality, is first of all the claim of historical phenomena to their own salvation, that is to say, their claim to a place within those "religious orders that are still coming into being"—even in the case of those phenomena where this claim seems to have the most questionable status. The reference to *das Fragwürdige* takes the place of what, in the writings from Benjamin's student days, is referred to as that which is "most endangered [*gefährdetste*], excoriated [*verrufenste*], and ridiculed [*verlachte*]."[189] The superlatives Benjamin uses here have the same function as the "also" (*auch*) in his reflections on the journal, which emphasizes that the *Zeitschrift* would have to show that even the most questionable elements in the *Geistesleben* of the epoch have an essential content that demands to be saved from its deformed shape in the present. If the messianic would involve the redemption of "the entire occurrence of history" (*alles historische Geschehen*) as Benjamin writes in the so-called "Theologico-Political Fragment," which is probably written in the same years, then the claim to this salvation would be most intense precisely in those phenomena where this claim is most questionable from the standpoint of historical existence itself. What is at stake in actuality is thus not the salvation of *Historie*; only the salvation of its *Anspruch*, the claim to its messianic completion. Nowhere is this claim that refers every phenomenon to a time that is yet to come more questionable, more tenuous, than in that which is "new or newest":

> Every journal must hold fast to that which, as something truly actual, takes shape under the infertile surface of that which is new or newest [*was als wahrhaft Aktuelles unter der unfruchtbaren Oberfläche jenes Neuen oder Neuesten sich gestaltet*], whose exploitation it should leave to the newspapers.[190]

What is here called "truly actual," and Benjamin describes later in the text as "true actuality" (*wahre Aktualität*), does not rely on the distinction between *Zeitschrift* and *Zeitung*; instead, it must be understood to revolve around the distinction between, on the one hand, the actuality to which both the *Zeitung* and the *Zeitschrift*—as the two exemplary forms of journalistic writing—must aspire and, on the other, the actuality proclaimed and demanded by the newspapers and journals in the plural, that is to say, in their given historical reality.[191] This actuality is not simply opposed to the "new or the newest" (*Neuen oder Neuesten*)—a phrase that evokes a novelty that is already surpassed and substituted by a newer one the moment after it has occurred and recalls the references in Benjamin's later writings to the temporality of the "landscape of hell" evoked in Kraus's writings as *das immer-wieder-Neue*.[192] The decisive distinction in this passage is rather between the "infertile surface" of the ever-same novelties and what struggles for life in them underneath this surface. If the vocation of a *Zeitschrift* is to strive for true actuality, this striving would exhaust itself at its highest level in its attempts to show that even the ever-same sensations of the newspapers—or what Benjamin elsewhere calls, with a similar formulation, the "most recent, journalistic actuality"[193]—contain something that struggles for life "in these days as in the first of an epoch."[194] Even though it is not mentioned by name, the model for the *Zeitschrift* that aspires to such actuality is unmistakable: it is the journal in which Kraus dissected the newspapers on a daily basis and found the whole of world history—as a single, uninterrupted catastrophe—pressing in on every single article, phrase, or advertisement, demanding to be redeemed in an unforeseeable future.[195] It is no accident that the image of uncountable throngs of angelic messengers, raising their voice before God in every now, expressing the possibility and demand for history to be brought to an end and completion, finds its closest counterpart in one of Benjamin's attempts to characterize the peculiar kind of journalism that he understood to be exemplified by Kraus. In a passage that echoes his earlier definition of the vocation of the *Zeitschrift*, Benjamin characterizes this journalism as follows: "Kraus knows no system. Every thought has its own cell. But every cell can, in the now [*Nu*], apparently occasioned by nothing, turn into a chamber—a legal chamber [*ein Gerichtskammer*]."[196]

Afterword
"Today"

The *day*, precisely, the question or reflection of the *day*, the resonance
of the word *today* . . .

—JACQUES DERRIDA, *THE OTHER HEADING*

The philosopher and the journalist: in the work of the three thinkers addressed
here, these two figures have been pitted against one another in a manner that
does not cease to recall the ancient polemic between the philosopher and the
sophist. In a reprise of the polemic between philosophy and sophistry, Kierkegaard, Nietzsche, and Benjamin will each propose to conceive of philosophy
itself precisely in and through its relation to journalism. Philosophy would, according to an origin myth that returns in their hyperbolic remarks on journalism, come into being exactly in the moment where it differentiates itself from
everything journalistic, just as philosophy in ancient times first emerges in its
polemical distinction and separation from sophistry.[1] In strict analogy with its
ancient counterpart, philosophy does not merely secure its own boundaries by
setting itself against everything journalistic, but would understand itself to be
constituted precisely in and through this distinction. It is Kierkegaard who
seems to suggest exactly this when he explicitly draws out the analogy between
philosophy's relation to its ancient and its contemporary opponents, the sophist and the journalist. In one of his journals of the mid-1840s, he will compare
the relation between philosophy and journalism to a lapse from philosophy
into sophistry. "If you were to think of a most eminent polemical author, the
likes of whom has never existed, and confront him with a journal," Kierkegaard writes here in characteristic hyperbole, "he cannot but lose unless he
himself is willing to publish a newspaper: and in that case he loses as well,

inasmuch as he has sunk from being a writer to being a journalist (which is just like a philosopher becoming a sophist)."[2] But it would be a mistake to assume that this analogy suggests that philosophical thought and writing, here captured in Kierkegaard's figure of the *Forfatter*, could simply be opposed to journalism. In Kierkegaard's own presentation of the ancient polemic between the philosopher and the sophist, the two figures are set against one another— but they are not placed in a relation of simple opposition. Quite the contrary: in Kierkegaard's account, philosophy comes into being precisely as a *radicalization* of sophistry.[3] The ancient philosopher, exemplified by the figure of Socrates, takes certain principles that lie at the root of sophistry—certain "secrets" harbored by their apothegm that "man is the measure of all things" of which they refuse to become conscious—and pushes this to an extreme, that is to say, beyond the point where sophistry is willing or able to go. If philosophy can place itself in the sharpest possible contrast to sophistry, this is not because the two can be neatly separated and opposed to one another: it is because philosophy takes up and radicalizes a question that sophistry fails to follow through to its end.[4] Understood in this sense, it is indeed possible to draw an analogy between the ancient couple of the philosopher and the sophist and the polemic between philosophy and journalism staged in different ways by Kierkegaard, Nietzsche, and Benjamin. As in the case of their ancient counterpart, the conflict between philosophy and journalism articulated here is not to be mistaken for one of simple opposition, even where the shrillest polemical tone may suggest so. To transpose the schema of Kierkegaard's interpretation of the ancient polemic onto the relation between philosophy and journalism would suggest instead that philosophy would have to be understood as a *radicalized* journalism: an attempt to take a concern that lies at the root of journalism, its *radix*, and to follow this through in the most uncompromising manner.[5]

Philosophy as a radicalized journalism: to understand philosophy in these terms would mean to grasp its relation to the word that is at the root of journalism itself—the *jour* of journalism, the day of today. If this word—*today*—is a cause for concern for philosophy, if philosophical thought is to concern itself with this word at all this is because it poses a challenge to it. It is perhaps this challenge that Derrida attempts to articulate when he defines the main concern of a series of newspaper articles written in the 1980s as a concern with the "resonance" of this word—a resonance that is brought out by its repeated iteration in the sentence that we have taken as our epigraph: "the *day*, precisely [*le* jour, *justement*], the question or reflection of the *day* [*la question ou la réflexion du* jour], the resonance of the word *today* [*la résonance du mot* aujourd'hui]."[6] The challenge that this word poses to thought would, then, not only be the challenge of treating precisely *justement* this word but also of treating this word *justement*—that is to say, of doing justice to it. To do justice to this word would be a matter of treating it not merely as a sign that one could well do without, a disposable means to refer to this or that day: it would require instead attending to that in the word which calls for a response in the first place. What calls for a response, what sets philosophy's work of questioning and reflecting into motion would, in other words, not be a conceptual problem or a logical contradiction: this movement would arise out of the word itself—or what is described here as its resonance. But what is the resonance of this word with which philosophy, as a radicalized journalism, would concern itself? And what does it mean to say that this word—*today*—resonates at all?

The moment philosophy begins to respond to this word—"today"—it would have already returned to the question with which this study began: that of the relation between thought and its time. It is not difficult to detect the echoes of a proposition which already appeared at the beginning of this study—Hegel's statement that "philosophy is its time, apprehended in thoughts" (*Philosophie ist ihre Zeit, in Gedanken erfaßt*)—in the encounter that Derrida stages with this word.[7] "Today" is a deictic—a word whose meaning is inseparable from the context in which it is uttered. Like other such time designators, it implies a relation between the time that is spoken of and the time in which it is spoken. The word "today" never ceases to refer thought to its own time; the day at stake here is always this day, here and now. For thought to attend to this word would thus mean for it to turn to this time, its own time—but not without dwelling on the word that had pointed it there, and with it, the conditions under which this time may be thought in the first place. If this word, "today," implies a question, it is always already a double one: the "question of the day" (*la question du jour*) would not only ask what constitutes this day, this time; it would also involve the question under what conditions it becomes possible to represent this day to ourselves, its supposed contemporaries, to ask questions about it and to begin responding to them—today.

The word "today" may seem to suggest that such questions are relatively unproblematic. The time to which thought is referred here is not some other time but simply this time, a time that presents itself to us in the here and now, the *present* day. This simple presence of the day is both emphasized and complicated by the exact word in which Derrida detects a challenge to thought: *aujourd'hui*, that is, *au jour de hui*, "on the day of today," or, if *hui* is traced back to its root in the Latin *hodie*—a word with the same semantic structure as the Old English *tō dæg*, "this day"—"on the day of this day." Is this word, *aujourd'hui*—if it is a single word—nothing but a tautology? Does it say the same thing twice, namely that *this* day is also *a* day? Or does this apparent tautology refer instead to a tension—a conflict between this day and the general concept of which it would be a mere instantiation? Is this day, the day of today, merely a day in general, a day that could be thought, grasped with the same concepts and rules as any other day? Or if there is something about this day that cannot be subsumed under already given concepts, something that resists analogy—something irreducibly singular? Is there then anything about this word that remains to be thought at all? The same tension that is implied in the conceptual dimension of the word *aujourd'hui* also marks its use as a metaphor. The word that is said to pose a challenge to thought is, in Derrida's newspaper articles, never merely this day in the literal sense; it never refers *only* to this day but always poses the challenge of thinking this "day and age." But what exactly is this relation between the day, *le jour d'aujourd'hui*, and the age? Can this day be understood to stand in for the age as a whole? Does the age, as an abstract totality, become manifest in this day, if it is only read properly? Can this day, in its particularity and concreteness, be shown to contain the entire age *in nuce*? Or is there something in this day that exceeds the age, something that cannot be reduced to its own time but announces a time that is yet to come?

If a "resonance" may be ascribed to this word, *aujourd'hui*, this could not simply be an expression of the fullness with which the day presents itself in the here and now, like the reverberating voice of a speaker who addresses us in the present. Just as the word "today," its *résonance* opens itself up to different readings. What exactly is resounding in this word—what is it that resonates in this day, here and now, and poses a challenge to thought? Are these days that have already happened—older days that now resound, repeat themselves in this day? Does philosophy, when confronted with its own day and age, not recognize in the "questions of the day" the resonance of other, older questions, which are destined to pose themselves again and again? Does it not detect in this day a return of questions that have been asked since time immemorial— those questions that precede the day of today but are nevertheless, as Derrida puts it in one of his articles, "always of current interest" (*toujours d'actualité*)? Are the "questions of the day," then, a reiteration of the same old questions— or is there something in this day that demands to be thought anew? Does something announce itself in the *résonance*; are these the tremors that indicate that, today, as Derrida asks in these same newspaper articles, "something is on its way" (*quelque chose est en course*)?[8] Would it be possible to read this epithet not as the expression of a complete presence but rather as the indication of a certain urgency, a pressure, that Derrida in these newspaper articles describes as an "imminence": not quite an immanence, in other words, but a state in which what happens today, in the here and now, cannot be reduced to the order of the present but rather announces something that is—perhaps—yet to come? If something announces itself in this day, is this yet another repetition of old days, of what has already happened and is fated to happen again and again—or does it harbor a promise of something genuinely new? Is it possible that something is *en course* in this day which is without precedent or precursor, something that refuses subsumption and analogy? If what is imminent in this day is to elude anticipation, even its novelty could not be of a familiar kind; it cannot be "new as always" (*nouvelle comme toujours*) but would have to be, to borrow an expression Derrida uses elsewhere in his newspaper articles, "newly new" (*nouvellement nouvelle*).[9] Because it couldn't bear the familiar marks of novelty, it would be difficult—perhaps even impossible—to recognize that which is *en course* today as something new. The challenge that the word "today" poses to thought would thus be to attend to an announcement that could never present itself as such, to detect in the resonance of this word not the expression of a fullness but rather a trembling—an anguished experience, hovering between fear and hope, of something that may be imminent but resists anticipation.

What would then be journalism's relation to this "today"? The writing that finds its proper place in the *journal* would seem to be propelled as much by the anguished experience of the day—an experience shaken by what is imminent, what announces itself in this day while eluding anticipation—as by the attempt to suppress the tremor in this experience, to bring it back under control, to render it productive or at least profitable. In the same newspaper articles that concern themselves with the "question of the day" Derrida also makes reference to the order challenged by this question—"the order of theoretical determination, of knowledge, certainty, judgment, and of statements in the form of 'this is that,' in other words, more generally and essentially, the order of the present or of presentation [*l'ordre du présent ou de la presentation*]."[10] The pages of the newspaper—the daily, the *journal*—would supposedly offer the stage on which the resonance of the word today, the experience shaken by what it cannot contain is to be subjected to this order, stabilized in the form of facts, made comprehensible through commentary, turned into a basis for well-informed, purposeful activity. The *jour* that takes on phenomenal form in the *journal* would already be structured by the assumption that what happens today can be rendered visible and comprehensible, that it could—at least in principle—become the object of an exhaustive overview. This "presentation" of the day, this attempt to make the *aujourd'hui* fully present, would be predicated on the assumption that what is happening today could be known completely and definitively in the moment in which it happens; that everything that takes place today is accessible to the witness and the camera, the reporter and the commentator—and by extension to "us," its contemporaries. If the word "today" poses a challenge, if it intimates a difficulty, this would here be reduced to the difficulty of stabilizing its meaning, of turning this word into a concept that gathers and comprehends everything that is happening here and now, at this moment in history, completely and definitively. And yet the writing of journalism would always retain the traces of the tremor in the word "today" and the experience it names: not least when its own forms, and most notably its oldest, most trusted form, the newspaper, turn out to be less stable than they appeared to be, lose their coherence and currency, and, in their own crisis and outdatedness, are themselves to be exposed to an uncertain and unforeseeable future—another day, and, perhaps, something other than the day. This crisis had, to be sure, always been at work within journalism. For Derrida, as for the three thinkers discussed here, journalistic reason always contains an element that breaks down the stability of its forms, interferes with the unity of its own rhythm, and interrupts its proper functioning. Precisely in its own crisis, in the elements that would silently but persistently disturb the work of presentation, journalism would retain something of the tremor that it never manages to bring under control completely and definitively.

"The resonance of the word today"—if philosophy may indeed be understood as a radicalized journalism, it would begin from its persistent refusal to petrify the tremor in this word while attempting to think it. In confronting *la question du jour*, philosophy would instead have to hold fast to that in the day which exceeds given concepts, resists being fixed and stabilized, known completely and definitively, but rather announces something that eludes anticipation. It is this gesture of refusal, in which the philosophical concern with the "today" would distinguish itself from journalism as its radicalized double, that is thematized in one of Derrida's last texts. This text stages a dialogue between a journalist and a philosopher—a dialogue that takes the form of a staged interview between a "passing journalist" and an unnamed philosopher, presumably the author himself.[11] The setting recalls not only the trope that we have seen recur in the preceding chapters, the polemical counterposition of philosophy and journalism; perhaps it also echoes the ancient dialogue between the philosopher and the sophist in which philosophy first forges a name for itself. But here it is not the philosopher who asks the questions, at least not in the first instance. In the questions of the journalist, the divergence between the philosopher and the journalist's relation to the word today, their different modes of thinking the occurrences of the day—not accidentally the publication of a book that deals precisely with the question of how thought takes place today—is thematized at the level of language. "Allow me to insist," the journalist says, "in the name of what I believe to be the ethics and deontology of journalism, that is to say my duty toward my readers. They ask you to be more concise and clearer, more spontaneous, more direct than usual, at least as much as possible."[12] "There is not much time and space left. Say what you want to say without delay and without detour. My readers, and even my editor . . ." Or, as he begins his following question: "Could you start by explaining to my readers, *in a nutshell* . . ."[13] At some point these demands turn into an insistent begging: "Couldn't you answer me with facts or short quotations, rather than with digressions?"[14] "Couldn't you explain yourself in a little more concrete, pedagogical, intelligible way? A little more communicative?"[15] Finally they are expressed as a command: "You, too, have duties," the journalist says. "You must communicate in an intelligible fashion and make yourself accessible in the public sphere."[16] The "passing journalist" that Derrida evokes here is not a particular person; his persistent demands may be taken as the cipher for a certain mode of speaking, a certain mode of orienting oneself in language toward what is happening to us today, what is happening right now. The language that he asks his interlocutor to speak is characterized by the demand for a certain clarity and directness, a certain conciseness and lack of excess, a certain spontaneity and comprehensibility—in short, a certain kind of communicability. The world that is presented in this language is always already structured and limited by this demand for communicability: it is a world where what is happening is thought to be immediately perceptible and readily comprehensible—at least in principle.

If the figure of the journalist emerges from these repeated demands to speak only of what is readily communicable, the figure of the philosopher comes into being in the persistent refusal to speak this language. The interviewee resists the demands of his interlocutor, sighs and complains—but it would be a mistake to think that philosophy here opposes itself to journalism. The relation between the two hinges on a phrase that is reiterated time and again by the philosopher in response to the journalist's questions: *vous voulez rire*—you must be joking. "You must be joking," the philosopher responds to the journalist whenever he is asked to speak this language. The phrase articulates a relation between philosophy and journalism in the form of a scolding reminder of what is disavowed in the journalist's questions. You must be joking: when Derrida's philosopher exclaims this phrase, he suggests there is something ridiculous about the seriousness of the journalist. Precisely the journalist, it suggests, that figure who reminds philosophy of the vanity of its claims to timeless truth, treats the language of its time as though it were eternal, and the occurrences of which it speaks as complete, fixed. In asking to speak of the occurrences of the day in a language that is direct and readily comprehensible, journalism turns into a faint version of itself: it inverts the principles of which it reminds philosophy and, in doing so, betrays the question that pulsates within it, its concern with the word today. Also here, in its confrontations with this interviewer, philosophy would, then, not come into being in an opposition to journalism but precisely where it radicalizes the question implied by this word. Philosophy would not distinguish itself from journalism by taking recourse to timeless values and eternal truths, but rather when it asks the question of the day with a certain persistence, when it holds fast to its concern with the word "today" with a rigor that exceeds its interlocutor's demands for clarity and comprehensibility. The philosophical concern with the word "today," the attempt to do right by its specific resonance, has to be accompanied by a resistance toward the tendency of this word to congeal, to assume a stable significance, to appear as if it were fully transparent: philosophy, insofar as it is concerned with the attempt to think its time, would always involve a resistance toward the presentism on which journalism and its presentation of the day necessarily relies. Such a thinking would involve a certain attentiveness to the conditions under which this today is rendered present in our time, the conditions under which it becomes possible for our time to assume a phenomenal form. Perhaps it is this same attentiveness to which Derrida may have alluded when he suddenly interrupts one of his newspaper articles to ask, in a play on one of the characteristic formulas of philosophy's ancient opponent, the sophist: "Has the day ever been the measure of all things, as one pretends to believe?"[17]

Acknowledgments

My gratitude goes out first of all to Julia Ng and Alberto Toscano for their careful reading and astute comments on the manuscript in its various stages. Special thanks are due to Rebecca Comay, whose rigorous feedback and generous support have proven invaluable as I prepared the manuscript for publication. I am also grateful to Werner Hamacher, whose comments and encouragement have been a driving force during an important phase of the project. In its early stages, my research benefited immensely from the commentary of Alexander Düttmann and Bernard Stiegler, as well as my other interlocutors at Goldsmiths, University of London, particularly at the Centre for Philosophy and Critical Thought. The editorial team at Fordham University Press has provided invaluable support and guidance during the publication process. I would especially like to thank my editors, Tom Lay and Eric Newman, and Nancy Rapoport for her meticulous copyediting.

Many of the ideas in this book emerged from conversations with friends and colleagues, especially Jacob Bard-Rosenberg, Sebastian Truskolaski, Sami Khatib, Nassima Sahraoui, Stefano Marchesoni, Chris Law, Ilit Ferber, and Caroline Sauter. Discussions with Arnd Wedemeyer, Christiane Frey, and Hannah Proctor also played an important role during the final stages of the project. The rigor, care, and thoughtfulness of Jan Sieber, who passed away much too early, have made their mark on the manuscript through our many conversations at the Staatsbibliothek.

I am most thankful to my friends and family, whose generous and unquestioning support was crucial as I worked on the project. But above all, my gratitude goes out to you, B., for being there when it counts most, and to you, Calderón, little comrade, for our moments of endless joy and laughter.

Notes

Morning News: Kant, Hegel

1. G. W. F. Hegel, *Werke* (Frankfurt am Main: Suhrkamp, 1970), 2: 547. Further references to this title will appear as GW.

2. The aphorism was published by Rosenkranz in 1842, together with other excerpts from the notebooks that were spread across different issues of the *Königsberger Literaturblatt*.

3. For an account of the complex role of aphorisms in Hegel's philosophical writings, especially the prefaces, see Yirmiyahu Yovel, *Hegel's Preface to the Phenomenology of Spirit* (Princeton: Princeton University Press, 1980), 14–19.

4. GW 12: 16; Hegel, *The Philosophy of History*, trans. J. Sibree (New York: Dover, 1956), 5.

5. GW 1: 422. A detailed account of the development of Hegel's thought in Frankfurt and Jena can be found in Dieter Henrich, *Hegel im Kontext* (Frankfurt am Main: Suhrkamp Verlag, 1967), 9–40, and Eckart Förster, *The Twenty-Five Years of Philosophy*, trans. Brady Bowman (Cambridge: Harvard University Press, 2012), 277–305.

6. GW 1: 422–23.

7. GW 3: 545–73; *Phenomenology of Spirit*, trans. A. V. Miller (Oxford: Oxford University Press, 1977), §748–87. (Hereafter cited as PS.) For an analysis of Hegel's concept of religion in the early writings and the *Phenomenology*, see Jean Hyppolite, *Introduction to Hegel's Philosophy of History*, trans. Bond Harris and Jacqueline Bouchard Spurlock (Gainesville: University Press of Florida, 1996), 1–19, and his *Genesis and Structure of Hegel's Phenomenology of Spirit*, trans. Samuel Cherniak and John Heckmann. (Evanston: Northwestern University Press, 1974), 529–72.

8. GW 3: 571; PS §784.

9. GW 2: 547.

10. GW 18: 38.

11. GW 18: 38.

12. That the two scenes in which this "discovery" is figured—*Morgensegen* and *Zeitungslesen*—are both implicitly but emphatically coded as European is, of course, no accident. For a detailed analysis of Hegel's exclusion of the non-European other from the trajectory of universal reason, see Gayatri Chakravorty Spivak, *A Critique of Postcolonial Reason* (Cambridge: Harvard University Press, 1999), 1–111; on the dynamics of racial subjection at work in an expansion of this universality that would "include the others of Europe," see Denise Ferreira da Silva, *Toward a Global Idea of Race* (Minneapolis: University of Minnesota Press, 2007).

13. That newspaper reading was, at the turn of the nineteenth century, still largely treated as a practice of "intensive" reading rather than the "extensive" reading with which it would quickly come to be associated, is reflected in Hegel's remark. On the distinction between intensive and extensive modes of reading, as well as the "reading revolution" in which these reading practices would play an important role, see Rolf Engelsing, *Der Bürger als Leser: Lesergeschichte in Deutschland, 1500–1800* (Stuttgart: J. B. Metzlersche Verlagsbuchhandlung, 1974).

14. An alternative reading is provided in Rebecca Comay's study *Mourning Sickness: Hegel and the French Revolution* (Stanford: Stanford University Press, 2011). In one of the footnotes of the book, Comay suggests that the aphorism may be read in light of Fichte's characterization of the print medium as the "most intimate means of connecting spirit and spirit"—a means of communication that would facilitate the collective isolation on which the possibility of an abstract and egalitarian *Publikum* is predicated. See *Mourning Sickness*, 165n.

15. GW 7: 26; PhR, 15. On the relation between these two propositions, both of which are found in the preface to the *Philosophy of Right*, see Joachim Ritter, *Hegel and the French Revolution: Essays on the Philosophy of Right*, trans. Richard Dien Winfield (Cambridge: MIT Press, 1982), 39–43.

16. For a detailed analysis of the motif of reading in Hegel and its status as a "fissure in the absolute," see Werner Hamacher, *Pleroma: Reading in Hegel*, trans. Nicholas Walker and Simon Jarvis (Stanford: Stanford University Press, 1998), 1–80 and 206–32.

17. Hegel was briefly editor of the *Bamberger Zeitung* from early 1807 to 1808, abandoning this role as soon as he was offered the rectorship of a gymnasium in Nürnberg. Rosekranz writes in his biography that, after his prospects in Jena became more desperate, he was considering other ways "to have a further influence on German intellectual life [. . .] perhaps through journalism." In a letter of 1806, Hegel remarks with regards to the newspaper trade: "this trade would interest me, since I, as you know, follow the world events with curiosity [*Neugierde*]," adding that the challenge would be to approximate the quality of French newspapers, but without abandoning what is expected by the German, namely "a kind of pedantry and impartiality with regards to the news." Under Hegel's editorship, the newspaper

did indeed not include so-called "reasoning articles" (*raisonnirenden Artikeln*) but seems to have restricted itself to the gathering of reliable information from correspondents and accurate description of events. See Karl Rosenkranz, *Georg Wilhelm Friedrich Hegel's Leben* (Berlin: Duncker und Humblot, 1844), 230–33.

18. Kant intended to publish the essay in the *Berliner Blätter*, but the publication was rejected by the *Stadtpräsident* and ended up being included in *The Conflict of the Faculties*. See Gerd Irrlitz, "Der Streit der Fakultäten," in *Kant Handbuch* (Stuttgart: J. B. Metzler, 2002), 435–39.

19. Immanuel Kant, *Gesammelte Schriften* (Berlin: De Gruyter, 1968), 7: 82; *The Conflict of the Faculties*, trans. Mary J. Gregor (New York: Abaris Books, 1979), 147. (Further references to these titles will appear as Ak and CF, respectively.) On the role of Kant's concept of the *Geschlecht* in his writings of this period, see Peter Fenves, *A Peculiar Fate: Metaphysics and World History in Kant* (Ithaca, N.Y.: Cornell University Press, 1991), 179–84. For a critical analysis of the tensions and co-implications of Kant's concepts of the human being, humankind (*das Menschengeschlecht*), and his theory of race, which had disappeared as an explicit concern in his writings of the 1790s but arguably still remain at work in these texts, see Emmanuel Chukwudi Eze, "The Color of Reason: The Idea of 'Race' in Kant's Anthropology," in *Postcolonial African Philosophy: A Critical Reader* (Oxford: Blackwell, 1997), 103–31, and Robert Bernasconi, "Kant as an Unfamiliar Source of Racism," in *Philosophers on Race: Critical Essays*, ed. Julie K. Ward and Tommy L. Lott (Oxford: Blackwell, 2002), 145–66.

20. An insightful discussion of this problem and its integration in the architectonic of Kant's system is found in Emile Fackenheim, "Kant's Concept of History," *Kant-Studien* 48 (1956–57): 381–98, and especially Yovel, *Kant and the Philosophy of History* (Princeton: Princeton University Press, 1980), 3–80.

21. See Ak 5: 45–46; *Critique of Practical Reason*, in *Practical Philosophy*, ed. and trans. Mary J. Gregor (Cambridge: Cambridge University Press, 1996), 64–65.

22. Ak 7: 83; CF, 147.

23. Ak 7: 80–81; CF, 141–43.

24. Ak 6: 51; *Religion Within the Boundaries of Mere Reason*, trans. George di Giovanni, in *Religion and Rational Theology*, ed. Allen W. Wood and George di Giovanni (Cambridge: Cambridge University Press, 1996), 58. Further references to the latter title will appear as RR.

25. Ak 6: 48; RR, 54–55.

26. Ak 7: 85; CF, 153. For a broader discussion of the fraught relation between German philosophy and the French revolution, see Stathis Kouvelakis, *Philosophy and Revolution: From Kant to Marx* (London: Verso, 2003), and Comay, *Mourning Sickness*, 8–54.

27. A glaring absence in Kant's essay is the other revolutionary event that had begun to unfold in the early 1790s, on the other side, not of the Rhine but of the Atlantic: the Haitian revolution. On the reception of this event in the centers of colonial power, which laid bare the contradictions that also traverse Kant's own

philosophy, see C. L. R. James, *The Black Jacobins: Toussaint L'Ouverture and the San Domingo Revolution* (New York: Random House, 1963), 118–45.

28. Ak 7: 85; CF, 153.

29. Ak 6: 101; RR, 111. For a discussion of this "wish" in the context of the second *Critique* and the *Religion*, see Förster, *The Twenty-Five Years of Philosophy*, 41–56 and 277–78.

30. Ak 7: 86; CF, 155. A more detailed analysis of Kant's concept of enthusiasm and its relation to his critical writings can be found in Jean-François Lyotard, *Enthusiasm: The Kantian Critique of History*, trans. Georges van den Abbeele (Stanford: Stanford University Press, 1986), and Peter Fenves, *A Peculiar Fate*, 258–89.

31. Ak 7: 85; CF, 153.

32. Ak 7: 84; CF, 151.

33. On the relation between Kant's account of the French revolution and the "newspaper fever" (*Zeitungsfieber*) of the 1790s—a term introduced by Goethe in "Die Reise der Söhne Megaprazons"—see Comay, *Mourning Sickness*, 52–54.

34. Ak 19: 604. Fenves offers an alternative reading of this passage in *A Peculiar Fate*, 252–53.

35. Cf. the section "On Assent from a Need of Pure Reason" in Ak 5: 142–46; CPrR 179–84. On the highest good as the "supreme interest of reason," see Yovel, *Kant and the Philosophy of History*, 14–22.

36. Ak 19: 604.

37. Ak 1: 419.

38. For a discussion of this transformation and its relation to Kant's analytic of the sublime, see Comay, *Mourning Sickness*, 31–35. A detailed discussion of the problem of history in Kant's natural-historical writings can be found in Fenves, *A Peculiar Fate*, 13–82.

39. Ak 7: 85; CF, 153.

40. Ak 7: 85; CF, 153; my emphasis.

41. Ak 7: 87; CF, 157.

42. For a detailed discussion of the distinction between *zuschauen* and *anschauen* in an earlier draft of the essay, see Peter Fenves, *A Peculiar Fate*, 244–55.

43. Kant already sets up a relation between the "progression of enlightenment" and the *Leserwelt* in his earlier essay "What is Enlightenment?," in Ak 8: 37.

44. Kant, Letter to Fichte, December 1797?, in *Correspondence*, ed. and trans. Arnuld Zweig (Cambridge: Cambridge University Press, 1999), 544.

45. Ak 7: 280; *Anthropology from a Pragmatic Point of View*, ed. and trans. Robert B. Louden (New York: Cambridge University Press, 2006), 181. Further references to the latter title will appear as APP.

46. Ak 7: 280; APP, 181.

47. Ak 7: 280; APP, 181.

48. Ak 5: 332; *Critique of the Power of Judgment*, trans. Paul Guyer and Eric Matthews (Cambridge: Cambridge University Press, 2000), 203.

49. Cf. Kant's recommendation to begin conversations with weather talk in Ak 7: 176; AP, 69.

50. One important exception that should already be mentioned here is Michel Foucault, who notes in his 1978 "What is Critique?": "There is much work to be done on the relationship between philosophy and journalism from the end of the 18th century on, a study . . . Unless it has already been done, but I am not sure of that . . ." Foucault, "What is Critique?" in *Politics of Truth*, ed. Sylvère Lotringer and Lysa Hochroth, trans. Lysa Hochroth (New York: Semiotext(e), 1997), 48.

51. Walter Benjamin, *Gesammelte Schriften*, ed. Rolf Tiedemann and Hermann Schweppenhäuser (Frankfurt am Main: Suhrkamp, 1972–91), 5: 60; *The Arcades Project*, trans. Howard Eiland and Kevin McLaughlin (Cambridge: Harvard University Press, 1999), 14. Further references to these titles will appear as GS and AP, respectively.

52. Benjamin uses the term *geschichtliche Erfahrung* in this double sense; see, for instance, the use of the term in his introduction to the last version of *Berlin Childhood* in GS 7: 387; *Selected Writings*, ed. Marcus Bullock and Michael W. Jennings, trans. Edmund Jephcott et al. (Cambridge: Harvard University Press, 1996), 4: 344. Future references to the latter title will appear as SW.

53. Søren Kierkegaard, *Samlede Værker*, ed. A. B. Drachman, J. L. Heiberg, and H. O. Lange (Copenhagen: Gyldendal, 1901–06), 2: 18; *Either/Or*, trans. D. F. and L. M. Swenson and D. W. Lowrie (Princeton: Princeton University Press, 1959), 2: 19. This remark will be discussed more extensively in the first chapter of the present study.

54. Here I am drawing especially on Hamacher's work on the relation between experience, history, and language in his "Disgregation of the Will," in *Premises: Essays on Philosophy and Literature from Kant to Celan*, trans. Peter Fenves (Cambridge: Harvard University Press, 1996), 145–48, and "Intensive Languages," trans. Ira Allen and Steven Tester, *MLN* 127 (2012): 489–99.

55. GS 2: 176; SW 1: 204.

56. This expression is borrowed from Lacoue-Labarthe, who introduces it in his essay on Nietzsche's early studies of language and rhetoric, "The Detour," in *The Subject of Philosophy*, trans. Thomas Trezise (Minneapolis: University of Minnesota Press, 1993), 14–36.

57. In the case of Benjamin, see, for instance, the use of this term in his essay on Baudelaire (GS 1: 611; SW 4: 316) and his claim, in the *Arcades Project*, that the form of the feuilleton is, from its birth, accompanied by a certain "feeling of space and time" (GS 5: 679; *The Arcades Project*, trans. Howard Eiland and Kevin McLaughlin [Cambridge: Harvard University Press, 1999], 546).

58. Karl Kraus, *Schriften*, ed. Christian Wagenknecht (Frankfurt am Main: Suhrkamp Verlag, 1994), 8: 77.

59. GS 2: 349; SW 2:443.

60. On this "exorbitant privilege of the present," see Derrida's commentary on the conceptions of time of Aristotle, Kant, Hegel, and Heidegger in *"Ousia* and

Grammē: Note on a Note from *Being and Time*," in *Margins of Philosophy*, trans. Alan Bass (Chicago: University of Chicago Press, 1982), 31–67.

61. GW 7: 26; *Elements of the Philosophy of Right*, ed. Allen Wood, trans. H. B. Nisbet (Cambridge: Cambridge University Press, 1991), 15.

1. Talking Machines: Kierkegaard

1. G. W. F. Hegel, *Werke* (Frankfurt am Main: Suhrkamp, 1970), 12: 11–28; *The Philosophy of History*, trans. J. Sibree (New York: Dover, 1956), 1–16. Further references to these titles will appear as GW and PhH, respectively.

2. GW 12: 22; PhH, 9.

3. GW 12: 75; PhH, 54. On *logos* and history in Hegel's lectures on the philosophy of history, see, for instance, Jean Hyppolite, *Introduction to Hegel's Philosophy of History*, trans. Bond Harris and Jacqueline Bouchard Spurlock (Gainesville: University Press of Florida, 1996), 20–34, and Joachim Ritter, *Hegel and the French Revolution: Essays on the Philosophy of Right*, trans. Richard Dien Winfield (Cambridge: MIT Press, 1982), 183–233.

4. For a discussion of the complicated relation of Kierkegaard's early writings to Hegel, see Jean Wahl, *Études kierkegaardiennes* (Paris: Librairie Philosophique J. Vrin, 1949), 86–158. The most thorough analysis of the problem of language and its role in Kierkegaard's engagement with the "whole newer development" can be found in Peter Fenves's *"Chatter": Language and History in Kierkegaard* (Stanford: Stanford University Press, 1993).

5. On the question of biography and the empirical-genetic interpretations of the relation between "philosophy" and "life" in Kierkegaard and Nietzsche, see the preliminary remarks of Jacques Derrida's "Otobiographies," in *The Ear of the Other: Otobiography, Transference, Translation*, ed. Christie V. MacDonald, trans. Peggy Kamuf (New York: Schocken Books, 1985), 3–7.

6. *Søren Kierkegaards Papirer*, ed. P. A. Heiberg, V. Kuhr, and E. Torsting (Copenhagen: Gyldendal, 1909–48), 10.2: A 314. Further references to this title will appear as Pap.

7. Cf. Julia Watkin's introduction to the standard English translation of the *Early Polemical Writings* (EPW, vii–xxxvi) and the *Writing Sampler* (WS, vii–xvii).

8. Søren Kierkegaard, *Samlede Værker*, ed. A. B. Drachman, J. L. Heiberg, and H. O. Lange (Copenhagen: Gyldendal, 1901–06), 13: 68; *Early Polemical Writings*, ed. and trans. Julia Watkin (Princeton: Princeton University Press, 1990), 76. Further references to these titles will appear as SV and EPW, respectively.

9. For a detailed analysis of the role of *Gestalt* in Hegel's account of the (re)presentation of thought, see Philippe Lacoue-Labarthe, "The Unpresentable," in *The Subject of Philosophy*, trans. Thomas Trezise (Minneapolis: University of Minnesota Press, 1993), 116–57.

10. This is the claim Lacoue-Labarthe elaborates in "The Unpresentable," 148–49.

11. On the problem of reappropriation and reinternalization in Hegel, see Hamacher, *Pleroma: Reading in Hegel*, trans. Nicholas Walker and Simon Jarvis (Stanford: Stanford University Press, 1998), 1–80.

12. See "On My Work as an Author," in *The Point of View: On My Work as an Author*, trans. Howard V. Hong and Edna H. Hong (Princeton: Princeton University Press, 1998), 1–20. Kierkegaard here has his "activity as a writer" commence with the publication of his first pseudonymous book, *Either/Or*. The term "early writings" will be used in this chapter to refer to Kierkegaard's work before the commencement of his authorship "proper," encompassing also the dissertation.

13. For a detailed survey and inventory of Kierkegaard's use of the term *Journaler*, see Peter Tudvad, "On Kierkegaard's *Journalism*," trans. Tod Alan Spoerl, *Kierkegaard Studies Yearbook* (2003): 214–33. Kierkegaard's unpublished play is included under the title "Battle between the Old and the New Soap-Cellars" in Pap. 2: B 1–22; EPW, 105–24.

14. The most important exception to mention here is the close reading of Kierkegaard's 1938 book review in Fenves's *"Chatter"*, which also includes a detailed analysis of his later essay "The Present Age." The early newspaper articles receive careful treatment in Joakim Garff's *Søren Kierkegaard: A Biography*, trans. Bruce H. Kirmmse (Princeton: Princeton University Press, 2005), 67–74, which provides a good overview of the context in which they were written but does not offer a study of the philosophical stakes of the texts.

15. Given the focus of this chapter on Kierkegaard's early newspaper articles and late pamphlet *The Instant*, his engagement with the theme of journalism at the time of the "Corsair Affair," in particular in his important text "The Present Age" and his *Journaler* from the mid 1840s, is considered only in passing.

16. Pap. 2: A 118; JN, DD: 28.

17. The *Kjøbenhavns flyvende Post*, the aesthetic periodical edited by J. L. Heiberg, described itself in those years as an *Interimsblad*—literally an "interim paper"—and was published around three times per week when Kierkegaard's text appeared there. Besides this text, published under the pseudonym "B.," the issue included a part of the serially published translation of Tieck's novella *Der Wassermensch*.

18. For a discussion of the context and development of the polemic, which unfolded in the wake of the French Revolution and the attempts of the Danish monarchy to curtail its effects through censorship, see Garff, *Søren Kierkegaard*, 60–67 and the historical introduction to EPW, vii–xxiii.

19. See Orla Lehmann, "Press Freedom Affair V," in EPW, 134–41.

20. In this respect, Kierkegaard's newspaper article radicalizes a gesture already implicit in the lecture "Our Journalistic Literature" he had given the year before at the Student Association in response to a plea for the merits of the emerging newspapers, periodicals, and even the "yellow journalism" of the time delivered by a fellow member, Johannes Ostermann. The position Kierkegaard took here, so his opponent remarked afterwards, was "more or less a matter of indifference." See Garff, *Søren Kierkegaard*, 62.

21. SV 13: 9; EPW, 6.

22. Pap. 11.1: A 342; *Kierkegaard's Journals and Notebooks*, ed. Niels Jorgen Cappelorn et al. (Princeton: Princeton University Press, 2011), NB 31: 14. Further references to the latter title will appear as JN.

23. Kierkegaard already used the term in this way in his lecture on "Our Journalistic Literature" of the preceding year. As was common practice at the time, the term *Journal-Litteratur* is employed not with reference to "journals" in the current sense but to all ephemera, ranging from more respectable newspapers to the pamphlets and tabloids circulating in Copenhagen in the early nineteenth century. Cf. for instance the use of the term in the lecture to which Kierkegaard responds here, Johannes Ostermann's "Our Latest Journalistic Literature," in EPW 189–99.

24. GW 3: 18–19; *Phenomenology of Spirit*, trans. A. V. Miller (Oxford: Oxford University Press, 1977), 6–7. The latter title will hereafter be cited as PS.

25. See GW 3: 45–46; PS, 27.

26. For an extensive discussion of the "preface" and its specific position in the context of Hegel's philosophical work, see Jacques Derrida, "Outwork, Prefacing", in *Dissemination*, trans. Barbara Johnson (London: Athlone Press, 1981), 1–59.

27. GW 3: 18–19; PS, 6–7.

28. Hegel's announcement of an *Aufgang* echoes the claim on the first pages of the *Phenomenology* that "now is the time for philosophy to be elevated to the status of a science" (GW 3: 14; PS, 3–4).

29. A recurrent problem of the (already sparse) interpretations of the early writings is the tendency to treat these texts as if they were written in Kierkegaard's "own" voice. Gillian Rose makes a persuasive claim against this possibility—even in the texts signed by "Kierkegaard"—in *The Broken Middle: Out of Our Ancient Society* (Oxford: Blackwell, 1992), 3–10.

30. See EPW, 135.

31. SV 13: 9; EPW, 6.

32. For an analysis of the role of contradiction in the "objectless" dialectic of Kierkegaard's later writings, see Theodor W. Adorno, *Kierkegaard: Construction of the Aesthetic*, trans. Robert Hullot-Kenter (Minneapolis: University of Minnesota Press, 1989), 30–32. For a critique of Adorno's treatment of the problem of language in Kierkegaard, see Fenves, "Image and Chatter: Adorno's Construction of Kierkegaard," *Diacritics* 22 (1992): 100–14.

33. SV 13: 9; EPW, 6.

34. Kierkegaard's double-length second piece was again published in the *Kjøbenhavns flyvende Post* and spread over the issues of March 12 and 15, 1936. This piece presents itself as a response to the article "On the Polemic in the Flying Mail," which was published by Johannes Hage, editor of another main newspaper, the *Fatherland*, and took aim at Kierkegaard's "Morning Observations," especially the personal attacks it includes. For a discussion of the context in which this second piece appeared, see Garff, *Søren Kierkegaard*, 63–64.

35. SV 13: 20; EPW, 15.

36. "World history is [. . .] the unfolding [*Auslegung*] of spirit in time" (GW 12: 96–97; LPH, 72).

37. GW 8: 247.

38. On the problem of manifestation and appropriation, see Lacoue-Labarthe, "The Unpresentable," 143–45.

39. GW 2: 37–38.

40. "This sentence contradicts the previous one" (GW 2: 38). It is noteworthy that Hegel does not initially introduce the concept of contradiction as a noun but as a verb whose subject is the *Satz* itself: for the sentences themselves inaugurate a movement of contradiction that is immanent to the *logos*.

41. GW 3: 57–60; PS, 36–39.

42. On the relation between the speculative proposition and the formal-grammatical sentence, see Hamacher, *Pleroma*, 5–7, and Jean-Luc Nancy, *The Speculative Remark*, trans. Céline Surprenant (Stanford: Stanford University Press, 2001), 75–101.

43. Here I draw on Peter Fenves's account of the movement of *logos* and the suspension of teleology in *"Chatter"*, 1–8.

44. Several years later, in the dissertation that marks the end of his "early writings," Kierkegaard will of course call this undecidability by its familiar name: irony. For a discussion of the theory of irony from Schlegel to Kierkegaard, see Paul De Man, "The Concept of Irony," in *Aesthetic Ideology*, ed. Andrzej Warminski (Minneapolis: University of Minnesota Press, 1996), 163–84.

45. SV 13: 9; EPW, 6.

46. The condition that is brought about in the mode of reading that is practiced in the early newspaper articles is, in this sense, closely related to the "permanent parabasis" described by Friedrich Schlegel, an undoing of the semantic function of language that is able to take place at all times. See Friedrich Schlegel, "Zur Philosophie," Fragment 668, in *Kritische Ausgabe*, ed. Ernst Behler (Paderborn: Ferdinand Schöningh, 1962), 18: 85.

47. SV 13: 20; EPW, 15.

48. On the difference between *logos* and *lexis*, *voulour dire* and *dire*, *das Gemeinte* and *Art des Meinens*, see Paul De Man's lecture on Walter Benjamin's theory of translation, "'Conclusions': Walter Benjamin's 'The Task of the Translator,'" in *The Resistance to Theory* (Minneapolis: University of Minnesota Press, 1986), 86.

49. SV 13: 20; EPW, 15.

50. SV 13: 9; EPW, 6.

51. GW 3: 61; PS, 39–40.

52. SV 13: 20; EPW, 15.

53. SV 13: 20; EPW, 15.

54. SV 13: 20; EPW, 15.

55. Pap. 1: A 328; JN, CC: 12.

56. Johann Georg Hamann, "Aesthetica in Nuce," in *Sämtliche Werke*, ed. Josef Nadler, vol. 2 (Vienna: Im Verlag Herder), 199. A helpful discussion of Hamann's engagement with the problematic relation between reason and language is found in Oswald Bayer's study *A Contemporary in Dissent: Johann Georg Hamann as Radical Enlightener* (Grand Rapids: Eerdmans, 2012), 156–70.

57. "Without word, no reason—no world." Hamann, "Biblische Betrachtungen," in *Sämtliche Werke*, 1: 322.

58. For an account of Babel as the figure not only of "the inadequation of one tongue to another" but "of language to itself and to meaning," see Derrida, "Des Tours de Babel," in *Acts of Religion*, ed. Gil Anidjar (New York: Routledge, 2002), 104–33. For an insightful commentary on the role of forgetting in the Babelic *confusion* (and thus of its relation to historical time), see the last section of Daniel Heller-Roazen, *Echolalias: On the Forgetting of Language* (New York: Zone Books, 2005), 219–31.

59. Pap. 1: A 328; JN, CC, 12.

60. John Durham Peters has noted the peculiar status of the concept of "communication" in Kierkegaard and pointed out how it is bound up with misunderstanding, arguing that "what Kierkegaard calls communication looks more like obfuscation or breakdown to those used to a technical or therapeutic understanding." See the chapter on Kierkegaard in *Speaking into the Air: A History of the Idea of Communication* (Chicago: University of Chicago Press, 1999), 127–35.

61. Genesis 11: 1–9. Derrida undertakes a close reading of the text in its relation to the problem of translation and incommensurability in "Tours de Babel," 104–8.

62. Hamann, Letter to Lindner, 9 August 1759, in *Briefwechsel*, ed. Arthur Henkel, vol. 1 (Frankfurt am Main, 1965), 394.

63. In his response to the "Morning Observations" and Kierkegaard's second article, Lehmann concedes that the writer of the article may have a "genuinely unmistakable talent for use of powerful language and spirited imagery" but complains that the "kernel is hidden within a very thick shell." See Orla Lehmann, "Reply to Mr. B. of the *Flyvende Post*," in EPW, 152–59.

64. Pap. 1: A 328; JN CC: 12.

65. GW 3: 13; PS, 2.

66. Pap. 2: A 583; JN FF: 34.

67. One is reminded here of Kierkegaard's later remark, in the reading of Genesis in *The Concept of Anxiety*, that "the speaker is language." For a discussion of this remark, see Fenves, *"Chatter"*, 77–84.

68. Pap. 1: A 328; JN CC: 12.

69. Pap. 1: A 328; JN CC: 12.

70. See Pap. 2: B 1–22; EPW, 105–24. For a detailed discussion of the context in which Kierkegaard wrote the play, which is known under its earlier title "The Battle between the Old and the New Soap-Cellars," see Garff, *Søren Kierkegaard*, 80–86. With regards to the character of "The Horn," Kierkegaard may have had in mind the lines that he cites in a note of the same period: "A hunter blew hard into his

horn,/Hard into his horn,/And everything he blew was/Lost." (Cited in Garff, *Søren Kierkegaard*, 78.)

71. Pap. 1: A 328; JN CC: 12.

72. See Pap. 2: B 1; EPW, 106. The character of Hastværksen is based on Orla Lehmann, the journalist under attack in the "Morning Observations"; the first name of the character, Holla, which was added at later stages of the manuscript, may be derived from the resemblance in sound and spelling to Orla.

73. The image of the talking machine is introduced in the section on "spiritlessness" of *The Concept of Anxiety*. See SV 4: 364; *The Concept of Anxiety*, trans. Reidar Thomte and Albert A. Anderson (Princeton: Princeton University Press, 1980), 95. Further references to the latter title will appear as CA.

74. John Durham Peters, in his history of the idea of communication, describes Kierkegaard—along with Marx—as one of the first thinkers who, despite his sparse remarks on media and technology, "make us face the clefts at the heart of what we too often want to dream of as the immediate sympathy of angels." See *Speaking into the Air*, 135.

75. Pap. 1: A 328; JN CC: 12.

76. For a detailed analysis of the role of "reading" in Hegel and its intimate relation to the figure of eating, see Hamacher, *Pleroma*, 1–80.

77. Peter Fenves offers an account of the relation between Kierkegaard's concept of "chatter" and the "newer development" that spans from Kant to Hegel in the introductory chapter to his *"Chatter,"* 14–18.

78. Pap. 1: A 328; JN CC: 12.

79. SV 13: 29; EPW, 30.

80. In his response to the "Morning Observations," Orla Lehmann complains precisely about the threat of such immobility. If the conflict staged in Kierkegaard's article were to be perpetuated, constructed as it is around a "system of taking particular articles, sometimes even particular phrases, from an article, in order to point out particular actual or supposed contradictions," so Lehmann warns, "the press would waste away without advancing a single step." Lehmann, "Reply to Mr. B.," in EPW, 152–53.

81. SV 13: 214; *The Concept of Irony*, trans. Howard V. Hong and Edna H. Hong (Princeton: Princeton University Press, 1989), 128. Hereafter cited as CI.

82. SV 2: 18; *Either/Or*, trans. D. F. and L. M. Swenson and D. W. Lowrie (Princeton: Princeton University Press, 1959), 2: 19.

83. Pap. 1: A 328; JN CC: 12.

84. SV 13: 15; EPW, 11.

85. In a diary entry from the same period, Kierkegaard distinguishes "philosophy" and "Christianity" on the basis of their relation to this "deficiency": "Christianity stipulates the deficiency of human cognition due to sin, which is then rectified in Christianity" (Pap. I A 94; AA, 13).

86. Pap. 1: A 94; JN AA: 13.

87. Pap. 1: A 328; JN CC: 12.

88. Pap. 1: A 328; JN CC: 12.

89. In a journal fragment from the same period, Kierkegaard referred to Hamann as an example of such "sparing" use of language. "Just as Socrates left no books, Hamann left only as much as the modern period's rage for writing [*den nyere Tids Skrivesyge*] made relatively necessary, and furthermore only occasional pieces [*Leilighedsskrifter*]" (Pap. 2: A 138; DD, 37).

90. Hamann, *Sämtliche Werke*, 2: 176.

91. Pap. 1: A 328; JN CC: 12.

92. Szondi touches on the relation between language and time harbored in Kierkegaard's theory of irony in his study of Romantic irony in *Satz und Gegensatz: Sechs Essays* (Frankfurt am Main: Suhrkamp, 1976), 5–18. An alternative account of this relation is provided by Paul de Man in his essay "The Rhetoric of Temporality," in *Blindness and Insight* (London: Routledge, 1983), 187–228.

93. The importance of the concept of the instant for Kierkegaard is often noted but curiously enough only rarely examined in detail. For a comprehensive discussion of the role of the concept throughout Kierkegaard's work, see David Kangas, *Kierkegaard's Instant: On Beginnings* (Bloomington: Indiana University Press, 2007).

94. Kierkegaard had begun his final polemic with several articles in the *Fatherland* but, in 1855, decided to start what a contemporary would describe as "a sort of journal." For a discussion of the broader context in which Kierkegaard began publishing this *Blad* and the development of his polemic, see Garff, 752–81.

95. The term occurs throughout *The Instant*; already in the first issue, for instance, Kierkegaard refers to his polemic as a "protest against the existing" (*Indsigelse mod det Bestaaende*). Apart from designating the "established order" against which Kierkegaard will direct his final polemic, the term can also be read in the more technical, philosophical sense, in which it is, as we will see, closely related to the concept of the instant.

96. SV 14: 115a.

97. SV 11: B 142.

98. See, for instance, SV 14: 358–63 and 217–19.

99. See SV 14: 189–90 and 211–14.

100. The relation between historicity, anxiety, and language is discussed in detail in the chapter on *The Concept of Anxiety* in Peter Fenves's *"Chatter"*, 75–84.

101. See, for instance, SV 4: 293; CA, 21 and SV 4: 341; CA, 7.

102. Kierkegaard cites the passage in a footnote to the last page of the book: "This anxiety in the world is the only proof of our heterogeneity. [. . .] This impertinent disquiet, this holy hypochondria is perhaps the fire with which we season sacrificial animals in order to preserve us from the putrefaction of the current *seculi*" (SV 4: 427; CA, 162).

103. This restlessness is articulated in an exemplary manner in the *Phenomenology*: "Consciousness [. . .] is something that goes beyond itself. [. . .] If it wishes to remain in a state of unthinking inertia, then thought troubles its thoughtlessness, and its own unrest disturbs its inertia" (GW 3: 75; PS, 51).

104. "As for time, it is the existent concept itself" (GW 3: 45–46; PS, 27). For a detailed discussion of Hegel's concept of time and its relation to the classical Aristotelian notion of time, see Derrida, "*Ousia* and *Grammē*: Note on a Note from *Being and Time*," in *Margins of Philosophy*, trans. Alan Bass (Chicago: University of Chicago Press, 1982), 206–19.

105. SV 4: 417; CA, 152.

106. Cf. SV 4: 360; CA, 90.

107. SV 4: 355; CA, 85.

108. SV 4: 355; CA, 85.

109. This aporia is already described in Aristotle's account of time in his *Physics*. "In one sense it has been and is no longer, and in another sense, it will be and is not yet." *Physics*, 217b.

110. SV 4: 355; CA, 85.

111. GW 3: 84; PS, 59–60.

112. GW 3: 84; PS, 60. Hegel introduces the model of writing by proposing a peculiar "experiment": "In order to test the truth of this sensuous certainty a simple experiment is all that is required. We write this truth down; a truth cannot be lost by writing it down; any more than it can be lost by our perceiving it. When we look again *now*, *today*, at the written truth, we shall have to say that it has become stale."

113. For a detailed discussion of the role of writing and reading in the dialectic of sense-certainty and Hegel's account of time consciousness, see Hamacher, *Pleroma*, 206–19.

114. SV 4: 355; CA, 85.

115. SV 4: 355; CA, 85.

116. GW 12: 204; PhH, 163.

117. Cf. SV 4: 357; CA, 87 and SV 4: 360; CA, 90.

118. SV 4: 359; CA, 89.

119. SV 4: 356; CA, 86.

120. SV 4: 359; CA, 89.

121. "The eternal, even though it is incommensurable with time, nevertheless preserves its commerce with time." SV 4: 359; CA, 89.

122. See, for instance, the references to Boethius's account of the divine foreknowledge of the future in various notebook entries of 1843–44, especially Pap. 4: C 62 and Pap. 5: B 15.

123. Boethius, *De Trinitate*, Chapter 5, in *Theological Tractates and The Consolation of Philosophy*, ed. H. F. Stewart, E. K. Rand, and S. J. Tester (Cambridge: Harvard University Press, 1973), 20.64–22.7; trans. Eleonore Stump and Norman Kretzmann, "Eternity," *The Journal of Philosophy* 78, no. 8 (August 1981), 430–31.

124. Boethius, *Philosophiae consolationis*, Book V, Prose 6, in *Theological Tractates and The Consolation of Philosophy*, 422.5–424.31, trans. Stump and Kretzmann, "Eternity," 430.

125. SV 4: 356; CA, 86.

126. SV 4: 356–57; CA, 87.

127. SV 4: 356; CA, 86.

128. SV 4: 90; CA, 90.

129. For a brief but insightful discussion of the eternal in Hegel, see Derrida, "*Ousia* and *Grammē*," 45–46.

130. SV 4: 358; CA, 88.

131. SV 4: 357; CA, 87. For an alternative reading of this passage, see the chapter on *The Concept of Anxiety* in Kangas, *Kierkegaard's Instant*, 185–86.

132. SV 4: 358; CA, 88.

133. SV 13: 279; CI, 198.

134. Pap. 1: A 73; JN AA: 12.

135. Aristophanes, *Plutus*, in *Lysistrata. Thesmophoriazusae. Ecclesiazusae. Plutus* (Cambridge: Harvard University Press), 1.210.

136. Johann Wolfgang Goethe, *Faust. Erster und Zweiter Teil* (Frankfurt am Main: Insel Verlag, 1998), 405–6. In 1835, Kierkegaard had begun working on a never finished study on Faust that was to rescue an older, medieval version of Faust from Goethe's rendering of the figure, which in Kierkegaard's reading ended up betraying its significance as a figure of irreconcilability, despair, and the limits of human comprehension. For a general outline of Kierkegaard's abandoned project, see Garff, *Søren Kierkegaard*, 74–80.

137. SV 4: 358–59; CA, 88–89.

138. The third section of the introduction consists of three sections—"The principle of development" (*Das Prinzip der Entwicklung*), "The beginning of history" (*Anfang der Geschichte*), and "The course of history" (*Gang der Geschichte*). See GW 12: 11–28; PhH, 54–79.

139. SV 4: 359; CA, 89.

140. Derrida discusses the radically unknowable and unforeseeable character of Kierkegaard's concept of the future in his essay "Whom to Give to (Knowing Not to Know)," in *Kierkegaard: A Critical Reader*, ed. Jane Chamberlain and Jonathan Rée (London: Wiley-Blackwell, 1997), 153–74.

141. SV 4: 359; CA, 89. For a discussion of the occurrence of the notion of interruption in Kierkegaard's early text *On the Papers of One Still Living*, see Peter Fenves, "*Chatter*", 61–63.

142. SV 4: 358; CA, 88.

143. SV 4: 358; CA, 88.

144. SV 4: 357; CA, 87.

145. SV 4: 355; CA, 85.

146. SV 4: 351; CA, 82. "Plato conceives of the instant purely abstractly. To orient oneself in its dialectic, one should keep in mind that the instant is nonbeing under the category of time. Nonbeing (*to mē on, to kenon* of the Pythagoreans) occupied ancient philosophers as much as it does modern philosophers."

147. SV 4: 358; CA, 88.

148. SV 4: 359; CA, 89.

149. SV 4: 359; CA, 89.

150. SV 4: 360; CA, 90.

151. SV 4: 360; CA, 90.

152. SV 13: 374; CI, 306.

153. See SV 13: 320; CI, 244.

154. Pap. 2: A 102; JN DD: 18.

155. SV 13: 349; CI, 277.

156. SV 13: 206; CI, 120.

157. SV 13: 206n; CI, 120.

158. SV 13: 249; CI, 165.

159. SV 13: 374; CI, 306.

160. SV 13: 374; CI, 306.

161. SV 13: 374; CI, 306.

162. SV 13: 334–35; CI, 260. The remarks stem from a passage discussing what it means to understand Socrates—who is for Kierkegaard, as for Hamann, the ancient polemicist par excellence—as a "historical turning point" (*historisk Vendepunkt*), which leads Kierkegaard to expound the difference between the "prophetic individual" and the "ironical subject" who exemplifies the specific temporal structure that Kierkegaard associates with the polemic.

163. SV 13: 334–35; CI, 260.

164. Pap. 1: A 340; JN CC: 25.

165. SV 4: 176; *Philosophical Fragments* and *Johannes Climacus*, trans. Howard V. Hong and Edna H. Hong (Princeton: Princeton University Press, 1985), 3.

166. Pap. 1: A 340; JN CC: 25.

2. Idolatry of Facts: Nietzsche

1. *Werke: Kritische Studienausgabe in 15 Bänden*, ed. Giorgio Colli and Mazzino Montinari (Berlin: Walter de Gruyter, 1988), 7: 27[20], Spring–Autumn 1873. Further references to this title will appear as KSA.

2. KSA 7: 35[12], Spring–Summer 1874.

3. KSA 7: 32[4], Early 1874–Spring 1874. The exact number of *Untimely Meditations* that Nietzsche planned to publish varies; the most elaborated outlines included in his notebooks refer to thirteen installments.

4. See KSA 4: 63 and 223; *Thus Spoke Zarathustra*, trans. Adrian del Caro (Cambridge: Cambridge University Press, 2006), 35 and 140–41. Further references to the latter volume will appear as Z. During the period in which he was working on his *Zarathustra*, Nietzsche still seems to have planned a philosophical work that would undertake an "attack" (*Attentat*)—the same word he would later use to describe his *Untimely Meditations*—on the press as a modern phenomenon. "An attack on the entire modern press (*Preßwesen*) lies in the domain of my future tasks," he writes in an 1884 letter. See *Sämtliche Briefe: Kritische Studienausgabe in 8 Bänden*, ed. Giorgio Colli and Mazzino Montinari (Berlin: Walter de

Gruyter, 1986), 4: §516, Letter to Malwide von Meysenbug, June 1884. (Cited hereafter as KSB.)

5. An exception to this widespread tendency among earlier readers of Nietzsche is provided by Martin Heidegger, who underlines the importance of understanding Nietzsche's preoccupation with journalism in relation to the major "rubrics" of his thought. See especially *Nietzsche*, ed. and trans. David Farrell Krell (San Francisco: Harper, 1991), 4: 240–43.

6. A typical case of these two common divisions of Nietzsche's work is provided by Walter Kaufmann's *Nietzsche: Philosopher, Psychologist, Antichrist* (Princeton: Princeton University Press, 1974).

7. See Heidegger, *Nietzsche*, 4: 241. The most important readers of Nietzsche on the other side of the Rhine—especially Derrida, Deleuze and Foucault—are undoubtedly aware of the philosophical significance of Nietzsche's polemic with journalism but never elaborate this as a theme in its own right. See, for instance, Jacques Derrida and Bernard Stiegler, *Echographies of Television*, trans. Jennifer Bajorek (Cambridge: Polity, 2002), 8–10; Gilles Deleuze, *Negotiations*, trans. Martin Joughin (New York: Columbia University Press, 1995), 137–38 and 153–54; Michel Foucault, *Dits et écrits*, ed. Daniel Defert and François Ewald, vol. 2 (Paris: Éditions Gallimard, 1994), 1302.

8. For a discussion of the role of typology and figurative language in Nietzsche's work, see Philippe Lacoue-Labarthe's study *Typography: Mimesis, Philosophy, Politics*, ed. and trans. Christopher Fynsk (Cambridge: Harvard University Press, 1989), 43–138.

9. See KSA 7: 27[20], Spring–Autumn 1873.

10. KSA 1: 362; *Untimely Meditations*, trans. R. J. Hollingdale (Cambridge: Cambridge University Press, 1995), 3: §3. Further references to the latter title will appear as UM.

11. KSA 6: 274; *Ecce Homo*, in *The Anti-Christ, Ecce Homo, Twilight of the Idols*, trans. Judith Norman (Cambridge: Cambridge University Press, 2007), "Why I Am So Wise," §7. Further references to the latter title will appear as EH.

12. KSA 1: 362; UM 3: §3.

13. KSB 5: §490, 1875; Letter to Erwin Rohde, October 7, 1875.

14. KSB 6: §66, 1880; Letter to Franz Overbeck.

15. KSB 6: §286, 1882; Letter to Theodor Curti.

16. "In Zürich the Barometer indicated 751; in Bern it was 765. 751 was the minimum in Europa, according to the newspapers" (KSB V: §849, 1879; Letter to Elisabeth Nietzsche); "I attach an excerpt from a Berlin newspaper, which may be interesting because of the different understanding of Carmen" (KSB 6: §311, 1882; Letter to Lou von Salomé, September 26, 1882).

17. Foucault formulates this question for the first time in a reflection on Nietzsche included in a short article of 1873 titled "Le monde est un grand asile," included in *Dits et écrits*, vol. 2, 1302. The formulation of the question cited here is taken from his later lecture series at the Collège de France, *The Government of Self*

NOTES TO PAGES 74–78

and Others, ed. Fréderic Gors, trans. Graham Burchell (Houndmills: Palgrave Macmillan), 2011.

18. Foucault, Dits et écrits, vol. 2, 1302.

19. KSA 1: 346; UM 3: §2.

20. Like Schopenhauer, Nietzsche's other "untimely type par excellence," Wagner was a virulent critic of journalism. In a 1966 text, Wagner holds "journalism" responsible for the "introducing the modern" into the "cultural development" of Germany (Richard Wagner, "'Modern,'" 178). The anti-Semitic dimension of Wagner's attacks on journalism—implicitly or explicitly it is always *jüdische Journalistik* that is guilty of the degeneration of German culture—is discussed in detail in the sections on the "case of Wagner" in Paul Reitter's book on Karl Kraus, *The Anti-Journalist: Karl Kraus and Jewish Self-Fashioning in fin-de-siècle Europe* (Chicago: University of Chicago Press, 2008), 53–59.

21. KSB 3: §22, Letter to Erwin Rohde, August 17, 1869.

22. See KSA 7: 19[330], Summer 1872–Early 1873 for an early plan of the *Untimely Meditations*.

23. KSA 1: 247; UM 2: Preface.

24. KSA 6: 316; EH, "Why I Write Such Great Books," "The Untimelies," §1. For a detailed analysis of Nietsche's later rereading of the *Untimely Meditations*, see Sarah Kofman, *Explosion II: Les enfants de Nietzsche* (Paris: Editions Galilée, 1993), 133–74.

25. KSA 6: 111–53; *Twilight of the Idols*, in *The Anti-Christ, Ecce Homo, Twilight of the Idols*, trans. Judith Norman (Cambridge: Cambridge University Press, 2007), "Wanderings of an Untimely," §1–51. Further references to the latter title will appear as TI.

26. The reference is to the full title of the book: *Twilight of the Idols, or How one Philosophizes with a Hammer*. (KSA 6: 55; TI, 1)

27. See for instance Deleuze, *Negotiations*, 137–38, and Derrida, *Echographies of Television*, 8–10 or, more recently, Giorgio Agamben, "What Is the Contemporary?," in *What Is an Apparatus?*, trans. David Kishik and Stefan Pedatella (Stanford: Stanford University Press, 2009), 39–40.

28. G. W. F. Hegel, *Werke* (Frankfurt am Main: Suhrkamp, 1970), 3: 26; *Elements of the Philosophy of Right*, ed. Allen Wood, trans. H. B. Nisbet (Cambridge: Cambridge University Press, 1991), 15.

29. KSA 1: 362; UM 3: §3.

30. KSA 7: 30[25], Autumn 1873–Winter 1873–74.

31. KSB 4: §313, 1873; Letter to Richard Wagner, September 18, 1873. See also the letters to Eugen Kretzen, Hugo von Senger, and Erwin Rohde from November 1873, where Nietzsche uses the same play of words in three letters.

32. "The journalist, the paper slave of the day" (KSA 1: 130; *The Birth of Tragedy and Other Writings*, trans. Ronald Speirs [Cambridge: Cambridge University Press, 1999], §20). "Helpless barbarian, slave of the day, put on the chain of the present moment, and thirsting for something, ever thirsting!" (KSA 1: 747, "On the Future

of Our Educational Institutions," in *Anti-Education: On the Future of Our Educational Institutions*, ed. Paul Reitter and Chad Wellmon, trans. Damion Searles (New York: New York Review of Books, 2015), §5. Further references to the latter title will appear as FE. "In the newspaper (*Journal*) the peculiar educational aims of the present culminate, just as the journalist, the servant of the moment, has stepped into the place of the genius, of the leaders for all time, of the deliverer from the tyranny of the moment" (KSA 1: 671; FE, §1). "The most important thing about wisdom is that it prevents human beings from being ruled by the moment. It is consequently not newspaperish (*zeitungsgemäss*) [. . .]" (KSA 7: 30[25], Autumn 1873–Winter 1873–74).

33. KSA 7: 32[4], Early 1874–Spring 1874.

34. On Nietzsche's remarks on colonialism and modern slavery, see Robert Bernasconi, "Nietzsche as a Philosopher of Racialized Breeding," in *The Oxford Handbook on Philosophy of Race*, ed. Naomi Zack (Oxford: Oxford University Press, 2017), 54–64.

35. See, for instance: KSB 4: §313, 1873; Letter to Richard Wagner, September 18, 1873.

36. This is overlooked when the *Untimely Meditations* are said to employ the "traditional form" of the numbered essay. Just as Nietzsche's later writings work within and against the book, so these early *Hefte* can be said to announce a writing within and against journalistic form, together with the relation between thought and its time that it exemplified for Nietzsche.

37. KSB 4: §313, 1873; Letter to Richard Wagner, September 18, 1873.

38. Cf. KSA 1: 222; UM 1: §11. "The fabricators of these newspapers are however [. . .] most accustomed to the slime of this newspaper language [*Zeitungs-Sprache*]."

39. KSA 1: 222; UM 1: §11.

40. KSA 7: 27[62], Spring–Fall 1873.

41. KSA 1: 671; FE, §1.

42. "Just like every human being has a physiognomy [. . .] so ever age has a physiognomy that is no less characteristic. For the spirit of a time is in each case like a sharp wind from the east that blows through everything." Schopenhauer, *Parerga und Paralipomena* (Frankfurt: Suhrkamp Verlag, 1986), 529–30.

43. KSA 7: 37[6], Late 1874: "The impoverishment and paling of language is a symptom of the waning universal soul [*der verkümmerten allgemeinen Seele*]." Cf. also the fourth *Untimely Meditation*: "Everywhere language is sick, and the oppression of this tremendous sickness now weighs on the whole of human development" (KSA 1: 455; UM 4: §5).

44. For a detailed exposition of Nietzsche's study of rhetoric and its impact on his early work, see especially Lacoue-Labarthe, "The Detour," in *The Subject of Philosophy*, trans. Thomas Trezise (Minneapolis: University of Minnesota Press, 1993), 14–18; and Kofman, *Nietzsche and Metaphor*, trans. Duncan Large (London: Athlone Press, 1993), 6–58. On the continued importance of the theory of rhetoric in Nietzsche's later work, see Paul de Man, *Allegories of Reading: Figural Language*

in Rousseau, Nietzsche, Rilke and Proust (New Haven: Yale University Press, 1979), 103–33.

45. KSA 1: 879; *Friedrich Nietzsche on Rhetoric and Language,* trans. Sander L. Gilman et al. (Oxford: Oxford University Press, 1989), 248–49. Further references to the latter title will appear as RL.

46. KSA 1: 879; RL, 248–49.

47. Kofman provides a detailed analysis of Nietzsche's critique of conceptuality and his account of the "metaphorical activity" that precedes it in her essay "The Forgetting of Metaphor," in *Nietzsche and Metaphor,* 23–39.

48. KSA 1: 880; RL, 249.

49. KSA 7: 37[7], Late 1874.

50. KSA 1: 877; RL, 247.

51. "Fragments sur le langage," trans. Philippe Lacoue-Labarthe and Jean Luc Nancy, *Poétique* 5 (1971): 133. Further references to this title will appear as FL.

52. FL, 133.

53. For a detailed discussion of the role of concept and metaphor in the understanding of the "proper," see Derrida, "White Mythology: Metaphor in the Text of Philosophy," in *Margins of Philosophy,* trans. Alan Bass (Chicago: University of Chicago Press, 1982), 207–72.

54. KSA 1: 887; RL, 254.

55. KSA 1: 887; RL, 254.

56. KSA 1: 455; UM 4: §5.

57. KSA 1: 877; RL, 247.

58. KSA 7: 37[7], Late 1874.

59. KSA 1: 455; UM 4: §5.

60. KSA 1: 889; RL, 256.

61. KSA 7: 37[7], Late 1874.

62. On the relation between uniformity and the opening up of history in Nietzsche's early writings, see Werner Hamacher, "'Disgregation of the Will': Nietzsche on the Individual and Individuality," in *Premises: Essays on Philosophy and Literature from Kant to Celan,* trans. Peter Fenves (Cambridge: Harvard University Press, 1996), 143–48.

63. KSA 1: 222; UM 1: §11.

64. For a discussion of the tension between Nietzsche's theory of the musical aspect of language and its rhetorical origin, see Lacoue-Labarthe, "The Detour," 30–31.

65. KSA 7: 27[68], Spring–Autumn 1873.

66. KSA 7: 37[7], Late 1874.

67. KSA 7: 37[6], Late 1874. Nietzsche explicitly returns to this point later in his notes for the unfinished *Untimely Meditation*: "The impoverishment and paling of language is a symptom of the languished general soul [. . .], even though the great uniformity in word and trope can appear to be the opposite, as the gaining of a common soul" (KSA 7: 36[7], Late 1874).

68. KSA 1: 462; UM IV: §6.

69. KSA 7: 35[12], Spring–Summer 1874.

70. This "haste" is a recurrent trope in Nietzsche's writings of the period, where it is often associated with journalism. In an earlier note, this haste is still characterized in organic terms as an "unripeness": "Haste, unripeness, the journalist" (KSA 7: 8[89], Winter 1870/71–Autumn 1872).

71. KSA 1: 684; FE, §2.

72. KSA 1: 329; UM 2: §10.

73. KSA 1: 329; UM 2: §10.

74. KSA 7: 27[68], Spring–Autumn 1873.

75. KSA 1: 889; RL, 256.

76. "But their critical pens never cease to flow, for they have lost control of them and instead of directing them are directed by them" (KSA 1: 285; UM 2: §5).

77. Lacoue-Labarthe examines the lingering opposition of speech and writing in Nietzsche's writings after his studies on rhetoric in his essay "Apocryphal Nietzsche," in *The Subject of Philosophy*, 47–55.

78. KSA 1: 222; UM 1: §11.

79. KSA 7: 27[62], Spring–Autumn 1873.

80. KSA 3: 480–82; *The Gay Science*, trans. Josephine Nauckhoff (Cambridge: Cambridge University Press, 2008), §125. Further references to the latter title will appear as GSC.

81. On the death of God as *Wort* and *Satz*, see Heidegger, "Nietzsches Wort 'Gott ist tot,'" in *Holzwege* (Frankfurt am Main: Klostermann, 1950), 209–68. For a general exposition of the death of God and Nietzsche's theory of nihilism, see Heidegger, *Nietzsche*, Vol. 4, 3–57.

82. KSA 3: 574; GSC, §343. In the later *Beyond Good and Evil*, Nietzsche also refers to the death of God as a "novelty" (*Neuigkeit*). See KSA 5: 238; *Beyond Good and Evil*, trans. Judith Norman (Cambridge: Cambridge University Press, 2007), §295.

83. In this respect, Nietzsche's messenger has a noteworthy affinity with the technology that he describes in a well-known aphorism as one of the "premises of the machine age" whose "thousand-year conclusion no one has yet dared to draw": the telegraph (KSA 2: 674; *Human, All Too Human: A Book for free Spirits*, trans. R. J. Hollingdale (Cambridge: Cambridge University Press, 1996), 2: §278). The telegraph, as the technique of writing at a distance that was central to the emergence of the modern news industry, did not require that its operators understood the meaning of the message conveyed, or even its grammatical or syntactical structure; in this sense, the telegraph demonstrates an indifference toward meaning not unlike the one that is, in Nietzsche's reflections on the rumorous news of the death of God, associated with language. On the role of the telegraph in the nineteenth-century transformation of the concept of "information," see John Durham Peters, "Information: Notes Toward a Critical History," *Journal of Communication Inquiry* 12, no. 9 (1988): 9–23; and Bernard Geoghegan, "Information," in Benjamin

Peters, ed., *Digital Keywords: A Vocabulary of Information Society & Culture* (Princeton: Princeton University Press, 2016), 175–77. Friedrich Kittler, of course, associates this moment in Nietzsche's thinking and writing not with the telegraph but with the typewriter in his study *Gramophone, Film, Typewriter*, trans. Geoffrey Winthrop-Young and Michael Wutz (Stanford: Stanford University Press, 1999), 183–214.

84. For an interpretation of the death of God as an "event of disappropriation" that plays out in language and must be understood as an "ongoing event" in all speaking, see Werner Hamacher, "'Disgregation of the Will': Nietzsche on the Individual and Individuality," 169–72.

85. KSA 3: 574; GSC, §343.

86. Blanchot refers to the "fragmentary speech" that for him characterizes Nietzsche's work as "barely speech—speech only at the limit." See Blanchot, "The Limit-Experience," in *The Infinite Conversation*, trans. Susan Hanson (Minneapolis: University of Minnesota Press), 159–60.

87. KSA 4: 14; Z, 5.

88. KSA 4: 167–71; Z, 102–5.

89. KSB 2: §480, Letter to Hermann Mushacke, September 20, 1865.

90. Tertullian, *Ad Nationes*, trans. Q. Howe, 1:7, 2007, Tertullian Project, accessed June 20, 2017, http://www.tertullian.org/articles/howe_adnationes1.htm.

91. KSA 3: 574; GSC, §343.

92. Heidegger discusses Nietzsche's understanding of idolatry in relation to the death of God in "Nietzsches Wort 'Gott ist tot,'" 209–68.

93. KSA 1: 309; UM 4: §8.

94. KSA 1: 309; UM 4: §8.

95. KSA 1: 309; UM 4: §8.

96. Nietzsche's remarks on the "idolatry of facts" may be read in the context of the nineteenth-century mystique of the telegraph and other new communication technologies. As John Durham Peters remarks, the electrical telegraph, as the technology bound up with the image of a factuality untouched by human interference, "seemed the latest in a long tradition of angels and divinities who spirit intelligence across vast distances." See *Speaking into the Air* (Chicago: University of Chicago Press, 1999), 94.

97. KSA 1: 309; UM 4: §8.

98. KSA 1: 309; UM 4: §8.

99. Rebecca Comay draws out the tension between the "idolatry of the factual" and the "plasticity of the moment" in the second *Untimely Meditation* in her essay "Redeeming Revenge: Nietzsche, Benjamin, Heidegger, and the Politics of Memory," in *Nietzsche as Postmodernist: Essays Pro and Contra*, ed. Clayton Koelb (New York: State University of New York Press, 1990), 28–30.

100. KSA 5: 399–400; GM 3: §24.

101. KSA 1: 308; UM 4: §8.

102. KSA 5: 399; GM 3: §24.

103. KSA 5: 400; GM 3: §24.

104. On the "presentism" characteristic of journalism, the "positive fact" and the fetishism of force that underpin it, see Hamacher, "Journals, Politics," in *Responses: On Paul de Man's Wartime Journalism*, ed. Werner Hamacher, Neil Hertz, and Thomas Keenan (Lincoln: University of Nebraska Press, 1989), 453–54.

105. KSA 7: 35[12].

106. KSA 10: 3[1] 250, Summer–Fall 1882. In his lecture series on Nietzsche, Heidegger cites this note in his exposition of the distinction between affect and passion, treating it as a mere paraphrase of Nietzsche's claim that "our age is an agitated one, and precisely for that reason not an age of passion" (*Nietzsche*, 1: 47).

107. KSA 10: 3[1] 248, Summer–Fall 1882.

108. KSA 1: 431; UM 4: §1.

109. KSA 1: 431; UM 4: §1.

110. KSA 5: 279; GM 1: §13.

111. KSA 5: 279; GM 1: §13. Hamacher offers a detailed interpretation of this example and the "doubling" by which language "separates the occurrence from itself" in his essay "The Promise of Interpretation," in *Premises: Essays on Philosophy and Literature from Kant to Celan*, trans. Peter Fenves (Cambridge: Harvard University Press, 1996), 117–19.

112. KSA 13: 15[90]—Spring 1888. For a detailed analysis of this "chronological reversal" and its relation to Nietzsche's theory of rhetoric, see De Man, *Allegories of Reading*, 107–8.

113. KSA 1: 279; UM 2: §5.

114. Cf. Lacoue-Labarthe, "The Detour," 14–18.

115. KSA 10: 16[78], Autumn 1883.

116. KSA 13: 11[411], November 1887—March 1888.

117. For a detailed discussion of Nietzsche's perspectivism, see Alexander Nehamas, *Nietzsche: Life as Literature* (Cambridge: Harvard University Press, 1985), 15–17.

118. De Man provides an exposition of this reversal of cause and effect in his study of metonymy in Nietzsche. See *Allegories of Reading: Figural Language in Rousseau, Nietzsche, Rilke and Proust* (New Haven: Yale University Press, 1979), 103–18.

119. KSA 3: 224–25; *Daybreak: Thoughts on the Prejudices of Morality*, trans. R. J. Hollingdale (Cambridge: Cambridge University Press, 1997), §307.

120. RL, 23.

121. KSB 6: §40, Letter to Heinrich Köselitz, August 14, 1880.

122. KSA 11: 34[65], April–June 1885.

123. KSA 11: 35[9], May–July 1885.

124. KSA 5: 255; *On the Genealogy of Morality*, trans. Carol Diethe (Cambridge: Cambridge University Press, 1997), Preface §8. Further references to the latter title will appear as GM.

125. KSB VI6: §190, Letter to Heinrich Köselitz, August 17, 1881.

126. For a detailed analysis of the relation between reading, rumination, and return in Nietzsche, see Hamacher, *Pleroma: Reading in Hegel*, trans. Nicholas Walker and Simon Jarvis (Stanford: Stanford University Press, 1998), 277–86.

127. On Nietzsche's "eternal return" as an impossible repetition of the same, see Pierre Klossowksi's seminal essay "The Experience of the Eternal Return," included in *Nietzsche and the Vicious Circle*, trans. Daniel W. Smith (Chicago: University of Chicago Press, 1979), 55–73. For a critique of the ontological interpretation of the eternal return as a new metaphysics of time or the totality of being—Heidegger's claim—see Derrida, *The Ear of the Other: Otobiography, Transference, Translation*, ed. Christie V. MacDonald, trans. Peggy Kamuf (New York: Schocken Books, 1985), 45–46.

128. KSA 1: 643; FE, Preface. For a brief commentary on this passage and the "anachronistic reading" demanded by it, see Derrida, *The Ear of the Other*, 22–26.

129. KSA 5: 255; GM, Preface §8.

130. On the "iterability" or "repeatability" of writing as a priori condition of the possibility of reading, see Derrida, "Signature Event Context," in *Margins of Philosophy*, 307–30. For Derrida, the "iterability" that must accompany the intelligibility of the mark is never a self-same repetition but implies both "repetition *and* alteration."

131. KSA 1: 832.

132. Schopenhauer, *Parerga und Paralipomena* (Frankfurt: Suhrkamp Verlag, 1986), 2: 657.

133. For an account of the relation between the motif of nausea, finitude, and reading, see Hamacher, *Pleroma*, 280–86. Derrida comments briefly on the role of "nausea" (*Ekel*) and the "want to vomit" in Nietzsche's early writings in *The Ear of the Other*, 23–24.

134. KSA 13: 11[17], November 1887–March 1888. Nietzsche's notes suggest that this is to be read as a general medical term, not as a reference to the morning sickness of the pregnant. For a discussion of morning sickness as a trope of historical experience, see Rebecca Comay, *Mourning Sickness: Hegel and the French Revolution* (Stanford: Stanford University Press, 2011), 138–39.

135. KSA 13: 11[218], November 1887–March 1888.

136. KSA 4: 63; Z, 35.

137. KSA 4: 223; Z, 140–41.

138. In his correspondence, Nietzsche finds it important to recall that the newspapers treat *Beyond Good and Evil*, the book he wrote immediately after his *Zarathustra*, as a threat: "my 'dangerous book,' as the newspapers like to call it" (*mein 'gefährliches Buch' wie es die Zeitungen nennen*). (KSB 7: §760, 1886; Letter to Franziska Nietzsche, October 10, 1886.)

139. KSA 13: 11[218], November 1887–March 1888.

140. A more detailed exposition of the figure of the *letzte Mensch* and its relation to the *Übermensch* is found in Blanchot, "The Limit-Experience," 143–51 and 155–56. "The thought of the overman does not first of all signify the advent of the overman, but rather the disappearance of something called man" (155).

141. KSA 4: 18–21; Z, 9–11.

142. KSA 4: 18; Z, 9.

143. When Nietzsche is asked by his publisher whether his forthcoming Zarathustra is to be advertised in the newspaper, he responds with caution: "A preliminary announcement [*vorläufige Anzeige*] I would find advisable. No promotion [*keine Reclame*], dear Mr. Schmeitzner—this would undermine the 'overhuman' nobility of the Zarathustra-tendencies" (KSB 6: §399, 1883; Letter to Ernst Schmeitzner, April 2, 1883).

144. Cf. Lacoue-Labarthe's analysis of the death of Dionysus—the god of presence that animated the work of the early 1870s—as such a "fact of language" in "The Detour," 31–36.

145. KSA 1: 365; UM 3: §4.

146. KSA 1: 462; UM 4: §6.

147. Cf. KSA 7: 19[36], Summer 1872–Early 1873 as well as late drafts for the *Philosophenbuch*, such as KSA 7: 19[318] and 19[320], also written in the same period as Nietzsche's course on rhetoric. The figure of the last philosopher is here introduced after a section on "truth and illusion."

148. See KSA 1: 889; RL, 256.

3. Last Days: Benjamin

1. Walter Benjamin, *Gesammelte Schriften*, ed. Rolf Tiedemann and Hermann Schweppenhäuser (Frankfurt am Main: Suhrkamp, 1972–91), 5: 60; *The Arcades Project*, trans. Howard Eiland and Kevin McLaughlin (Cambridge: Harvard University Press, 1999), 14. Further references to these titles will appear as GS and AP, respectively.

2. GS 5: 1255.

3. On the relation between "essence" and "philosophy," see the "Epistemo-Critical Prologue" to Benjamin's *Origin of the German Mourning Play*, especially the sections on the relation between idea and phenomenon. GS 1: 214–18; *The Origin of German Tragic Drama*, trans. John Osborne (London: Verso, 1998), 34–38. Further references to the latter title will appear as O.

4. GS 5: 60; AP, 14.

5. In his 1922 essay on reification and historical consciousness—a text that Benjamin became familiar with in the period he was working on his *Habilitationsschrift*—Georg Lukács cites Marx in a passage on the "unexplained and inexplicable facticity of the here and now": "Thus history existed once upon a time, but it does not exist anymore." Cf. Lukács, *History and Class Consciousness: Studies in Marxist Dialectics*, trans. Rodney Livingstone (Cambridge: MIT Press, 1971), 156–57.

6. See GS 1: 237; O, 56.

7. For Benjamin's presentation of the concept of "origin" (*Ursprung*), see the relevant section in the prologue to his *Origin of the German Mourning Play* (GS 2:

225–27; O, 44–46). For an earlier and more recent analysis of the concept, see Rolf Tiedemann, *Studien zur Philosophie Walter Benjamins* (Frankfurt am Main: Suhrkamp Verlag, 1973), and Samuel Weber, "Genealogy of Modernity: History, Myth and Allegory in Benjamin's *Origin of the German Mourning Play*," in *Benjamin's -abilities* (Cambridge: Harvard University Press, 2010), 131–63.

8. Benjamin also understood Kracauer's work of the late 1920s as a writing within and against journalistic form. See Benjamin's review of *Die Angestellten*, Kracauer's study of the "salaried masses," which initially appeared in twelve installments in the feuilleton section of the *Frankfurter Zeitung* in 1929–30. In this review, published in May 1930, Benjamin compares Kracauer—whom he calls, like Kraus, a *Störenfried*, a "disturber of the peace"—to "the grumbler from the only great drama of the world war," Kraus's *The Last Days of Mankind* (GS 3: 219–25); *Selected Writings*, ed. Marcus Bullock and Michael W. Jennings, trans. Edmund Jephcott et al. (Cambridge: Harvard University Press, 1996), 2: 355–57. Further references to the latter title will appear as SW.

9. For a discussion of the genesis and reception of Benjamin's essay on Kraus, see Alexander Honold, "Karl Kraus," in *Benjamin-Handbuch*, ed. Burkhardt Lindner (Stuttgart & Weimar: Verlag J. B. Metzler, 2006), 522–38. Although Benjamin had been familiar with Kraus since 1916, the Viennese journalist appears for the first time in Benjamin's writings in his correspondence of 1920. See Letter to Scholem, December 29, 1920, in *Briefe*, ed. Theodor Adorno and Gerschom Scholem (Frankfurt am Main: Suhrkamp, 1978), 250–51; *The Correspondence of Walter Benjamin, 1910–1940*, ed. Gerschom Scholem and T. W. Adorno, trans. M. R. Jacobson et al. (Chicago: University of Chicago Press, 1994), 171. Further references to these titles will appear as B and CB, respectively.

10. Among the wide range of secondary literature on Karl Kraus and his polemic against journalism, see especially Helmut Arntzen, *Karl Kraus und die Presse* (München: Wilhelm Fink, 1975), and Paul Reitter, *The Anti-Journalist: Karl Kraus and Jewish Self-Fashioning in Fin-de-Siecle Europe* (Chicago: University of Chicago Press, 2008), which also includes a chapter on Benjamin and Scholem as readers of *Die Fackel*.

11. Kraus founded *Die Fackel* in 1899, when he was twenty-five years old; from 1911 onwards he was its only contributor. For a good general introduction to Kraus's work and life, see Chris Timms, *Apocalyptic Satirist: Culture and Catastrophe in Habsburg Vienna* (New Haven: Yale University Press, 1989) and his more recent *Apocalyptic Satirist, Volume 2: The Postwar Crisis and the Rise of the Swastika* (New Haven: Yale University Press, 2013).

12. During his time in Paris, Benjamin planned a "cycle of lectures" on the "German avant-garde" that would each revolve around "a figure in whom the present situation finds expression in a decisive way [*sich maßgebend ausprägt*]." Cf. B, 603; CB, 438.

13. GS 2: 241; "Announcement of the Journal *Angelus Novus*," in *Selected Writings*, 1: 292. Further references to the latter title will appear as AJ.

14. Karl Kraus, *Schriften*, ed. Christian Wagenknecht (Frankfurt am Main: Suhrkamp Verlag, 1994), 8: 209. Hereafter cited as S.

15. S 8: 216. For a lucid account of the place of Kraus's critique of journalism as one of the key protagonists in his diagnosis of the crisis of modernity, see Paul Reitter, *The Anti-Journalist*, 1–30.

16. See, for instance, Thomas Birkner, *Das Selbstgespräch der Zeit. Die Geschichte des Journalismus in Deutschland* (Köln: Herbert von Halem Verlag, 2012), and Frank Bösch, *Mass Media and Historical Change: Germany in International Perspective, 1400 to the Present*, trans. Freya Buechter (New York: Berghahn, 2015). A good indication of the state of the socio-historical study of journalism at the time Benjamin was preparing his essay on Kraus is Dieter Paul Baumert, *Die Entstehung des deutschen Journalismus. Eine sozialgeschichtliche Studie* (Leipzig: Duncker & Humblot, 1928).

17. For a detailed account of the impact of both events on Benjamin's working life, see Howard Eiland and Michael W. Jennings, *Walter Benjamin: A Critical Life* (Cambridge: Harvard University Press, 2014), 173–234.

18. After *Angelus Novus*, the projected journal he worked during the early 1920s, other references to planned journals are found in his letters of the mid-1920s; the most important project that testifies to his continued preoccupation with the form of the *Zeitschrift* is, however, *Krisis und Kritik*, the journal he prepared with Bertolt Brecht, Bernard von Brentano, and Herbert Ihering in 1930, the year before his essay on Kraus was published. Benjamin withdrew from this project on the grounds that his collaborators failed to see how the project would be threatened by succumbing to the "exigencies of journalistic actuality [*journalistische Aktualität*]"—the concept to which the last part of this chapter will be dedicated (Letter to Brecht, Late February 1931, in B, 520–21; CB, 370–71). On the *Krisis und Kritik* project, see Erdmut Wizisla, *Benjamin and Brecht: The Story of a Friendship*, trans. Christine Shuttleworth (New Haven: Yale University Press, 2009), 66–96.

19. See, for example, Benjamin's "Descriptive Analysis of the German Decline," a collection of fragments on the present situation on which he began to work in 1923 and to which we will return later in this chapter (GS 4: 916–935). Benjamin's experiments with what he later called, in *One-Way Street*, the "prompt language" found in "fly sheets, brochures, journal articles and advertisements" may even be traced back to the journal articles from his student days, which will be discussed in the last part of this chapter (GS 2: 56–60; EW, 120–25).

20. Letter to Scholem, December 22, 1924, in B, 368; CB, 257.

21. GS 2: 1115. The note is included in the convolute "Paralipomena zum Kraus" in which Benjamin gathered thirty pages of schemata, notes, and fragments.

22. The importance of this rescue operation is suggested by an important unpublished text written in the months after the publication of his essay on Kraus, titled "Diary from the Seventh of August, Nineteen Hundred Thirty One Until the Day of my Death." Several pages after discussing Kraus's response to his essay, Benjamin writes: "It is on the stage [*Schauplatz*] of the deepest degradation of the

printed word, the newspaper, where, in a new society, its restoration will take place" (GS 6: 446).

23. Kraus, *Die Fackel* 1 (1899): 1.

24. GS 2: 334–35; "Karl Kraus," in *Selected Writings*, 2: 433. Further references to the latter title will appear as KK.

25. GS 2: 335; KK, 434.

26. See the typescript for Benjamin's radio broadcast "Carousel of Professions" (*Karussel der Berufe*), in GS 2: 670–73. The reference is to Peter Suhrkamp's article "Der Journalist," in *Deutsche Berufskunde*, ed. Ottolenz v. d. Gablentz and Carl Mennicke (Leipzig: Bibliographisches Institut, 1930), 382–86.

27. GS 2: 335; KK, 434.

28. GS 5: 1255. In his critique of the reified view of history exemplified by the *journalistischen Mensch*, Benjamin differs markedly from Hannah Arendt, who treats the reporter as one of the privileged representatives of the "existential modes of truthtelling" and places this figure alongside the philosopher, scientist, artist, historian, judge, fact-finder, and witness. See: Arendt, "Truth and Politics," in *Between Past and Future: Six Exercises in Political Thought* (New York: Penguin Books, 1968), 255.

29. GS 2: 335; KK, 434.

30. A reference to *Verzweiflung* also appears in an important early sketch that has a close relation to the essay on Kraus: the fragment "Capitalism as Religion." Here Benjamin speaks of despair as a *Weltzustand* that marks the extreme accomplishment of the guilt history described in this fragment but also the only state out of which the possibility of another history might arise (GS 6: 101).

31. GS 2: 334; KK, 433.

32. See, for instance, the cupper engravings and etchings of Hans Ulrich Frank and Jacques Callot made during the Thirty Years War, in particular the latter's *Les misères et les malheurs de la guerre*, a series of eighteen etchings documenting events such the pillaging of a house, the destruction of a monastery, or the suffering of the poor and the sick.

33. See Thomas Schröder, "The Origins of the German Press," in *The Politics of Information in Early Modern Europe*, ed. Brendan Dooley and Sabrina A. Baron (London: Routledge, 2001), 123–50, and Johannes Weber, "Der große Krieg und die frühe Zeitung: Gestalt und Entwicklung der deutschen Nachrichtenpresse in der ersten Hälfte des 17. Jahrhunderts," *Jahrbuch für Kommunikationsgeschichte* (1999): 23–61.

34. For a good overview of the place of the *Neue Zeitungen* in relation to the periodical newspapers emerging at the start of the seventeenth century, see Thomas Schröder, "The Origins of the German Press," 123–50. The standard work on the subject is Emil Weller, ed., *Die ersten deutschen Zeitungen* (Tübingen: Laupp, 1872).

35. Benjamin cites Kraus's remark—"*Shakespeare hat alles vorausgewußt*"—in the last section of the essay, which develops a reading of the figure of Timon as misanthrope (*Menschenfeind*) (GS 2: 357; KK, 449–50). On Benjamin's reading of

Shakespeare in the essay on Karl Kraus, see Julia Ng, "Each Thing a Thief: Walter Benjamin on the Agency of Objects," *Philosophy and Rhetoric* 44, no. 4 (2011): 382–402.

36. GS 1: 242–43; O, 62.

37. GS 1: 242; O, 62.

38. GS 1: 242; O, 62.

39. For a broader discussion of Benjamin's concept of "myth," see Eli Friedlander, *Walter Benjamin: A Philosophical Portrait* (Cambridge: Harvard University Press, 2012), and Samuel Weber, "Genealogy of Modernity," 144–49.

40. The concepts of myth and fate also play an important role in Benjamin's first published text on Kraus, the one-page fragment "Monument to a Warrior" (*Kriegerdenkmal*) included in *One-Way Street*. For a more detailed discussion of this fragment, see Tom Vandeputte, "Karl Kraus. Die Sprache rächen," in *Entwendungen: Walter Benjamin und seine Quellen*, ed. Jessica Nitzsche and Nadine Werner (Paderborn: Verlag Wilhelm Fink, 2019), 263–80.

41. For an insightful discussion of the relation between myth and religion in Benjamin's earlier reflections on history, see Hamacher, "Guilt History: Benjamin's Sketch Capitalism and Religion," trans. Kirk Wetters, *Diacritics* 32, no. 3–4 (2002): 82–85.

42. See especially "Fate and Character" (GS 2: 171–79; SW 1: 201–6), where Benjamin describes the mythical system of fate as a *natürliche Verfassung* and demarcates it both from the sphere of ethics and that of religion.

43. Cf. especially the first paragraph of "The Life of Students" of 1915 (GS 2: 75; EW, 197–98).

44. GS 6: 202, and GS 5: 1010; AP, 842.

45. In "Fate and Character," Benjamin writes that the mythical "nexus of guilt" (*Schuldzusammenhang*) is "improperly temporal" (*uneigentlich Zeitlich*) (GS 2: 176; SW 1: 204).

46. GS 2: 341; KK, 437.

47. GS 2: 171–79; SW 1: 204.

48. The most important instance of this image is undoubtedly found in the "Epistemo-Critical Prologue," where the concept of origin is likened to a vortex whose movement is distinguished strictly from that of the "river of becoming" (GS 1: 226; O, 45).

49. Cf., for instance, the note on the "time of hell" in the early sketches for the *Passagenwerk* and its subsequent elaboration in the convolute on the Eternal Return (GS 5: 1010–11; AP, 843 and GS 5: 178; AP, 119).

50. S 19: 144.

51. S 19: 144.

52. GS 2: 335; KK, 433.

53. S 19, 144.

54. GS 2: 341; KK, 437.

55. See Lukács, *The Theory of the Novel*, trans. Anna Bostock (Cambridge: MIT Press, 1971), 62.

56. This phrase appears in the later essay on reification, in the same passage where Lukács cites Marx's claim that, for bourgeois economics, "history existed once upon a time, but it does not exist any more." See Lukács, *History and Class Consciousness*, 157.

57. GS 1: 267; O, 88.

58. A more detailed analysis of the concept of natural history in Benjamin's *Trauerspiel* book is found in Weber, "Genealogy of Modernity," 138–39. For a discussion of its relation to Lukács's theory of second nature, see Adorno, "The Idea of Natural History," trans. Robert Hullot-Kenter, *Telos* 60 (1984): 112–17, and Rose, *The Melancholy Science* (London: Verso Books, 2014), 35–39.

59. This point is made by Eric Santner in the insightful discussion of the concept of natural history and creaturely life in Benjamin included in *On Creaturely Life: Rilke, Benjamin, Sebald* (Chicago: University of Chicago Press, 2006).

60. Lukács makes this point in his essay on reification and the consciousness of the proletariat: "The problems of consciousness arising from wage-labour were repeated in the ruling class in a refined and spiritualised, but, for that very reason, more intensified form. This phenomenon can be seen at its most grotesque in journalism. Here it is precisely subjectivity itself, knowledge, temperament and powers of expression that are reduced to an abstract mechanism functioning autonomously and divorced both from the personality of their 'owner' and from the material and concrete nature of the subject matter in hand" (*History and Class Consciousness*, 100).

61. For a general discussion of Benjamin's understanding of the relation between nature, natural history, creation and creaturely life, see Santner, *On Creaturely Life*, 1–41, and Sigrid Weigel, *Walter Benjamin: Images, the Creaturely, and the Holy* (Stanford: Stanford University Press, 2012).

62. That Benjamin, like Kraus, draws on the "inherent duplicity or ambiguity of the term *Kreatur* [. . .] [signaling] the lowliest form of animality as well as human depravity" has been pointed out by Beatrice Hanssen in *Walter Benjamin's Other History* (Berkeley: University of California Press, 2000).

63. GS 2: 341; KK, 437–38.

64. See, for instance, GS 1: 259; O, 80.

65. GS 1: 343; O, 166.

66. GS 1: 267; O, 88.

67. See GS 1: 263–64; O, 85–86.

68. Kraus, *No Compromise: Selected Writings of Karl Kraus* (New York: Ungar, 1977), 69.

69. Kraus, *No Compromise*, 69.

70. "Die Zeitung," in *Worte in Versen* (München: Kösel, 1959), 360. "Do you, who reads the newspaper, know / how many trees must bleed / for you see your face in the mirror / blinded by currencies / in order to hurry back to your business? / Do you, who reads the newspaper, know / how many people die / so that a few can have their pleasure / and so that the creature can enjoy himself / the creature of unspeakable perversion?"

71. See GS 2: 246; O, 80.

72. GS 2: 339–40; KK, 437. For a closer reading of this passage and its relation to passages on Stifter in Benjamin's essay on Kraus, see Weigel, *Walter Benjamin*, 4–18.

73. GS 2: 437; KK, 339.

74. For a discussion of the disappearance of eschatology and the distinction between empty and fulfilled time in Benjamin's studies of tragedy and *Trauerspiel*, see Peter Fenves, "Tragedy and Prophecy in Benjamin's *Origin of the German Mourning Play*," in *Arresting Language: From Leibniz to Benjamin* (Stanford: Stanford University Press, 2001), 227–48.

75. GS 1: 257; O, 78

76. GS 1: 259; O, 80.

77. GS 1: 260; O, 81.

78. See Fenves, "Tragedy and Prophecy," 234–35.

79. GS 1: 317; O, 138–39.

80. "Der Sterbende Mensch," in *Worte in Versen*, 57.

81. GS 4: 85; OWS, 144.

82. S 10: 193.

83. See Harry Zohn, introduction to *In These Great Times*, ed. Harry Zohn (Manchester: Carcanet, 1976), 24–27.

84. S 10: 192.

85. Kraus, "Der Sterbende Mensch," 57.

86. GS 2: 345; KK, 440. On Benjamin's concept of lament (*Klage*), see Rebecca Comay, "Paradoxes of Lament: Benjamin and Hamlet," in *Lament in Jewish Thought*, ed. Ilit Ferber and Paula Schwebel (Berlin: De Gruyter, 2014), 257–61, and Ilit Ferber, *Philosophy and Melancholy* (Stanford: Stanford University Press, 2013), 118–62.

87. GS 5: 114; AP, 65 and GS 5: 679; AP, 546.

88. GS 5: 1010–11; AP, 842–43.

89. GS 5: 1011; AP, 843.

90. GS 5: 679; AP, 546.

91. GS 5: 679; AP, 546.

92. The description of capitalism as "cult religion" appears in Benjamin's unpublished fragment of 1921, "Capitalism as Religion" (GS 6: 100–3; SW 1: 288–91). For a more detailed analysis of the relation between Christianity and capitalism, see Hamacher, "Guilt History: Benjamin's Sketch Capitalism and Religion," 82–85.

93. GS 1: 683; SW 4: 184.

94. Benjamin probably began working on his "Descriptive Analysis of the German Decline" in February 1923 when traveling through Germany. In September of the same year, Benjamin gives Scholem the manuscript, written on a scroll, of a text on Germany during the inflation; a reworked version of the text that Benjamin initially planned to publish in September 1924 in the *Red Guard*, a Moscow-based journal, was later published as the "Kaiserpanorama" fragments in *One-Way Street* (GS 4: 916–35).

95. For a broader discussion of this thesis and its role in Benjamin's work of the 1920s, see Rebecca Comay, "Benjamin's Endgame," in *Walter Benjamin's Philosophy*, ed. Andrew Benjamin and Peter Osborne (London: Routledge, 1993), 262–63.

96. GS 2: 348; KK, 443.

97. Cf. Benjamin's early note on "world history" and "divine history" in GS 6: 91–92. For a detailed interpretation of this note and its claim that guilt is "the highest category of world history," see Hamacher, "Guilt History," 82–85.

98. A closer examination of the peculiar logic of compression at stake here would require a discussion of Benjamin's reception of Leibniz. For a general account of the role of Leibniz's monadology in Benjamin's theory of interpretation, see Paula Schwebel, "Intensive Infinity: Walter Benjamin's Reception of Leibniz and Its Sources," *MLN* 127 (2012): 589–610.

99. Cf. also one of the entries included in his *Passagen-Werk*: "The authentic concept of universal history is a messianic concept" (GS 5: 608; AP, 485). Michael W. Jennings rightly interprets this as a note referring to the structural incompleteness—and thus impossibility—of any universal history. See "The Will to Apokatastasis: Media, Experience and Eschatology in Walter Benjamin's Late Theological Politics," in *Walter Benjamin and Theology*, ed. Colby Dickinson and Stéphane Symons (New York: Fordham University Press, 2016), 93–111.

100. GS 2: 348; KK, 443.

101. For a discussion of the motif of the "will of Joshua"—the will to arrest time and bring history to a standstill—in Benjamin's writings of the 1920s and 1930s, see Rebecca Comay, "Benjamin's Endgame," 264–65, and Tom Vandeputte, "Resistance," in *Re-: An Errant Glossary*, ed. Christoph F. E. Holzhey and Arnd Wedemeyer, *Cultural Inquiry* 15 (Berlin: ICI Berlin, 2019), 127–32.

102. Immanuel Kant, *Gesammelte Schriften* (Berlin: De Gruyter, 1968), 6: 101; *Religion Within the Boundaries of Mere Reason*, trans. George di Giovanni, in *Religion and Rational Theology*, ed. Allen W. Wood and George di Giovanni (Cambridge: Cambridge University Press, 1996), 111.

103. GS 2: 365; KK, 455.

104. GS 2: 349; KK, 443.

105. See, for instance, "Tourist Trips to Hell," in *No Compromise*, 69. Kraus's meticulous analysis of the use of punctuation marks in the writings of his contemporaries is exemplified, in particular, by the texts collected under the title *Worte in Versen*.

106. That the ultimate concern of this philology would be to retrieve from petrified phenomena what Benjamin describes as their "origin" is suggested by one of Benjamin's sparse reflections on philology in a letter to Scholem of February 1921 in B, 257; CB 175–76. "Philology," Benjamin writes here, "promises to historical investigation the pleasures that the neoplatonics sought in the ascesis of contemplation." For an insightful reading of this letter and the nexus of philology and history, see Thomas Schestag, "Interpolationen: Benjamins Philologie" in *Philo:zenia*, ed. Thomas Schestag (Basel: Engeler, 2009), 35–93.

107. GS 2: 337; KK, 435.

108. GS 6: 100; SW 1: 288.

109. GS 6: 101; SW 1: 289.

110. See Tom Vandeputte, "Constellation and Configuration: Language and Reading in the 'Epistemo-Critical Prologue,'" in *Thinking in Constellations: Walter Benjamin in the Humanities*, ed. Nassima Sahraoui and Caroline Sauter (Cambridge: Cambridge Scholars, 2018), 83–102.

111. For a helpful overview of Kraus's concept and critique of language, see Joseph Quack, *Bemerkungen zum Sprachverständnis von Karl Kraus* (Bonn: Bouvier, 1976), and Jay F. Bodine, "Karl Kraus's Conception of Language," *Modern Austrian Literature* 8, no. 1/2 (1975): 268–314. On the relation of Kraus's work to the nineteenth-century tradition of *Sprachkritik*, see Hannelore Ederer, *Die literarische Mimesis entfremdeter Sprache. Zur sprachkritischen Literatur von Heinrich Heine bis Karl Kraus* (Köln: Pahl Rugenstein, 1979).

112. S 8: 235.

113. Kraus returns to the impossibility to "have" thoughts in another aphorism in *Pro Domo*, which has a remarkable affinity with Benjamin's own reflection on this matter in the "Epistemo-Critical Prologue": "The thought is in the world, but one does not possess it [*aber man hat ihn nicht*]" (S 8: 236).

114. See Scholem, *Story of a Friendship*, 64.

115. For more detailed expositions of Benjamin's early philosophy of language, see amongst others Rodolphe Gasché, "Saturnine Vision and the Question of Difference: Reflections on Walter Benjamin's Theory of Language," in *Benjamin's Ground: New Readings of Walter Benjamin*, ed. Rainer Nägele (Detroit: Wayne State University Press, 1988), 83–104; Hamacher, "Intensive Languages," 485–541; Wilfried Menninghaus, *Walter Benjamins Theorie der Sprachmagie* (Frankfurt am Main: Suhrkamp, 1995).

116. GS 2: 144; SW 1: 65.

117. GS 2: 144; SW 1: 65.

118. GS 2: 145–46; SW 1: 66–67.

119. For a detailed discussion of Benjamin's concept of *Mitteilbarkeit* ("communicability" or "impartability") see Weber, "Impart-ability: Language as a Medium," in *Benjamin's -abilities*, 31–52.

120. *Die Fackel*, 1: 1.

121. S 8: 117.

122. GS 2: 337; KK, 435.

123. GS 2: 336–37; KK, 435. See Suhrkamp, "Der Journalist," 386.

124. GS 2: 335; KK, 440.

125. S 8: 224.

126. GS 2: 337; KK, 435.

127. GS 2: 349; KK, 444.

128. GS 2: 352; KK, 446.

129. GS 2: 352; KK, 446.

130. GS 2: 153; SW 1: 71. A close reading of this essay and the concept of "chatter" is found in Fenves, *"Chatter": Language and History in Kierkegaard*, 191–242.

131. GS 2: 153; SW 1: 71.

132. GS 2: 154; SW 1: 72.

133. Hamann, Letter to Lindner, August 9, 1759, in *Briefwechsel*, ed. Arthur Henkel (Frankfurt am Main: Insel, 1965), 1: 394. For a discussion of Benjamin's reception of Hamann, see Winfried Menninghaus, *Walter Benjamins Theorie der Sprachmagie*, 22–32 and 205–14.

134. GS 2: 144; SW 1: 65.

135. For a comprehensive study of the role of this suffix throughout Benjamin's work and its origins in Kant, see Weber, *Benjamin's -abilities*, esp. 3–10.

136. S 8: 256.

137. GS 2: 356; KK, 448.

138. GS 2: 362–63; KK, 453.

139. GS 4: 10; TT, 254.

140. The reference is to the fragment on world history of the late 1910s, where Benjamin writes, "Guilt is the highest category of world history for guaranteeing the uni-directionality [*Einsinnigkeit*] of what occurs" (GS 6: 92).

141. GS 2: 363; KK, 454.

142. GS 2: 363; KK, 454.

143. GS 2: 362–63; KK, 453.

144. See Weber, "Citability—of gesture," in *Benjamin's -abilities*, 95–114 and the discussion of "impartibility" and "translatability" in Hamacher, "Intensive Languages," 487–91.

145. GS 2: 363; KK, 454.

146. GS 2: 367; KK, 457. For a discussion of the relation of this angel to the eponymous painting by Klee that Benjamin owned, see Scholem, "Walter Benjamin and His Angel," in *On Walter Benjamin: Critical Essays and Recollections*, ed. Gary Smith (Cambridge: MIT Press, 1988), 198–236, and Sigrid Weigel, "Angelus Novus," in *Enzyklopädie jüdischer Geschichte und Kultur*, ed. Dan Diner (Stuttgart: Verlag J. B. Metzler, 2011), 94–100. The figure also plays an important role in Stéphane Moses's book *The Angel of History, Rosenzweig, Benjamin, Scholem*, trans. Barbara Harshaw (Stanford: Stanford University Press, 2009).

147. In his comments on Benjamin's "new angel," Scholem refers to the "talks about Jewish angelology, especially of the Talmudic and Kabbalistic kind" he had with Benjamin in the early 1920s and stresses the importance of "the Talmudic theme of the formation and disappearance of angels before God, of whom it is said in a Kabbalistic book that they 'pass away as the spark on the coals'" ("Walter Benjamin and His Angel," 210 and 213).

148. GS 2, 246; AJ, 296.

149. GS 2: 1106–7.

150. GS 2: 367; KK, 457.

151. For an exposition of the complex relation between Benjamin's early writings and Cohen's conception of the messianic, see Hamacher, "Das Theologisch-politische Fragment," in *Benjamin-Handbuch*, ed. Burkhardt Lindner (Stuttgart & Weimar: Verlag J. B. Metzler, 2006), 175–78. On Benjamin's later messianism, see Wohlfarth, "On the Messianic Structure of Walter Benjamin's Last Reflections," *Glyph* 3 (1978): 148–212, and Hamacher, "Now! Walter Benjamin and Historical Time," trans. N. Rosenthal, in *Walter Benjamin and History*, ed. Andrew Benjamin (New York: Continuum, 2005), 38–68. A good general discussion of the messianic as a "profane figure" is found in Sami Khatib, "The Messianic Without Messianism: Walter Benjamin's Materialist Theology," in *Anthropology & Materialism* 1 (2013): 1–17.

152. GS 2: 246; AJ, 296.

153. GS 2: 96; SW 1: 10.

154. B, 444; CB, 314.

155. GS 2: 96; SW 1: 10.

156. GS 2: 98; SW 1: 12.

157. GS 2: 56–60; EW, 120–25. Like the other important early *Artikel* Benjamin published in this year, "Experience," this text was written under the pseudonym "Ardor" and appeared in *Der Anfang*.

158. The first fragment of Benjamin's *One-Way Street* calls for a "prompt language that shows itself actively able to cope with the instant [*dem Augenblick wirkend gewachsen*]" (GS 4: 85).

159. GS 2: 59; EW, 123.

160. GS 6: 91.

161. GS 2: 59; EW, 123. Even though Benjamin's terminology here is undoubtedly Kantian, Benjamin's break with Kant and Cohen can be located precisely in his concept of *Zukunft*. See Hamacher, "Das Theologisch-politische Fragment," 175–78. On the place of the *Aufgabe* in Benjamin's philosophical project, see Jan Sieber and Sebastian Truskolaski, "The Task of the Philosopher," *Anthropology & Materialism* 1 (2017): 1–16.

162. GS 2: 60; EW, 123.

163. The *Life of Students* was published in *Der Neue Merkur. Monatsschrift für geistiges Leben* in September 1915.

164. GS 2: 75; EW, 197.

165. GS 2: 75; EW, 197–98.

166. GS 2: 75; EW, 198.

167. The most thorough account of this story, interwoven with the publication of two texts that Benjamin planned to be his own contributions to the first two issues of *Angelus Novus*—his "Task of the Translator" and "Elective Affinities"—is found in Eiland and Jennings, *Walter Benjamin: A Critical Life*, 150–73.

168. GS 2: 241; AJ, 292.

169. GS 2: 241; AJ, 292. On the relation between "life," language, and criticism, which is touched upon in this passage, as well as the "Life of Students," see Kevin McLaughlin, "Biophilology: Walter Benjamin's Literary Critical Legacy," *MLN* 133, no. 3 (2018): 562–84.

170. In his *Critique of Violence*, written and published the year before the announcement of his journal, Benjamin writes that Sorel, whose *Reflections on Violence* provides an important point of reference for his own text, "in taking up occasional statements by Marx, rejects every kind of program, of utopia [. . .] for the revolutionary movement" (GS 2: 194).

171. GS 2: 75; EW, 197.

172. GS 2: 241; AJ, 292.

173. For an account of the problems of justice and judgment and an analysis of the motifs of the complaint, claim, and trial in Benjamin's early writings, see Irving Wohlfarth, "On Some Jewish Motifs in Benjamin," 167–205.

174. GS 2: 353; KK, 446.

175. Elsewhere in the essay, Benjamin writes: "For this is the last official act [*Amtshandlung*] of this zealot: to place the legal order itself under accusation" (GS 2: 349; KK, 444).

176. GS 2: 337; KK, 435.

177. GS 2: 75; EW, 197.

178. GS 2: 75; EW, 197.

179. Cf. Jacob and Wilhelm Grimm, *Deutsches Wörterbuch*, "Anspruch."

180. GS 2: 75; EW, 197.

181. GS 2: 246; AJ, 296.

182. It is in this sense that the term *Aktualität* is also used in the opening paragraph of one of Benjamin's first published newspaper articles, the brief text "The Weapons of Tomorrow: Wars with Chlorazetophenol, Diphenylaminchlorasine and Dichlorathylsulfide," published pseudonymously in the *Vossische Zeitung* on June 29, 1925. In this text, written in the wake of the rejection of his *Habilitation* thesis, Benjamin discusses how, in "the war to come," the "convenient acronyms [*Abkürzungen*] for the tongue-breaking words indicating chemicals" will "over the course of a few hours gain a never suspected actuality [*nie geahnter Aktualität*]." See GS 4: 473.

183. GS 2: 244; AJ, 294.

184. GS 2: 244; AJ, 294.

185. GS 2: 56; EW, 120.

186. On the radically unassimilable character of *Zukunft* in Benjamin, see Hamacher, "Das Theologisch-politische Fragment," 175–78, and Comay, "Benjamin's Endgame," 265–66.

187. GS 2: 244; AJ, 294.

188. GS 2: 241; AJ, 292.

189. GS 2: 75; EW, 197.

190. GS 2: 241–42; AJ, 293.

191. The continued importance of this distinction between true actuality and the actuality demanded by journalism is suggested by the fact that Benjamin motivated his withdrawal from the other major journal project he was involved in an odd decade later, *Krisis und Kritik*, by pointing out the failure of his fellow editors to observe the incommensurability between the journal's task to "present something

fundamentally new" and the "exigencies of journalistic actuality." Letter to Brecht, Late February 1931, in B, 520–21; CB, 370–71.

192. GS 5: 1011; AP, 843.

193. GS 2: 1198.

194. GS 2: 244; AJ, 294.

195. Benjamin's work on the founding of his *Angelus Novus* begins in the same period in which the first traces of his life-long preoccupation with Kraus appear in his writings. See, in particular, his Letter to Scholem, December 29, 1920, in B, 251; CB, 171. Kraus, who delivered a series of lectures in Berlin in 1921 that Benjamin probably attended, was also an important reference in Benjamin's discussions with collaborators about his *Angelus Novus* in the same year. See Eiland and Jennings, *Walter Benjamin: A Critical Life*, 154.

196. GS 2: 349; KK, 443.

Afterword: "Today"

1. For an extensive discussion of the conflict between philosophy and sophistry, see Barbara Cassin, *L'Effet Sophistique* (Paris: Gallimard, 1995).

2. *Søren Kierkegaards Papirer*, ed. P. A. Heiberg, V. Kuhr, and E. Torsting (Copenhagen: Gyldendal, 1909–48), 7.1: A 122; *Kierkegaard's Journals and Notebooks*, ed. Niels Jorgen Cappelorn et. al. (Princeton: Princeton University Press, 2011), NB: 30.

3. Søren Kierkegaard, *Samlede Værker*, ed. A. B. Drachman, J. L. Heiberg, and H.O. Lange (Copenhagen: Gyldendal, 1901–06), 13: 223; *The Concept of Irony*, trans. Howard V. Hong and Edna H. Hong (Princeton: Princeton University Press, 1989), 138. (Hereafter cited as SV and CI, respectively.) Kierkegaard develops this hypothesis in his reading of Aristophanes's account of Socrates, which identifies him as a sophist. Such an identification is possible precisely when "one bears in mind that in a certain sense Socrates and the Sophists held the same position and that Socrates actually struck at their very roots by carrying through their position, by destroying the halfness in which the Sophists set their minds at ease, so that Socrates by defeating the Sophists was thereby in a certain sense himself the greatest Sophist" (SV 13: 223; CI, 138).

4. SV 13: 286; CI, 207. "The Sophists' pompous, confident parading, their matchless self-sufficiency (all of which we learn from Plato), is proof enough that they thought themselves able to satisfy the demands of the times, not by shaking the foundations of everything but, after having shaken the foundations, by making it all secure again."

5. The term "radicalized journalism" also appears in a brief newspaper article that Michel Foucault wrote in 1973, where it is also related to the question of the "today." "If we want to be masters of our future," Foucault writes here, "we must fundamentally pose the question of the today [*la question de l'aujourd'hui*]. This is why, for me, philosophy is a sort of radical journalism [*une espèce de journalisme radical*]" (Foucault, *Dits et ecrits*, vol. 1, 1302).

6. Derrida, *L'autre cap. Suivi de La démocratie ajournée* (Paris: Les Éditions de Minuit, 1991), 8; *The Other Heading*, trans. Pascale-Anne Brault and Michael B. Naas (Bloomington: Indiana University Press, 1992), 3.

7. G. W. F. Hegel, *Werke* (Frankfurt am Main: Suhrkamp, 1970), 7: 26; *Elements of the Philosophy of Right*, ed. Allen Wood, trans. H. B. Nisbet (Cambridge: Cambridge University Press, 1991), 15.

8. Derrida, *L'Autre Cap*, 5; *The Other Heading*, 12.

9. Derrida, *L'Autre Cap*, 22; *The Other Heading*, 17.

10. Derrida, *L'Autre Cap*, 79; *The Other Heading*, 81.

11. For a sociological analysis of the fraught relationship between philosophy and journalism in post-war French intelligentsia, which also touches on the increasingly prominent form of the interview, see Geoffroy De Lasagnerie, *L'Empire de l'université. Sur Bourdieu, les intellectuels et le journalisme* (Paris: Éditions Amsterdam, 2007).

12. Derrida, "Vous Voulez Rire! Interview with a Passing Journalist," in *Points of Departure: Samuel Weber between Spectrality and Reading*, ed. Peter Fenves, Kevin McLaughlin, and Marc Redfield (Evanston: Northwestern University Press, 2016), 220.

13. Derrida, "Vous Voulez Rire!," 220.

14. Derrida, "Vous Voulez Rire!," 247.

15. Derrida, "Vous Voulez Rire!," 253.

16. Derrida, "Vous Voulez Rire!," 256.

17. Derrida, *L'Autre Cap*, 124; Derrida, *The Other Heading*, 109.

Bibliography

Adorno, Theodor. "The Idea of Natural History." Translated by Robert Hullot-Kenter. *Telos* 60 (1984): 111–24.

———. *Kierkegaard: Construction of the Aesthetic.* Translated by Robert Hullot-Kenter. Minneapolis: University of Minnesota Press, 1989.

Adorno, Theodor, et. al. *Über Walter Benjamin.* Frankfurt am Main: Suhrkamp Verlag, 1968.

Agamben, Giorgio. *Infancy and History: The Destruction of Experience.* Translated by Liz Heron. London: Verso, 1993.

———. *Potentialities: Collected Essays in Philosophy,* ed. and tr. Daniel Heller-Roazen. Stanford: Stanford University Press, 1999.

———. "What Is the Contemporary?" In *What Is an Apparatus?*, translated by David Kishik and Stefan Pedatella, 39–54. Stanford: Stanford University Press, 2009.

Arendt, Hannah. "Truth and Politics." In *Between Past and Future: Six Exercises in Political Thought,* 223–59. New York: Penguin Books, 1968.

Arntzen, Helmut. *Karl Kraus und die Presse.* München: Wilhelm Fink, 1975.

Baumert, Dieter Paul. *Die Entstehung des deutschen Journalismus. Eine sozialgeschichtliche Studie.* Leipzig: Duncker & Humblot, 1928.

Bayer, Oswald. *A Contemporary in Dissent: Johann Georg Hamann as Radical Enlightener.* Grand Rapids: Eerdmans, 2012.

Benjamin, Andrew, ed. *Walter Benjamin and History.* Continuum: London, 2005.

Benjamin, Andrew, and Peter Osborne, eds. *Walter Benjamin's Philosophy: Destruction and Experience.* London: Routledge, 1993.

Benjamin, Walter. *The Arcades Project.* Translated by Howard Eiland and Kevin McLaughlin. Cambridge: Harvard University Press, 1999.

———. *Briefe.* Edited by Theodor Adorno and Gerschom Scholem. 2 vols. Frankfurt am Main: Suhrkamp, 1978.

——. *The Correspondence of Walter Benjamin, 1910–1940*. Edited by Gerschom Scholem and T. W. Adorno. Translated by M. R. Jacobson et al. Chicago: University of Chicago Press, 1994.

——. *Early Writings 1910–1917*. Edited by Howard Eiland. Cambridge: Harvard University Press, 2011.

——. *Gesammelte Schriften*. Edited by Rolf Tiedemann and Hermann Schweppenhäuser. 7 vols. Frankfurt am Main: Suhrkamp, 1972–91.

——. *The Origin of German Tragic Drama*. Translated by John Osborne. London: Verso, 1998.

——. *Selected Writings*. Edited by Marcus Bullock and Michael W. Jennings. Translated by Edmund Jephcott et al. 4 vols. Cambridge: Harvard University Press, 1996.

Bernasconi, Robert. "Kant as an Unfamiliar Source of Racism." In *Philosophers on Race: Critical Essays*, edited by Julie K. Ward and Tommy L. Lott, 145–66. London: Blackwell, 2002.

——. "Nietzsche as a Philosopher of Racialized Breeding." In *The Oxford Handbook on Philosophy of Race*, edited by Naomi Zack, 54–56. Oxford: Oxford University Press, 2017.

Birkner, Thomas. *Das Selbstgespräch der Zeit. Die Geschichte des Journalismus in Deutschland 1605–1914*. Köln: Herbert von Halem, 2012.

Blanchot, Maurice. *The Infinite Conversation*. Translated by Susan Hanson. Minneapolis: University of Minnesota Press, 1993.

Bodine, Jay F. "Karl Kraus's Conception of Language." *Modern Austrian Literature* 8, no. 1/2 (1975): 268–314.

Boethius. *Theological Tractates and The Consolation of Philosophy*. Edited by H. F. Stewart, E. K. Rand, and S. J. Tester. Cambridge: Harvard University Press, 1973.

Bösch, Frank. *Mass Media and Historical Change: Germany in International Perspective, 1400 to the Present*. Translated by Freya Buechter. New York: Berghahn, 2015.

Cassin, Barbara. *L'Effet sophistique*. Paris: Gallimard, 1995.

Caygill, Howard. "Benjamin, Heidegger and the Destruction of Tradition." In *Walter Benjamin's Philosophy*, edited by Andrew Benjamin and Peter Osborne, 1–31. London: Routledge, 1993.

——. "Non-Messianic Political Theology in Benjamin's 'On the Concept of History.'" In *Walter Benjamin and History*, edited by Andrew Benjamin, 215–26. Continuum: London, 2005.

——. *Walter Benjamin: The Colour of Experience*. London: Routledge, 1998.

Comay, Rebecca. "Benjamin and the Ambiguities of Romanticism." In *Cambridge Companion to Walter Benjamin*, edited by David Ferris, 134–51. Cambridge: Cambridge University Press, 2004.

——. "Benjamin's Endgame." In *Walter Benjamin's Philosophy*, edited by Andrew Benjamin and Peter Osborne, 251–91. London: Routledge, 1993.

———. *Mourning Sickness: Hegel and the French Revolution*. Stanford: Stanford University Press, 2011.

———. "Paradoxes of Lament: Benjamin and Hamlet." In *Lament in Jewish Thought*, edited by Ilit Ferber and Paula Schwebel, 257–75. Berlin: De Gruyter, 2014.

———. "Redeeming Revenge: Nietzsche, Benjamin, Heidegger, and the Politics of Memory." In *Nietzsche as Postmodernist: Essays Pro and Contra*, edited by Clayton Koelb, 21–38. New York: SUNY Press, 1990.

De Lasagnerie, Geoffroy. *L'Empire de l'université. Sur Bourdieu, les intellectuels et le journalisme*. Paris: Éditions Amsterdam, 2007.

De Man, Paul. *Allegories of Reading: Figural Language in Rousseau, Nietzsche, Rilke and Proust*. New Haven: Yale University Press, 1979.

———. "The Concept of Irony." In *Aesthetic Ideology*, edited by Andrzej Warminski, 163–84. Minneapolis: University of Minnesota Press, 1996.

———. "'Conclusions': Walter Benjamin's 'The Task of the Translator.'" In *The Resistance to Theory*, 73–105. Minneapolis: University of Minnesota Press, 1986.

———. "The Rhetoric of Temporality." In *Blindness and Insight*. London: Routledge, 1983.

———. "The Temptation of Permanence." In *Critical Writings 1953–1978*, edited by Lindsay Waters. Minneapolis: University of Minnesota Press, 1988.

Deleuze, Gilles. *Difference and Repetition*. Translated by Paul Patton. London: Continuum, 1994.

———. *Negotiations*. Translated by Martin Joughin. New York: Columbia University Press, 1995.

———. *Nietzsche and Philosophy*. Translated by Hugh Tomlinson. New York: Columbia University Press, 1983.

Derrida, Jacques. "Above All, No Journalists!" In *Religion and Media*, edited by Hent de Vries and Samuel Weber, 56–93. Stanford: Stanford University Press, 2002.

———. "Des tours de Babel." In *Acts of Religion*, edited by Gil Anidjar, 104–33. New York: Routledge, 2002.

———. *Dissemination*. Translated by Barbara Johnson. London: The Athlone Press, 1981.

———. *The Ear of the Other: Otobiography, Transference, Translation*. Edited by Christie V. MacDonald. Translated by Peggy Kamuf. New York: Schocken Books, 1985.

———. "Loving in Friendship: Perhaps—the Noun and the Adverb." In *Politics of Friendship*, translated by Georg Collins, 26–48. London: Verso Books, 1997.

———. *Margins of Philosophy*. Translated by Alan Bass. Chicago: University of Chicago Press, 1982.

———. *Of Grammatology*. Translated by Gayatri Spivak. Baltimore: Johns Hopkins University Press, 1998.

———. *The Other Heading: Reflections on Today's Europe*. Translated by Pascale-Anne Brault and Michael B. Naas. Bloomington: Indiana University Press, 1992.

———. "*Ousia* and *Grammē*: Note on a Note from *Being and Time*." In *Margins of Philosophy*, 29–68.

———. "Signature Event Context." In *Margins of Philosophy*, 307–30.

———. "Vous Voulez Rire! Interview with a Passing Journalist." In *Points of Departure: Samuel Weber between Spectrality and Reading*, edited by Peter Fenves, Kevin McLaughlin, and Marc Redfield, 211–68. Evanston: Northwestern University Press, 2016.

———. "White Mythology: Metaphor in the Text of Philosophy." In *Margins of Philosophy*, translated by Alan Bass, 207–72. Chicago: University of Chicago Press, 1982.

———. "Whom to Give to (Knowing Not to Know)." In *Kierkegaard: A Critical Reader*, edited by Jane Chamberlain and Jonathan Rée, 153–74. London: Wiley-Blackwell, 1997.

———. *Writing and Difference*. Translated by Alan Bass. London: Routledge, 2001.

Derrida, Jacques, and Bernard Stiegler, *Echographies of Television*. Translated by Jennifer Bajorek. Cambridge: Polity, 2002.

Deuber-Mankowsky, Astrid. *Der frühe Walter Benjamin und Hermann Cohen: Jüdische Werte, Kritische Philosophie, vergängliche Erfahrung*. Berlin: Verlag Vorwerk, 2000.

Düttmann, Alexander Garcia. "For and Against the Contemporary: An Examination." In *Art and Contemporaneity*, edited by Frank Ruda and Jan Völker, 9–22. Berlin: Diaphanes, 2017.

———. *The Memory of Thought: An Essay on Heidegger and Adorno*. Translated by Nicholas Walker. London: Continuum, 2002.

———. *Philosophy of Exaggeration*. Translated by James Philips. London: Continuum, 2007.

Ederer, Hannelore. *Die literarische Mimesis entfremdeter Sprache. Zur sprachkritischen Literatur von Heinrich Heine bis Karl Kraus*. Köln: Pahl Rugenstein, 1979.

Eiland, Howard, and Michael W. Jennings, eds. *Walter Benjamin: A Critical Life*. Cambridge: Harvard University Press, 2014.

Engelsing, Rolf. *Der Bürger als Leser: Lesergeschichte in Deutschland, 1500–1800*. Stuttgart: J. B. Metzlersche Verlagsbuchhandlung, 1974.

Eze, Emmanuel Chukwudi. "The Color of Reason: The Idea of 'Race' in Kant's Anthropology." In *Postcolonial African Philosophy: A Critical Reader*, 103–31. Oxford: Blackwell, 1997.

Fackenheim, Emile. *Encounters Between Judaism and Modern Philosophy: A Preface to Future Jewish Thought*. New York: Schocken Books, 1973.

———. "Kant's Concept of History." *Kant-Studien* 48 (1956–57): 381–98.

Fenves, Peter. *"Chatter": Language and History in Kierkegaard*. Stanford: Stanford University Press, 1993.

———. "The Genesis of Judgment: Spatiality, Analogy, and Metaphor in Benjamin's 'On Language as Such and on Human Language.'" In *Walter Benjamin:*

Theoretical Questions, edited by David S. Ferris, 75–93. Stanford: Stanford University Press, 1996.

———. "Image and Chatter: Adorno's Construction of Kierkegaard." *Diacritics* 22 (1992): 100–14.

———. *The Messianic Reduction: Walter Benjamin and the Shape of Time*. Stanford: Stanford University Press, 2011.

———. "The Paradisal *Epochē*: On Benjamin's First Philosophy." In *Arresting Language: From Leibniz to Benjamin*, 174–225. Stanford: Stanford University Press, 2001.

———. *A Peculiar Fate: Metaphysics and World History*. Ithaca, N.Y.: Cornell University Press, 1991.

———. "Tragedy and Prophecy in Benjamins *Origin of the German Mourning Play*." In *Arresting Language: From Leibniz to Benjamin*, 227–48. Stanford: Stanford University Press, 2001.

Ferber, Ilit. *Philosophy and Melancholy: Benjamin's Early Reflections on Theater and Language*. Stanford: Stanford University Press, 2013.

Ferreira da Silva, Denise. *Toward a Global Idea of Race*. Minneapolis: University of Minnesota Press, 2007.

Fink, Eugen. *Nietzsche's Philosophy*. Translated by Goetz Richter. London: Continuum, 2003.

Förster, Eckart. *The Twenty-Five Years of Philosophy: A Systematic Reconstruction*. Translated by Brady Bowman. Cambridge: Harvard University Press, 2012.

Foucault, Michel. *Dits et écrits*. Edited by Daniel Defert and François Ewald. 2 vols. Paris: Éditions Gallimard, 1994.

———. *The Government of Self and Others: Lectures at the Collège de France 1982–1983*. Edited by Fréderic Gors. Translated by Graham Burchell. Houndmills: Palgrave Macmillan, 2011.

———. "What Is Critique?" In *Politics of Truth*, edited by Sylvère Lotringer and Lysa Hochroth, translated by Lysa Hochroth, 41–82. New York: Semiotext(e), 1997.

Friedlander, Eli. *Walter Benjamin: A Philosophical Portrait*. Cambridge: Harvard University Press, 2012.

Garff, Joakim. *Søren Kierkegaard: A Biography*. Translated by Bruce H. Kirmmse. Princeton: Princeton University Press, 2005.

Gasché, Rodolphe. "Saturnine Vision and the Question of Difference: Reflections on Walter Benjamin's Theory of Language." In *Benjamin's Ground: New Readings of Walter Benjamin*, edited by Rainer Nägele, 83–104. Detroit: Wayne State University Press, 1988.

Geoghegan, Bernard. "Information." In *Digital Keywords: A Vocabulary of Information Society & Culture*, edited by Benjamin Peters, 175–77. Princeton: Princeton University Press, 2016.

Geulen, Eva. *The End of Art: Readings in a Rumor After Hegel*. Translated by James McFarland. Stanford: Stanford University Press, 2006.

Goethe, Johann Wolfgang. *Faust. Erster und Zweiter Teil.* Frankfurt am Main: Insel Verlag, 1998.

Hale, Geoffrey A. *Kierkegaard and the Ends of Language.* Minneapolis: University of Minnesota Press, 2002.

Hamacher, Werner. "Afformative, Strike." Translated by Dana Hollander. *Cardozo Law Review* 13, no. 4 (1991): 1133–56.

——. "Das Theologisch-politische Fragment." In *Benjamin-Handbuch,* edited by Burkhardt Lindner, 175–92. Stuttgart & Weimar: Verlag J. B. Metzler, 2006.

——. "The End of Art with the Mask." In *Hegel After Derrida,* edited by Stuart Barnett, 105–30. London: Routledge, 1998.

——. "Guilt History: Benjamin's Sketch 'Capitalism as Religion.'" Translated by Kirk Wetters. *Diacritics* 32, no. 3–4 (2002): 81–106.

——. "Intensive Languages." Translated by Ira Allen and Steven Tester. *MLN* 127 (2012): 485–541.

——. "Journals, Politics." In *Responses: On Paul de Man's Wartime Journalism,* edited by Werner Hamacher, Neil Hertz, and Thomas Keenan, 438–67. Lincoln: University of Nebraska Press, 1989.

——. "'Now': Walter Benjamin on Historical Time." Translated by N. Rosenthal. In *Walter Benjamin and History,* edited by Andrew Benjamin, 38–68. New York: Continuum, 2005.

——. *Pleroma: Reading in Hegel.* Translated by Nicholas Walker and Simon Jarvis. Stanford: Stanford University Press, 1998.

——. *Premises: Essays on Philosophy and Literature from Kant to Celan.* Translated by Peter Fenves. Cambridge: Harvard University Press, 1996.

——. "The Word Wolke—If It Is One." In *Benjamin's Ground: New Readings of Walter Benjamin,* edited by Rainer Nägele, 147–76. Detroit: Wayne State University Press, 1988.

Hamann, Johann Georg. *Briefwechsel.* Edited by Arthur Henkel. 7 vols. Frankfurt am Main: Insel, 1965–79.

——. *Johann Georg Hamanns Hauptschriften Erklärt.* Edited by Fritz Blanke und Karlfried Gründer. 4 vols. Gütersloh: Mohn, 1963.

——. *Sämtliche Werke.* Edited by Josef Nadler. 6 vols. Vienna: Im Verlag Herder, 1949–1957.

Hannay, Alistair. *Kierkegaard: A Biography.* Cambridge: Cambridge University Press, 2001.

Hanssen, Beatrice. *Walter Benjamin's Other History: Of Stones, Animals, Human Beings, and Angels.* Berkeley: University of California Press, 2000.

Hegel, G. W. F. *Elements of the Philosophy of Right.* Edited by Allen Wood. Translated by H. B. Nisbet Cambridge: Cambridge University Press, 1991.

——. *Phenomenology of Spirit.* Translated by A. V. Miller. Oxford: Oxford University Press, 1977.

——. *The Philosophy of History.* Translated by J. Sibree. New York: Dover, 1956.

——. *Werke.* 20 vols. Frankfurt am Main: Suhrkamp, 1970.

Heidegger, Martin. *Being and Time*. Translated by J. Macquarrie and E. Robinson. San Francisco: Harper and Row, 1962.

———. *Hegel's Phenomenology of Spirit*. Translated by Parvis Emad and Kenneth Maly. Bloomington: Indiana University Press, 1988.

———. "Nietzsches Wort 'Gott ist tot.'" In *Holzwege*, 209–68. Frankfurt am Main: Klostermann, 1950.

———. *Nietzsche. Volumes One and Two: The Will to Power as Art; The Eternal Recurrence of the Same*. San Francisco: Harper, 1991.

———. *Nietzsche. Volumes Three and Four: The Will to Power as Knowledge and as Metaphysics; Nihilism*. Edited and translated by David Farrell Krell. San Francisco: Harper, 1991.

Heller-Roazen, Daniel. *Echolalias: On the Forgetting of Language*. New York: Zone Books, 2005.

Henrich, Dieter. *Hegel im Kontext*. Frankfurt am Main: Suhrkamp Verlag, 1967.

Honold, Alexander. "Karl Kraus." In *Benjamin-Handbuch*, edited by Burkhardt Lindner, 522–38. Stuttgart & Weimar: Verlag J. B. Metzler, 2006.

Houlgate, Stephen. *An Introduction to Hegel: Freedom, Truth, and History*. Malden, Mass.: Blackwell, 2005.

Hyppolite, Jean. *Genesis and Structure of Hegel's Phenomenology of Spirit*. Translated by Samuel Cherniak and John Heckmann. Evanston, Ill.: Northwestern University Press, 1974.

———. *Introduction to Hegel's Philosophy of History*. Translated by Bond Harris and Jacqueline Bouchard Spurlock. Gainesville: University Press of Florida, 1996.

Irrlitz, Gerd. *Kant Handbuch*. Stuttgart: J. B. Metzler, 2002.

James, Cyril Lionel Robert, *The Black Jacobins: Toussaint L'Ouverture and the San Domingo Revolution*. New York: Random House, 1963.

Jennings, Michael W. "The Will to Apokatastasis: Media, Experience, and Eschatology in Walter Benjamin's Late Theological Politics." In *Walter Benjamin and Theology*, edited by Colby Dickinson and Stéphane Symons, 93–111. New York: Fordham University Press, 2016.

Kangas, David J. *Kierkegaard's Instant: On Beginnings*. Bloomington: Indiana University Press, 2007.

Kant, Immanuel. *Anthropology from a Pragmatic Point of View*. Edited and translated by Robert B. Louden. New York: Cambridge University Press, 2006.

———. *The Conflict of the Faculties*. Translated by Mary J. Gregor. New York: Abaris Books, 1979.

———. *Correspondence*. Edited and translated by Arnuld Zweig. Cambridge: Cambridge University Press, 1999.

———. *Critique of Practical Reason*. In *Practical Philosophy*. Edited and translated by Mary J. Gregor. Cambridge: Cambridge University Press, 1996.

———. *Critique of the Power of Judgment*. Translated by Paul Guyer and Eric Matthews. Cambridge: Cambridge University Press, 2000.

——. *Gesammelte Schriften* (facsimile of the standard "Akademie" edition published by the Königlich Preußische Akademie der Wissenschaften, 1902–). 29 vols. Berlin: De Gruyter, 1968–.

——. *Religion Within the Boundaries of Mere Reason.* Translated by George di Giovanni. In *Religion and Rational Theology.* Edited by Allen W. Wood and George di Giovanni. Cambridge: Cambridge University Press, 1996.

Kaufmann, Walter. *Nietzsche: Philosopher, Psychologist, Antichrist.* Princeton: Princeton University Press, 1974.

Khatib, Sami. "The Messianic Without Messianism: Walter Benjamin's Materialist Theology." In *Anthropology & Materialism* 1 (2013): 1–17.

——. *"Teleologie ohne Endzweck": Walter Benjamin's Ent-stellung des Messianischen.* Marburg: Tectum Verlag, 2013.

Kierkegaard, Søren. *The Concept of Anxiety.* Translated by Reidar Thomte and Albert A. Anderson. Princeton: Princeton University Press, 1980.

——. *The Concept of Irony.* Translated by Howard V. Hong and Edna H. Hong. Princeton: Princeton University Press, 1989.

——. *The Corsair Affair.* Translated by Howard V. Hong and Edna H. Hong. Princeton: Princeton University Press, 1982.

——. *Early Polemical Writings.* Edited and translated by Julia Watkin. Princeton: Princeton University Press, 1990.

——. *Either/Or.* 2 vols. Translated by D. F. and L. M. Swenson and D. W. Lowrie. Princeton: Princeton University Press, 1959.

——. *Gesammelte Werke.* Edited by Ingrid Jacobsen and Harmut Waechter. Vol. 27. Düsseldorf: Eugen Diederichs, 1969.

——. *Kierkegaard's Journals and Notebooks.* Edited by Niels Jorgen Cappelorn et al. Princeton: Princeton University Press, 2011–.

——. *Philosophical Fragments* and *Johannes Climacus.* Translated by Howard V. Hong and Edna H. Hong. Princeton: Princeton University Press, 1985.

——. *The Point of View: On My Work as an Author.* Translated by Howard V. Hong and Edna H. Hong. Princeton: Princeton University Press, 1998.

——. *Prefaces/Writing Sampler.* Edited and translated by Todd W. Nichol. Princeton: Princeton University Press, 1997.

——. *Søren Kierkegaards Papirer.* Edited by P. A. Heiberg, V. Kuhr, and E. Torsting Copenhagen: Gyldendal, 1909–48.

——. *Søren Kierkegaards Samlede Værker,* I–XIV. Edited by A. B. Drachman, J. L. Heiberg, and H. O. Lange. Copenhagen: Gyldendal, 1901–06.

——. *Two Ages: A Literary Review.* Edited and translated by Howard. V. Hong and Edna H. Hong. Princeton: Princeton University Press, 1978.

Kittler, Friedrich A. *Gramophone, Film, Typewriter.* Translated by Geoffrey Winthrop-Young and Michael Wutz. Stanford: Stanford University Press, 1999.

Klossowski, Pierre. *Nietzsche and the Vicious Circle.* Translated by Daniel W. Smith. Chicago: University of Chicago Press, 1979.

Kofman, Sarah. *Explosion II: Les enfants de Nietzsche.* Paris: Editions Galilée, 1993.

———. *Nietzsche and Metaphor*. Translated by Duncan Large. London: Athlone Press, 1993.

Kouvelakis, Stathis. *Philosophy and Revolution: From Kant to Marx*. London: Verso, 2003.

Kraus, Karl. *In These Great Times*. Edited by Harry Zohn. Manchester: Carcanet, 1976.

———. *No Compromise: Selected Writings of Karl Kraus*. Edited and translated by Frederick Ungar. New York: Ungar, 1977.

———. *Schriften*. Edited by Christian Wagenknecht. 20 vols. Frankfurt am Main: Suhrkamp Verlag, 1994.

———. *Worte in Versen*. Edited by Heinrich Fischer. München: Kösel, 1959.

Lacoue-Labarthe, Philippe. *The Subject of Philosophy*. Translated by Thomas Trezise. Minneapolis: University of Minnesota Press, 1993.

———. *Typography: Mimesis, Philosophy, Politics*. Edited and translated by Christopher Fynsk. Cambridge: Harvard University Press, 1989.

Lacoue-Labarthe, Philippe, and Jean-Luc Nancy. *The Literary Absolute*. Translated by Philip Barnard and Cheryl Lester. Albany, N.Y.: SUNY Press, 1988.

La Vopa, Anthony. *Fichte: The Self and the Calling of Philosophy, 1762–1799*. Cambridge: Cambridge University Press, 2001.

Leslie, Esther. *Walter Benjamin*. London: Reaktion Books, 2007.

———. *Walter Benjamin: Overpowering Conformism*. London: Pluto Press, 2000.

Lindner, Burkhardt, ed. *Benjamin-Handbuch*. Stuttgart & Weimar: Verlag J. B. Metzler, 2006.

Löwith, Karl. *From Hegel to Nietzsche: The Revolution in Nineteenth-Century Thought*. Translated by David E. Green. New York: Columbia University Press, 1991.

———. *Nietzsche's Philosophy of the Eternal Recurrence of the Same*. Trans. by J. Harvey Lomax. Berkeley: University of California Press, 1997.

Löwy, Michael. *Redemption & Utopia: Jewish Libertarian Thought in Central Europe*. Translated by Hope Heaney. London: The Athlone Press, 1992.

Lukács, Georg. *History and Class Consciousness: Studies in Marxist Dialectics*. Translated by Rodney Livingstone. Cambridge: MIT Press, 1971.

———. *Soul and Form*. Translated by Anna Bostock. London: Merlin, 1974.

———. *The Theory of the Novel*. Translated by Anna Bostock. Cambridge: MIT Press, 1971.

Lyotard, Jean-François. *Enthusiasm: The Kantian Critique of History*. Translated by Georges van den Abbeele. Stanford: Stanford University Press, 1986.

———. *The Inhuman: Reflections on Time*. Translated by Geoffrey Bennington and Rachel Bowlby. Cambridge: Polity, 1991.

McLaughlin, Kevin. "Biophilology: Walter Benjamin's Literary Critical Legacy." *MLN* 133, no. 3 (2018): 562–84.

Menninghaus, Winfried. *Walter Benjamins Theorie der Sprachmagie*. Frankfurt am Main: Suhrkamp, 1995.

Mosès, Stéphane. *The Angel of History: Rosenzweig, Benjamin, Scholem.* Translated
    by Barbara Harshaw. Stanford: Stanford University Press, 2009.
Müller-Lauter, Wolfgang. *Nietzsche: His Philosophy of Contradictions and the
    Contradictions of his Philosophy.* Translated by David J. Parent. Chicago:
    University of Illinois Press, 1971.
Nägele, Rainer, ed. *Benjamin's Ground: New Readings of Walter Benjamin.* Detroit:
    Wayne State University Press, 1988.
———. "Das Beben des Barock in der Moderne: Walter Benjamins Monadologie."
    MLN 106, no. 3 (1991): 501–27.
Nancy, Jean-Luc. *The Speculative Remark.* Translated by Céline Surprenant.
    Stanford: Stanford University Press, 2001.
Nehamas, Alexander. *Nietzsche: Life as Literature.* Cambridge: Harvard University
    Press, 1985.
Ng, Julia. "Each Thing a Thief: Walter Benjamin on the Agency of Objects."
    Philosophy and Rhetoric 44, no. 4 (2011): 382–402.
Nietzsche, Friedrich. *The Anti-Christ, Ecce Homo, Twilight of the Idols.* Translated
    by Judith Norman. Cambridge: Cambridge University Press, 2007.
———. *Beyond Good and Evil.* Translated by Judith Norman. Cambridge:
    Cambridge University Press, 2007.
———. *The Birth of Tragedy and Other Writings.* Translated by Ronald Speirs.
    Cambridge: Cambridge University Press, 1999.
———. *Daybreak: Thoughts on the Prejudices of Morality.* Translated by R. J.
    Hollingdale. Cambridge: Cambridge University Press, 1997.
———. "Fragments sur le langage." Translated by Philippe Lacoue-Labarthe and
    Jean Luc Nancy. *Poétique* 5 (1971): 99–142.
———. *Friedrich Nietzsche on Rhetoric and Language.* Translated by Sander L.
    Gilman et al. Oxford: Oxford University Press, 1989.
———. *The Gay Science.* Translated by Josephine Nauckhoff. Cambridge:
    Cambridge University Press, 2008.
———. *Human, All Too Human: A Book for free Spirits.* Translated by R. J.
    Hollingdale. Cambridge: Cambridge University Press, 1996.
———. "On the Future of Our Educational Institutions." In *Anti-Education: On the
    Future of Our Educational Institutions,* edited by Paul Reitter and Chad
    Wellmon, translated by Damion Searles, 3–96. New York: New York Review of
    Books, 2015.
———. *On the Genealogy of Morality.* Translated by Carol Diethe. Cambridge:
    Cambridge University Press, 1997.
———. *Sämtliche Briefe: Kritische Studienausgabe in 8 Bänden.* Edited by Giorgio
    Colli and Mazzino Montinari. Berlin: Walter de Gruyter, 1986.
———. *Thus Spoke Zarathustra.* Translated by Adrian del Caro. Cambridge:
    Cambridge University Press, 2006.
———. *Untimely Meditations.* Translated by R. J. Hollingdale. Cambridge:
    Cambridge University Press, 1995.

——. *Werke: Kritische Studienausgabe in 15 Bänden*. Edited by Giorgio Colli and Mazzino Montinari. Berlin: Walter de Gruyter, 1988.

Osborne, Peter. *The Politics of Time: Modernity and Avant-Garde*. London: Verso, 2011.

——. "Small-scale Victories, Large-scale Defeats: Walter Benjamin's Politics of Time." In *Walter Benjamin's Philosophy*, edited by Andrew Benjamin and Peter Osborne, 59–109. London: Routledge, 1993.

Peters, John Durham. *Speaking into the Air: A History of the Idea of Communication*. Chicago: University of Chicago Press, 1999.

Quack, Joseph. *Bemerkungen zum Sprachverständnis von Karl Kraus*. Bonn: Bouvier, 1976.

Reitter, Paul. *The Anti-Journalist: Karl Kraus and Jewish Self-Fashioning in fin-de-siècle Europe*. Chicago: University of Chicago Press, 2008.

Ricoeur, Paul. "Philosophy after Kierkegaard." In *Kierkegaard: A Critical Reader*, ed. Jane Chamberlain and Jonathan Rée. London: Wiley-Blackwell, 1997.

Ritter, Joachim. *Hegel and the French Revolution: Essays on the Philosophy of Right*. Translated by Richard Dien Winfield. Cambridge: MIT Press, 1982.

Ronell, Avital. "Street Talk." In *Benjamin's Ground: New Readings of Walter Benjamin*, edited by Rainer Nägele, 119–45. Detroit: Wayne State University Press, 1988.

Rose, Gillian. *The Broken Middle: Out of Our Ancient Society*. Oxford: Blackwell, 1992.

——. *Hegel Contra Sociology*. London: Verso Books, 2009.

——. *The Melancholy Science: An Introduction to the Work of Theodor W. Adorno*. London: Verso Books, 2014.

Rosenkranz, Karl. *Georg Wilhelm Friedrich Hegel's Leben*. Berlin: Duncker und Humblot, 1844.

Rosenzweig, Franz. *The Star of Redemption*. Madison: University of Wisconsin Press, 2005.

Santner, Eric. *On Creaturely Life: Rilke, Benjamin, Sebald*. Chicago: University of Chicago Press, 2006.

Schestag, Thomas. "Interpolationen: Benjamins Philologie." In *Philo:zenia*, edited by Thomas Schestag, 35–93. Basel: Engeler, 2009.

Schlegel, August Wilhelm. *Vorlesungen über dramatische Kunst und Literatur*. Stuttgart: W. Kohlhammer Verlag, 1966.

——. "Vorlesungen über philosophische Kunstlehre." In *Komödientheorie*, edited by Ulrich Profitlich, 109–11. Reinbek bei Hamburg: Rowohlt, 1998.

Schlegel, Friedrich. *Philosophical Fragments*. Translated by Peter Firchow. Minneapolis: University of Minnesota Press, 1991.

——. "Zur Philosophie," Fragment 668, in *Kritische Ausgabe*, edited by Ernst Behler, vol. 18, 85. Paderborn: Ferdinand Schöningh, 1962.

Scholem, Gerschom. "Walter Benjamin and his Angel." In *On Walter Benjamin: Critical Essays and Recollections*, edited by Gary Smith, 198–236. Cambridge: MIT Press, 1988.

———. *Walter Benjamin: The Story of a Friendship*. London: Faber, 1981.
Schopenhauer, Arthur. *Parerga und Paralipomena*. Frankfurt: Suhrkamp Verlag, 1986.
Schröder, Thomas. "The Origins of the German Press." In *The Politics of Information in Early Modern Europe*, edited by Brendan Dooley and Sabrina A. Baron, 123–50. London: Routledge, 2001.
Schwebel, Paula. "Intensive Infinity: Walter Benjamin's Reception of Leibniz and Its Sources." *MLN* 127 (2012): 589–610.
Sieber, Jan, and Sebastian Truskolaski. "The Task of the Philosopher: In Place of an Introduction." *Anthropology & Materialism* 1 (2017): 1–16.
Spivak, Gayatri Chakravorty. *A Critique of Postcolonial Reason*. Cambridge: Harvard University Press, 1999.
Stump, Eleonore, and Norman Kretzmann. "Eternity." *The Journal of Philosophy* 78, no. 8 (August 1981): 429–58.
Suhrkamp, Peter. "Der Journalist." In *Deutsche Berufskunde. Ein Querschnitt durch die Berufe und Arbeitskreise der Gegenwart*, edited by Ottolenz v. d. Gablentz and Carl Mennicke, 382–86. Leipzig: Bibliographisches Institut, 1930.
Swenson, David F. "A Danish Thinker's Estimate of Journalism." *Ethics* 1 (1927–28): 70–87.
Szondi, Peter. *An Essay on the Tragic*. Translated by Paul Fleming. Stanford: Stanford University Press, 2002.
———. *Satz und Gegensatz: Sechs Essays*. Frankfurt am Main: Suhrkamp, 1976.
Tiedemann, Rolf. *Dialektik im Stillstand: Versuche zum Spätwerk Walter Benjamins*. Frankfurt am Main: Suhrkamp Verlag, 1983.
———. *Studien zur Philosophie Walter Benjamins*. Frankfurt am Main: Suhrkamp Verlag, 1973.
Timms, Chris. *Apocalyptic Satirist: Culture and Catastrophe in Habsburg Vienna*. New Haven: Yale University Press, 1989.
———. *Apocalyptic Satirist, Volume 2: The Postwar Crisis and the Rise of the Swastika*. New Haven: Yale University Press, 2013.
Tudvad, Peter. "On Kierkegaard's *Journalism*." Translated by Tod Alan Spoerl. *Kierkegaard Studies Yearbook* (2003): 214–33.
Vandeputte, Tom. "Constellation and Configuration: Language and Reading in the 'Epistemo-Critical Prologue.'" In *Thinking in Constellations: Walter Benjamin in the Humanities*, edited by Nassima Sahraoui and Caroline Sauter, 83–102. Cambridge: Cambridge Scholars, 2018.
———. "Karl Kraus. Die Sprache rächen." In *Entwendungen: Walter Benjamin und seine Quellen*, edited by Jessica Nitzsche and Nadine Werner, 263–80. Paderborn: Verlag Wilhelm Fink, 2019.
———. "Resistance." In *Re-: An Errant Glossary*, edited by Christoph F. E. Holzhey and Arnd Wedemeyer, 127–32. *Cultural Inquiry* 15. Berlin: ICI Berlin, 2019.
Wagner, Richard. ""Modern."" In *Richard Wagners Gesammelte Schriften*, edited by Julius Kapp, vol. 3, 177–83. Leipzig: Hesse und Becker, 1911.

Wahl, Jean. *Études Kierkegaardiennes*. Paris: Librairie Philosophique J. Vrin, 1949.

Weber, Johannes. "Der große Krieg und die frühe Zeitung: Gestalt und Entwicklung der deutschen Nachrichtenpresse in der ersten Hälfte des 17. Jahrhunderts." *Jahrbuch für Kommunikationsgeschichte* (1999): 23–61.

Weber, Samuel. *Benjamin's -abilities*. Cambridge: Harvard University Press, 2010.

———. "Kierkegaard's Posse." In *Theatricality as Medium*, 200–28. New York: Fordham University Press, 2004.

———. "Religion, Repetition, Media." In *Religion and Media*, edited by Hent de Vries and Samuel Weber, 43–55. Stanford: Stanford University Press, 2002.

Weigel, Sigrid. "Angelus Novus." In *Enzyklopädie jüdischer Geschichte und Kultur*, edited by Dan Diner, 94–100. Stuttgart: Verlag J. B. Metzler, 2011.

———. *Walter Benjamin: Images, the Creaturely, and the Holy*. Stanford: Stanford University Press, 2012.

Weller, Emil, ed. *Die ersten deutschen Zeitungen*. Tübingen: Laupp, 1872.

Witte, Bernd. *Walter Benjamin: An Intellectual Biography*. Translated by James Rolleston. Detroit: Wayne State University Press, 1991.

Wizisla, Erdmut. *Walter Benjamin and Bertolt Brecht: The Story of a Friendship*. Translated by Christine Shuttleworth. New Haven: Yale University Press, 2009.

Wohlfarth, Irving. "No-Man's Land: On Walter Benjamin's 'Destructive Character.'" In *Walter Benjamin's Philosophy*, edited by Andrew Benjamin and Peter Osborne, 59–109. London: Routledge, 1993.

———. "On Some Jewish Motifs in Walter Benjamin." In *Problems of Modernity: Adorno and Benjamin*, edited by Andrew Benjamin, 157–215. London: Routledge, 1989.

———. "On the Messianic Structure of Walter Benjamin's Last Reflections." *Glyph* 3 (1978): 148–212.

Yovel, Yirmiyahu. *Hegel's Preface to the Phenomenology of Spirit*. Princeton: Princeton University Press, 1980.

———. *Kant and the Philosophy of History*. Princeton: Princeton University Press, 1980.

Index

TOM VANDEPUTTE is head of Critical Studies at the Sandberg Institute in Amsterdam, where he teaches continental philosophy and critical theory. He is also a fellow at the Institute for Cultural Inquiry (ICI) Berlin, where he is preparing a book on the political thought of Walter Benjamin.